Tips

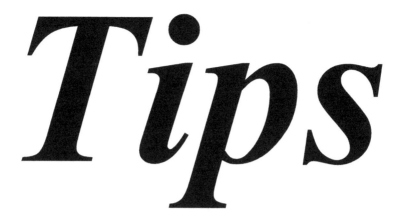

Tips

A Guidebook for Teaching Excellence in ESL

A sampler of ideas and resources for the mind, the heart, and the classroom

DAN MANOLESCU

gatekeeper press

Columbus, Ohio

Tips: A Guidebook for Teaching Excellence in ESL

Published by Gatekeeper Press
2167 Stringtown Rd, Suite 109
Columbus, OH 43123-2989
www.GatekeeperPress.com

ISBN (hardcover): 9781642374056
ISBN (paperback): 9781642374049
eISBN: 9781642374032

Printed in the United States of America

To My Alma Mater

Contents

Acknowledgements

MY HEARTFELT THANKS go to all my students, especially those who attended my classes in various places in New Jersey (LIFE Program in Rutherford, Berlitz on Campus in Madison and Teaneck, New Jersey City University in Jersey City) and in New York City (Summer Programs at The Juilliard School and ELS at Adelphi University).

First and foremost, the educator who left an indelible imprint in my early apprenticeship was Valeria Magda, who left us long ago but will remain in my affectionate memory for many years to come. Ms. Magda, with her encyclopedic knowledge, was the one who convinced me that teaching is the best and the most rewarding profession in the world.

I spent the most productive—and most intense—10 years of my teaching career at our LIFE Program in Rutherford, New Jersey, between 1984 and 1994, before our language center moved to Madison, New Jersey. During those 10 years, my fellow teachers and good friends made me feel like I was part of a family. After all these years, I consider myself lucky and blessed to have worked side by side with John Coyman, Madgid Hannoucene, Ward Morrow, Ted Stazeski, Peggy Street, and Darinka Zaharieff, to name a few. A member of the extended family indeed I was, and I took this concept with me when I became the Academic Director at ELS Manhattan, where I did my best to re-create the same atmosphere in the classroom and in the office between 1997 and 2017. This was possible mainly because we all had Mr. Mark W. Harris at the helm, our CEO, knowledgeable educator and efficient businessman par excellence, who welcomed and empowered the dedicated teacher as well as the motivated student.

The supervisor who spent time with me in her office and listened to all my questions, good, bad or otherwise, was Rosemary Rowlands. In 1991, before we opened our summer program at The Juilliard School in New York City, where I taught and worked in the office as well, Rosemary shared with me the secrets of the administrative side of ESL. She also checked the first baby steps of this project and offered excellent advice as well as much needed encouragement. After all these years, Rosemary remains for me the quintessential Academic Coordinator, and I am lastingly indebted.

My collective gratitude goes to all my friends and colleagues who shared with me, with a daily dose of good humor, their passion, their ideas, as well as their concerns regarding the process of teaching ESL. I am grateful to have worked with people like John Artise, who helped me with valuable suggestions when I started this project. I must also add Danielle DeKoker and Melissa Kaufman, who worked with me in the Academic Office, as well as Laura Lee Lafortezza, who was the heart and soul of the teaching staff at ELS Manhattan during our years at Adelphi University in New York City.

I am also deeply grateful for the 25 years I taught, among other things, EC I and EC II (English Composition 101 and 102) on Saturdays at New Jersey City University (formerly known as Jersey City State College), where I was surrounded by professionals and worked with some of the best ESL educators: Dr. Clyde Coreil, Professor Emeritus, and Dr. Anne Mabry, who provided their unflinching support and were always available to discuss with me the challenges and intricacies of the ESL Program at New Jersey City University.

I am particularly grateful to Sarah Spencer at Gatekeeper Press for her understanding and patience with my manuscript in its various stages before printing and publication.

Last but not least, I wish to express my devoted thanks to the friendly folks at Clarence Dillon Public Library in Bedminster, New Jersey, where I researched and compiled most of the material in this sampler.

> "The English language is the sea which receives tributaries from every region under heaven."
>
> Ralph Waldo Emerson

Foreword

HOW CAN YOU describe ESL (English as a Second Language)? It's very hard to put it in words, but you can feel it because it is all MAGIC. How can you discover its MYSTERIES? Well, you will have to go into the classroom and meet your students.

This book is the result of decades of ESL teaching experience in both public and private schools. As a teacher, you will need at least two very important skills: one is the ability to **read ESL sources and continue doing research**, and the other one is the ability to **translate your information into knowledge** presented to your students.

Reading and researching ESL material can be done during the break, before class, after class, over the weekend, but these are necessary tools that will keep you afloat among your peers. That is why most chapters in this guidebook contain information for teachers to absorb and digest. However, that is not enough. For every topic, you will have to devise lesson plans and find a way to **make students aware that they must make a mental effort** if they want to learn the language. ESL teachers can resort to specialized materials, journals, and online resources. That is part of what each section of this book presents. Separately, students and teachers also have textbooks covering the basic academic skills with graphs, rules, and exercises to address those skills. This book has collected various concepts into one solid source of information and practical exercises to match.

Why put everything in one book? Teachers do not have time to prepare for the classroom. They have to be familiar with a curriculum per level of study, they have to compile quizzes and tests, grade papers, and at the same time, make sure their students also do their part. We read on the bus, on the train, waiting in line at the stores, we read everywhere we find the right place and the right moment.

You can open the book and you will find something interesting to read. Certain chapters have longer explanations, others have shorter presentations, but they should all appeal to the ESL teachers' taste and **provide the motivation to know how to discover new things** all the time. And that is not for teachers alone, because whatever we accumulate and discover, our students are the ultimate goal. THEY should be able to benefit. STUDENTS should learn from us to do the same: **read** and **learn** and **practice**.

In a nutshell, this book is a combination of **extensive ESL research** and **practical information** for the ESL teachers and students.

WHAT?	HOW?
What are we teaching?	How are we delivering the information?
	How are we motivating and empowering the students?

Both concepts are very IMPORTANT, especially HOW we approach our students.

> Open the long closed doors and let your mind wander freely. Feast your eyes and "let knowledge grow from more to more." Information is at your fingertips.
>
> Adapted from Alfred Tennyson (1809-1892)

What This Guidebook Is All About

Rationale - ESL is tinged with **magic** and rich in **mysteries**. You need to **discover** them. Four strategies for **success** in ESL classes will help teachers deliver high quality instruction:

Lessons should be

Interesting
Informative
Communicative
Motivating

The English Language - Quick overview of how English developed over the centuries

The English Alphabet – English letters and their history

Language and Culture - Language grows out of culture and represents that culture.

Methodology – General overview of students' needs, followed by various strategies and methods:

The Grammar-Translation Method
The Direct Method
Audiolingual Methodology
The Communicative Language Teaching Approach

Vocabulary - This section includes theoretical and practical knowledge about teaching **vocabulary in context**, dealing with **homonyms, similar sounding**

words, silent letters, onomatopoeic words, eponyms, and **oxymora.** A **successful approach** to vocabulary also relates to how words are formed, and how students can enrich their own vocabulary by looking at context, analyzing words, working with synonyms, and using dictionaries.

Denotation, Connotation, and Inference

From denotation to connotation
Why connotation is so important
Research and examples of inference

Figurative Meaning Euphemisms, Metaphors, Similes

Mnemonics – Memory training techniques from Greek and Roman orators to present-day ESL

Reading – The history of reading
Why we should develop the reading skill

Writing – Why **writing is a form of magic**
What is a sentence, a paragraph, a topic sentence, a thesis statement, an essay, a research paper, a book report, a book review
Scanning, skimming, paraphrasing, summarizing, quoting

Grammar – *Glamour* and *grammar* were once one and the same word. Students need to understand the English grammar by integrating all skills into one. Teachers need to guide them by looking at morphology and syntax, by analyzing examples, and by empowering students to teach each other what they discover. Once a structure is acquired, **practice** will consolidate and cement it in our knowledge reservoir. Practical exercises in every grammar section

Speaking – Public speaking in social contexts - Conversation styles

Literature – "Values in literature are the same as values in life."

Examples of short stories with specific tasks and assignments

Appendix – Extra information for in-depth knowledge

Rationale

ENGLISH AS A Second Language (ESL) is a special breed. In the United States, it started in Dade County, Florida in 1963 as a government-supported bilingual program, but it soon attracted the attention of educators who wanted to see the example set by the original program. In 1966, the first national organization was founded: TESOL – Teachers of English to Speakers of Other Languages – and in time, it grew into an international professional organization.

There is something special about teaching ESL, and you can detect it as soon as you walk into a classroom and meet your students. This kind of special is called **MAGIC**. It is difficult to describe it, but you can feel it, you can sense it, and you can experience it alone or together. **ESL is tinged with magic** and **rich in mysteries**. The magic of the classroom activities and the style of each academic skill create an aura of magic with consequences behind the walls of the building and after the class hours. Schools and educators create curricula and syllabi to stream the huge volume of information and resources, but the ultimate goal is to teach each other and to learn from each other. **Very few disciplines include the reciprocal rapport** and **the bridge between the classroom and the community**. ESL does it 24/7, and it competes with industries and world economies with a speed that does not show any signs of stopping.

"The present-day teacher of English is a far cry from the old-time schoolmaster who taught by parsing and diagramming sentences on the board and by reading to the class pieces of abstruse poetry that the class could not understand and appreciate. He (or she) is today a very practical-minded person, who is fully aware of the pitfalls of the language and the latest scientific and educational devices for circumventing them. He seldom tries to teach English in a vacuum, but relates the subject to all of life's manifold activities, as well as to the other subjects of the curriculum. Above all, he is no longer a stuffy grammarian of the prescriptive school, but a broadminded person who realizes that language is perpetually changing, and allowances must be made for this fact." (Mario Pei, *The Story of the English Language*, J. B. Lippincott Company, Philadelphia and New York, 1967, p. 373)

Dealing with ESL students means dealing with students from various cultures. Teachers should be aware of the **differences and nuances of the language character** and make sure they approach their students with respect and understanding. The etiquette of communication can easily be acquired by accepting that **each student is a separate entity** and that they all come from different backgrounds. Here are some generalities to keep in mind from Sundem, Krieger & Pickiewicz (2008):

1. "Many cultures see eye contact as aggressive or intimate (especially between the genders).

2. Spanish-speaking, Arabic-speaking, and Asian students may be comfortable with less personal space and more physical contact than students (and teachers) experienced with American culture. [...]

3. Korean families may place extreme importance on education and can become upset by the appearance of their child's underachievement.

4. Parents of Asian students relate to teachers more formally than do their American counterparts.

5. Spanish-speaking students might offer immediate respect for females in authority roles while withholding respect form female peers.

6. Arabic-speaking students may have difficulties with female making decisions and exercising authority.

7. Nodding and saying 'yes' in Asian cultures demonstrates hearing but not necessarily agreement.

8. Spanish-speaking students may prioritize family obligations over education.

9. Copying schoolwork may be acceptable to students from former Eastern-bloc countries.

Students from Asian countries might excel in memorization but have difficulties with reading comprehension." (introduction, p. XX)

In other words, ESL instructors should be able **to walk the fine line between cultures.** Before we look a little deeper into the unique characteristics and facets of ESL, let us admire this "marvelous invention" called **language.**

"Of all mankind's manifold creations, language must take pride of place. Other inventions – the wheel, agriculture, sliced bread – may have transformed our material existence, but the advent of language is what made us human. Compared to language, all other inventions pale in significance, since everything we have ever achieved depends on language and originates from it. Without language, we could never have embarked on our ascent to unparalleled power over all other animals, and even over nature itself." (Guy Deutscher, *The Unfolding of Language,* Henry Holt and Company, New York, 2005, p. 2)

Let us remember that **language is a miracle itself**, and one of its most important assets is the fact that language allows us to put sounds together "into an infinite variety of subtle senses." The same author says, "The wheels of language run so smoothly that one rarely bothers to stop and think about the resourcefulness and expertise that must have gone into making it tick." (2)

What is the magic of ESL? What is so attractive and appealing is the wide scope of learning ESL and **the vision of being able to speak, read, and write like a native**. And if, in some cases, students still keep a part of their own culture and vocabulary, so much the better. This is what **each mystery reveals** when approached properly, with **respect and mutual understanding**. Each new reading passage or listening exercise is a mystery in itself, and nobody knows better than those involved in the teaching process day in and day out. The rewards are endless when teachers and students discover together the minutiae of a lesson objective, or when after weeks, months, or even years of learning, we go back and reflect. The accomplishments are great, and words cannot express the gratitude of those who open the door and let English enter their lives. It's not only the language; it entails basic beliefs, assumptions and values, body language, face expressions – they are all ingrained in the native speakers and ESL students should be made aware of that.

After studying English as a Second Language and teaching it for decades, I would like to share some of my best classroom experiences so other teachers do not have to re-invent the wheel. Teachers do not have enough time to keep in touch with new developments or to stay updated. There is so much information and so many resources but very little time. I have collected so much and learned so much over the years, but now I think it is the time to share.

There are no secrets, but there are lots of small details that come into action when we start looking at the whole ESL concept. Let's start with **four basic principles** that education in general and ESL in particular would recommend.

Interesting

The first and most important unwritten rule, I think, is to find the teaching material that presents itself as **attractive and very, very interesting**. No matter if we delve into vocabulary, grammar, reading techniques, listening exercises, or writing assignments, students should be somehow attracted not only by the main focus but also by the inherent and interesting quality of what they face for the first time. The subject matter and the way we present the information in the classroom should lure the students into the classroom instruction. ESL students are learning English for various reasons, but when they sit in a classroom, they expect to learn new things and the visual aspect, the combination of several classroom activities, (in other words, *everything*) should entertain and **provide food for thought**.

Informative

Knowledge comes in many facets, and the impact of the new material in the classroom should delight but also inform the learner. The teacher is the guide who organizes and empowers the students to make the instruction process meaningful. On a daily basis, we acquire information about the weather, politics, travel, sports, business, family matters, or entertainment. By the same token, every day in school is a day students learn to perform a certain task, practice new vocabulary, listen to dialogues, mini speeches or conversations, and in doing so improve their skills. At the end of each class period, students should be able to say, "**I learned something today. My classroom experience was worth my effort, and I left empowered with something new, more interesting and more informative than I expected.**" Our goal is to **exceed** the **student's expectations** – which seems quite challenging for any educator, but which makes teaching a rewarding experience. If the feedback we provide is clear and positive, students will build on what they already know. A college professor once said that, the human mind, once expanded by knowledge, can never go back to its original shape.

Communicative

With so much to **learn, absorb, and process**, students should be able to take their recently acquired knowledge and apply it right away, be it in a casual conversation, or in another class with a different or similar focus. The need to exchange information should be instilled in the learner's mind so they can find a useful application but also test the depth and width of the previously learned experience. **Practice** is the most obvious segue to the next step, which is always inter-human communication.

"Good instruction teaches students to do something." This is the main idea behind *Teaching for Competence* by Howard Sullivan and Norman Higgins (1983). The act of teaching does not consist of simply presenting information; we teach our students to do something with that knowledge. (2)

How do we go about communicating with our students? In some cases, this is an art, and it takes some time to communicate the learning objectives to the students, but at the same time find a motivator. The best way to achieve this would be to inform the students of the value of what they will be learning. We should "explain why the knowledge or skill is important in its own right and/ or as a necessity for learning other knowledge or skills. It is helpful to relate the usefulness of the new learning to life outside the school, as well as the previous or future school work. Whenever possible, you should also emphasize the importance of the objective for students' immediate needs or interests, rather than for more remote, long-range matters." (53)

In other words, your (teacher's) role is to "provide conditions that help all students learn as well as possible, rather than one in which you simply make information and resources available for students to learn according to their abilities. If you present the information for performing a task but do not provide appropriate practice, the top students may still perform quite well because of their better ability to interpret and apply the information. Less able students, however, are unlikely to be able to perform the task without an opportunity to practice it. Good instruction will include practice of the exact task stated in the objective because such practice helps students learn." (41-42)

Motivating

When we decide **what skills we teach**, we have handbooks, manuals, textbooks, websites, our own experience as teachers, and sometimes the students' previous classroom experience. We also have curricula, and we can develop our own objective sheets for each separate skill. What we do NOT have is the student's motivation. This is something we need to think about very seriously and find ways to make the ESL students aware that learning also involves their own motivation. A quick walk through *Motivating Learning* by Jill Hadfield and Zoltan Dornyei (2011) will give you a chance to see the multiple ways we can resort to when it comes to **motivation.** According to the authors, teachers must create a vision for the ESL students. The goals are not good enough and instead they must be replaced by a clear vision. The example they give is that young people can set the goal of becoming a doctor, but the vision will make them aware of what they will feel during their first day in the professional life of doctors. Extrapolating this idea, we might say that the ESL students' goal is to learn English, but the vision would involve them in conversations with native speakers at the airport, the bank, or the department store, and would make them feel comfortable in the new culture using English as a Second Language.

The vision would give them a feeling of accomplishment. The skills they learn in the classroom would enable them to do certain things in English.

"Doing describes what a person does to express himself in action of some kind. [...] Americans insist on identifying an agent who can take purposeful and sequential action. The concepts of *motive* and *motivation* provide the link between action on one hand and the agent (and his purposes) on the other hand. Motives are attributes of the individual which arouse him to action. The **concept of motivation** reveals the connection and direction in a sequence of actions and, in everyday life, provides a convenient explanation for performance. It is appropriate to say someone succeeds or excels because he is well motivated." (Stewart, 1997, p. 60)

> "Darwin believed that language was half art, half instinct, and he made the case that using sound to express thoughts and be understood by others was not an activity unique to humans."
>
> Christine Kenneally, *The First Word*, 2007, p. 21

The English Language

ACCORDING TO CHARLES Berlitz, there were 2,796 languages in the world in 2005. In his *Native Tongues*, he mentions that "the world's languages are divided into 12 important languages families and 50 lesser ones. The Indo-European language family, to which English belongs, is one of the 12 most important – and among languages importance is measured by the number of speakers around the world."(2) Sam Leith (2018), on the other hand, says "There are about seven thousand languages spoken worldwide. Less attention is paid to the fact that when we talk about 'English,' we are not talking about a single thing either; we're talking about a huge, messily overlapping mass of dialects and accents and professional jargons and slangs - some spoken, some written – that have their own vocabularies and grammatical peculiarities and resources of tone and register." (7)

After talking about the existence of dialects, Berlitz goes on to say:

> "English, in its earliest form, Anglo-Saxon, was the dialect of powerful Wessex; modern English, which developed after the Normans conquered England in 1066, grew out of the dialect of London, the capital city." (2)

The rise of the English language is considered by many linguists **a mystery**, while others rate it as a success story. When the Romans conquered Britain, English did not exist. In time, the language grew out of its original territory and slowly but surely became international.

Certain historical events, like the Hundred Years War with France (1337-1454), the outbreak of the plague called the Black Death, which in itself made labor scarce, accelerated the rise of the English language. After the plague, schools started to teach English grammar, not French or Latin. In 1325, William of Nassyngton (a village in Northamptonshire in England) made the following statement, which rendered into contemporary English would be like this:

In the English tongue I shall tell you,
If you with me so long will dwell,
No Latin will I speak nor waste,
But English, that men use most,
That is able each man to understand,
That is born in England;
For that language is most displayed,
As much among the learned as unread.
Latin, as I believe, know none
Except those who have it in school done.
And some know French and not Latin,
Who have used it at court and there remain.
And some know of Latin partly
Who know of French but feebly.
And some understand well English
Who know neither Latin nor French.
Both learned and unread, old and young,
All understand the English tongue.

(Quoted by David Crystal in *The Stories of English*, 2004, p. 131)

In the companion to the PBS TV series, *The Story of English*, R. McCrum, W. Cran, and R. MacNeil (1986) continue the story after William of Nassyngton, the chronicler whose statement was read before senior staff at Cambridge University in 1384.

"English now appears at every level of society. In 1356, the mayor and aldermen of London ordered the court proceedings there be heard in English; in 1362, the Chancellor opened Parliament in English. During Wat Tyler's rebellion in 1381, Richard II spoke to the peasants in English. In the last year of the century the proceedings for the deposition of Richard II (together with the document by which he renounced the throne) were in English. Henry IV speeches claiming the throne and later accepting it were also in English." (78)

Spoken English was different from county to county, and the five main speech areas – Northern, West Midlands, East Midlands, Southern and Kentish – are similar to contemporary English speech areas.

The same authors also mentioned that, towards the end of his life, Walt

Whitman defined language as "something arising out of the work, needs, ties, joys, affections, tastes, of long generations of humanity" and having "its basis broad and low, close to the ground." (351)

In his highly entertaining and informative book, *The Stories of English*, David Crystal opened his exploration of English with two stories, the standard and the real story. Let's see what he said about the former:

"The standard history of the English language usually goes something like this:

- In the year 449 Germanic tribes arrived in Britain from the European mainland, and displaced the native British (Celtic) population, eventually establishing a single language which was Anglo-Saxon in character.

- Most writings of the period are shown to be preserved in the West Saxon dialect, the language of King Alfred, spoken in the politically and culturally dominant region of southern England around Winchester. Descriptions of the language, known as Anglo-Saxon or Old English, therefore reflect the dominance.

- Fundamental changes began to affect Old English grammar during the later Anglo-Saxon period, and these, along with changes in pronunciation, innovative spelling conventions, and a huge influx of new words after the Norman Conquest, led to the language evolving a fresh character, known as Middle English.

- During the Middle English period, the literary language began to evolve, culminating in the compositions of Chaucer, and we see the first signs of a Standard English emerging in the work of the Chancery scribes of London.

- The introduction of printing by Caxton in 1476 brought an enormous expansion in the written resources of the language, and was the major influence of the development of s standardized writing system. Spelling began to stabilize, and thus became less of a guide to pronunciation, which continued to change.

- Further changes in pronunciation and grammar, and another enormous increase in vocabulary stimulated by the Renaissance, led to the emergence of an Early Modern English. Its character was much influenced by Elizabethan literature, notably by Shakespeare, and by the texts of many Bibles, especially those of Tyndale (1525) and King James (1611).

- The unprecedented increase in the language's range and creativity brought a reaction, in the form of a climate of concern about the unwelcome pace and character of language change. This led to the writing of the first English dictionaries, grammars, and manuals of pronunciation, in an attempt to bring the language under some measure of control.

- As a result, there emerged a sharpened sense or correctness in relation to a standard form of English, and this came to be encountered worldwide, as speakers of educated British English gained global influence throughout the British Empire. At the same time, the question of standards became more complex, with the arrival of American English as an alternative global presence.

- By the end of the eighteenth century, the standard language had become so close to that of the present day, at least in grammar, pronunciation, and spelling, that it is safely described as Modern English. But there continued to be massive increases in vocabulary, chiefly as a consequence of the industrial and scientific revolutions, and of the ongoing globalization of the language – a process which would continue throughout the twentieth century and into the twenty-first." (3-4)

Besides the standard story, David Crystal also takes into consideration what he calls "the real story." It is not what the orthodox histories include which is the problem; it is what they omit, or marginalize.

"'The' story of English, as it has been presented in the mainstream tradition, is the story of a single variety of the language, Standard English, its special status usually symbolized through capitalization. But this variety is only a small part of the kaleidoscopic diversity of dialects and styles which make up 'the English language.'"(5)

At a certain point, David Crystal is ready to get into conversational English, although he says its story is 'patchy.'

This is "a casual style, with its half-formed thoughts, loosely constructed sentences, unfinished utterances, interruptions, changes of subject, vagueness, repetitiveness, and a general 'play it by ear' attitude to interaction, is somewhat intrinsically inferior to a style where everything is carefully thought out, sentences are tightly organized and complete, the progression of meaning is logical and coherent, and conscious effort is made to be relevant, clear, and precise. This is a message which prescriptive grammarians and purist commentators have been drumming into us for the past 250 years. It may take another 250 to forget it, though the signs are that it will take much less." (10)

From our perspective as language instructors, we need to look at both aspects. What needs to be done is a concerted effort to unite the "standard" English with the spoken language of today. No matter how much we read and write and teach these skills together or separately, the spoken aspect is an integral part of the teaching process. I would venture to say that **even grammar, vocabulary, or listening, for that matter, should be done as a conversation activity.** Whatever is taught as new material should be practiced and reviewed so students can get a feeling of what a new grammar point, for example, sounds like in a real life situation.

As far as **the written form** is concerned, after the grand master of the Elizabethan era left us the legacy of Shakespearean drama and poetry, English moved slowly but gradually towards other parts of the known and little explored world. When the *Mayflower* left Plymouth in 1620, the written form that was recorded in those days gave us "one of the finest and earliest examples of prose written in America." (McCrum, Cran and McNeill, 1986)

William Bradford, the Mayflower's historian and the first Governor of the Massachusetts Colony, described the whole situation in this short passage:

> "Being thus passed the vast ocean, and a sea of troubles . . . they had now no friends to welcome them, nor inns to entertaine or refresh their weather-beaten bodyes, no houses or much less townes to repair to . . . it was muttered by some that if they got not a place in time they would turn them and their goods ashore [and return] . . . But may not and ought not the children of these fathers rightly say – Our Fathers were Englishmen which came over this great ocean, and were ready to perish in the wilderness, but they cried unto the Lord, and he heard their voice and looked on their adversities." (116)

From the approximately thirty different communities representing England on the *Mayflower,* "the sea voyage across the stormy Atlantic provided a kind of language melting pot in which the regional differences of speech began to intermingle. In the settlement that followed the voices of Kent and Yorkshire and Devon, as well as those of the East Anglian majority, blended together to mark the beginning of American English." (117)

Then came the American Revolution, and the people of this country wanted to separate themselves from those in the old country in every way possible. In 1782, the United States Congress for the first time used the phrase "the American language." The Declaration of Independence is living proof that those who signed it meant every word when they wrote the following:

> "When in the course of human events it becomes necessary for one people to dissolve the political bands which have connected them with another, and to assume among the Powers of the Earth, the separate and

equal station to which the Laws of Nature and of Nature's God entitle them, a decent respect to the opinions of mankind requires that they should declare the causes which impel them to the separation.

We hold these truths to be self-evident: that all men are created equal; that they are endowed by their Creator with certain unalienable rights, that among these are life, liberty and the pursuit of happiness . . ."

California, which became the 31st state in the Union in 1850, "reminds us of the gold-rush words that are now part of everyday speech":

Bonanza: originally a Spanish word meaning *fair weather.*

Diggings: the place where the prospectors mined for gold, abbreviated to *digs.*

El Dorado: the name of the legendary Indian Kingdom of Gold sought by the Spanish in the sixteenth century.

Pan out: the gold would be *panned* in a river, and it was accumulated by *panning out*, which came to mean, generally, *to produce, to be successful.*

Prospector: this was first recorded in 1846, derived from a prospect, a *promising place to search for gold.*

Stake a claim: the process of establishing exclusive rights to mining land, a phrase which goes back, referring to land generally, to the earliest days of White America.

Strike: the Californian Gold Rush spawned a whole family of *strike* phrases – *strike it rich, big strike, lucky strike.*" (Crum et at., 1986, pp. 252-253)

We should also remember that "Language has always been – as the phrase goes – the mirror to society. English of today is no exception. In its world state, it reflects very accurately the crises and contradictions of which it is a part. In Britain, its first home, it has become standardized and centralized in the South, apparently cautious of change. The English of the United States (heard on television, films and radio through the world) has become the voice of the First World in finance, trade and technology."

In the words of Emerson, [. . .] 'Language is a city, to the building of which every human being brought a stone.' " (351)

The English of today is being spread all over the world through mass media, emails, Twitter, LinkedIn, and any other types of electronic messages and social media that people use to communicate with each other and this is the language that ESL is also teaching and propagating.

The English Alphabet

THE ORIGINAL ALPHABET was developed around 2000 B.C. by a Semitic people living in or near Egypt.

A a   The first letter and the first vowel of the alphabet in most of the known languages of the earth. It is the first because it represents the first vocal sound naturally formed by the human organs, being the sound pronounced by a mere opening of the mouth without constraint. It is found in many words uttered by infants. In Hebrew, *am* is "mother" and *ab* is "father." In Arabic, *aba* is "father." In Welsh, *tad* is "father" – from whence we derive "Dad." It is similar to the ancient Greek letter *alpha*, from which it is derived. An earlier ancestor was *aleph*, the first letter of the Phoenician alphabet - also called an *abjad* to be distinguished from a true alphabet. In turn, the ancestor of *aleph* may have been **an ox's head** in scripts influenced by Egyptian hieroglyphs.

B b   The second letter and the first consonant as it is in other languages of the Aryan family spoken in Europe. The sound and character corresponding to the English *b* and the Greek *beta* is the second letter and the first consonant in Phoenician, Arabic, and Coptic. The Greek letter was an adaptation from the Phoenician *beth* meaning **house.** In Hebrew, the letter was called *beth, bet,* or *bayt,* which also means **house.** *B* is called a bilabial from the Latin *labia* for lips. The Semitic *beth,* like the corresponding word in Hebrew, signifies **a house,** to which it has some faint resemblance. Our lowercase *b* shape emerged around the year 500 A.D., when scribes began omitting *B*'s upper loop for the sake of speed.

C c   The third letter and the second consonant came from the Latin, where
        it had the sound of *k*, through the French. The Latin borrowed it from
        the Greek alphabet, where it was represented by *gamma* in the sound of
        /*g*/. The Greeks took it from the Phoenician alphabet, where the letter
        was called *gamel* which meant **camel**. In the Latin alphabet, *c* with its /k/
        sound, was transferred to Anglo-Saxon in all positions: *Cicen* – "chicken"
        – pronounced /kiken/ and *Cild* – "child" – pronounced /kild/.

D d   The fourth letter and the third consonant holds the same place in the
        Hebrew, Samaritan, Greek, and Latin alphabets. In Arabic, it is the
        eighth and in Russian, it is the fifth. The letter was derived from the
        Semitic *daleth* from the logogram of a **fish** or a **door**. The equivalent
        Greek letter is *Delta*. D is a dental articulation formed by placing the end
        of the tongue against the gum just above the upper teeth.

        In Roman times, *D* was called *da* or *de,* but the great English vowel
        shift of the 1400s and 1500s turned the name into "*dee.*"

E e   This letter (developed from the Semitic *he*) is the second vowel and the
        fifth letter. It has the same positions in our alphabet as the corresponding
        sign or character as it had in the Latin, Greek, and Phoenician alphabets,
        from which ours is derived. In Greek *epsilon* – or *e psilon* – means "a
        simple *e.*"

        E is the most common letter (or has the highest frequency) in the
        English language. In the story *The Gold-Bug* by Edgar Allan Poe, a
        character figure deciphers a code by remembering that *e* is the most
        common letter.

F f   The sixth letter (and the fourth consonant) of the alphabet was taken
        from the Latin in both sound and form. The Latin F is derived from Old
        Greek *digamma*, so-called because it resembles two *gammas* in form. The
        Greek *digamma* came from the Phoenician *vav* or *waw*, meaning **peg**
        or **hook**, equivalent in sound to English /w/. The Phoenician form of
        the letter was Y in Greek (also called *upsilon*), which became U, V and
        W in Latin. When the Romans adopted the alphabet, they used V from
        Y not only for the vowel /*u*/ but also form the semivowel /*w*/, leaving F
        available for f.

G g   The seventh letter and the fifth consonant came from the Latin C, which
        had the same power as G, as in *Caius* pronounced *Gaius*. The Latin G or
        C came from the Greek *gamma*, which in its turn came from the Assyrian
        gimel or *gomel*, meaning **camel**, so-called because of its resemblance to
        the neck of a camel. In the Etruscan adaptation of the Greek alphabet,
        this letter was used for both voiceless and voiced /k/ and /g/. When the
        letter came to be used in Latin, the two sounds had to be distinguished
        and, therefore, a stroke was added to the lower curve of C.

H h   The eighth letter and the sixth consonant came into English through the Greek and Latin from the Phoenician, where it has the same position and order as in English. In the Phoenician, the sound is of a rough guttural aspirate, and the letter *Heth* may have been used to stand for a **fence** or **posts**. The Latin and Greek used it as an open breathing before a vowel. In the Greek alphabet, it was first used to express rough breathing (*spiritus asper*) and later became the letter *eta* (H). The name *aitch* is from the French *ache*.

I i   The ninth letter and the third vowel (derived from the Semitic consonant letter *yodh*) came through the Latin and Greek from the Phoenician and probably originated in the Egyptian alphabet. In the Phoenician, the value of *i* was that of a consonant rather than a vowel. The absence of an equivalent consonant in Greek led to its reevaluation to the vowel letter *iota*, I. The dot on the small letter came into use in Greek in the 14th century because other letters were also written with simple vertical strokes, like *n* II and *m* III.

One of the four main vowel letters, *I* is considered the fourth most frequent letter, after E, T, and A. *I* shows up in words like *I*, *is*, and the *–ing* ending, as well as combinations with the letter *e*. No genuine English word ends with *i*, this sound when occurring at the end of a word changing into *y*. It is written, however, in foreign words introduced into English like *alkali*.

J j   The sound of the tenth letter and seventh consonant coincides exactly with that of *g* in *genius*. The sound does not occur in Anglo-Saxon and was introduced through the French. As a character, it was formerly used interchangeably with *i*, both letters having originally the same sound. The separation of these two letters is of comparatively recent date, being brought about through the influence of the Dutch printers.

K k   The eleventh letter and the eighth consonant came from the Semitic *kaph* through the Greek *kappa*, K. It is said to be literally the "**hollow of the hand**" so-called because of its shape. Since it was used interchangeably with *c* in Etruscan, it fell into disuse in Latin. In English, it was introduced after the Norman Conquest, its main function being to distinguish native from Romance origin words. This is how *cyng* became *king*, and *cnif* became *knife*. In the middle and at the end of a word, *ck* represents /*k*/, as in *back*. Before *n*, *k* is silent: *knife, knee*, etc.

L l   This is the twelfth letter and the ninth consonant, derived from the Phoenician **crook** or **goad**, which stood for /l/. It began as a picture of a **stick** or **goad**, a traditional farming tool, used to guide stock, usually oxen. The letter goes back to the Semitic *lamedh* through the Greek *lambda* and may have been based on an Egyptian hieroglyph. The Romans adopted it as the letter L. There is only one sound in English for this letter: *l*ook, *l*ike, cana*l*, etc.

M m The thirteenth letter and the tenth consonant derived from the Phoenician *mem,* via the Greek *mu.* The Semitic *mem* came most likely from a Bronze Age adoption of MEM – the **water** graphic symbol used in Egyptian writing. In Indo-European and Semitic languages, M refers to the principles of **water** and **birth.**

N n The fourteenth letter and the second most frequent consonant comes from one of the Egyptian hieroglyphs: the **fish,** which may have been an **eel** or a **snake.** The Greeks used it for *nu* (N), which derived from *nun* – "fish" in Phoenician, Hebrew, Aramaic, and Arabic. It was introduced to Greek in 740 B.C., and the Romans started to use it around 540 B.C. The snake was used in Egyptian writing to stand for a sound like English /j/ because the Egyptian word for "snake" was *djet.*

O o The fifteenth letter and the fourth vowel, *ayiu* – **the eye** – was a deep throat consonant re-evaluated in Greek to become a vowel they called *omicron.* This vowel is currently used in most languages. The letter O/o looks like the sun disk and symbolizes perfection in many cultures.

P p The sixteenth letter and the twelfth consonant, *Pe* – the **mouth** may have originally been a symbol for the **corner.** The Greeks used it for Pi, and the Romans turned it into P. Most English words beginning with the letter P are of foreign origin, mostly French, Latin, Greek, and Slavic.

Q q The seventeenth letter and the thirteenth consonant came from the Semitic *qop,* which may have been a representation of the **eye of a needle,** a **knot,** or a **monkey** with its tail hanging down. *Qaf* in Arabic meant "nape," and some linguists transcribed this letter as *k.* Q's pairing with *u* is a Latin invention. Q's shape may have come from an Egyptian hieroglyph for a **cord of wool** pronounced *qaw.*

R r The eighteenth letter and the fourteenth consonant, originally came from the Semitic *resh,* the **head.** The Greeks used it for Rho (P), and the Romans added a line to differentiate it from Rho (P) and made it R.

R's growling sound has been associated with dogs. "Geofrey Tory observes in his 1529 book on the alphabet, *Champ Fleury:* 'When dogs are angry, before they begin to bite each other, contracting their throats and grinding their teeth, they seem to be saying R.' " (Sacks, *Language Visible,* 2003, p. 280)

S s The nineteenth letter and the fifteenth consonant came from the Semitic *shin,* the **tooth.** It may have been initially represented by a **bow,** and it was originally pronounced /sh/. The Greeks used it sideways for Sigma (Σ), and the Romans rounded it to make it S. Among the 26 letters, S is considered number 8 in frequency and number 1 as an initial letter. "The shape of the letter 'S' [. . .] was often used as a decorative motif in ancient and primitive art and many examples survive from India, Greece, Rome and elsewhere. Like the spiral, it would appear to symbolize movement in the direction of oneness, whether seen as horizontal or vertical, between Heaven and Earth, the male and female principle, the mountain and the valley, the waves of the sea, gusts of wind, waterspouts and whirlwinds." (J. Chevalier and A. Gheerbant, *The Penguin Dictionary of Symbols*, p. 817)

T t   The twentieth letter is also the most commonly used consonant and the second most common letter in English. Its origin goes back to Semitic *Taw, tav, or taf*, and the Egyptian hieroglyph meaning **mark** that was used by the Greeks for *tau* (T) and by the Romans for *T*. A common digraph is *th*, which occasionally represents the /t/ sound as in *Thomas* or *thyme*. *T* occurs more often at the middle or end of words than at the beginning. That is why the *T* section of a dictionary isn't especially thick.

U u   The twenty-first letter and the fifth vowel of the English alphabet came from the Semitic *waw* through the Greek *upsilon* (Y). Etruscan had its own letter for the same sound, a more pointed V, which came to be used in Latin interchangeably with U. The differentiation between the two developed sometime in Medieval Latin.

V v   The twenty-second letter and the seventeenth consonant comes from the Semitic *waw*, a letter which as Greek *upsilon* (Y) rendered the vowel /u:/ as in "moon." During the Middle Ages, two forms of "v" were used: the more pointed "v" was used at the beginning of a word, while a more rounded "u' appeared in the middle or end of word, no matter how it sounded. After the Norman Conquest of England, it was used to distinguish the /w/ sound of English from the French /v/.

V was born from U (so was W), while J was born from I. The histories of V and J run parallel. Back in A.D. 100 or so, the Romans were doing just fine with 23 letters. The three letters absent were J, W, and V. Around the year 1650, the letters U and V began to be used separately, and by 1700 they were standardized. English 'vee" comes from the letter's French name, *vé*.

W w   The twenty-third letter of the modern English alphabet was created in the Middle Ages to distinguish UU from UV. Different names were used earlier for the same letter: *double u* in English and *double v* in French. The change from VV to W happened gradually, and the new letter was a separate entity by the end of the 14th century. W represents a sound that goes back to the ancient Germanic roots of English. It is a voiced bilabial semivowel – one of the two consonants, the other being Y.

X x The twenty-fourth letter of the English alphabet is derived from the Semitic *waw*, where it had a /t/-like value. This letter represents the /ks/ sound in Etruscan and Latin and is the only letter of the English alphabet to stand for a combination of sounds: /ks/ in words like *text*, /gz/ in words like *example*, and /z/ at the beginning of words like *xenophobia*. In 1895, when German physicist Wilhelm Konrad Rontgen discovered a new radiation, he called it the X-ray because he did not know what it contained. The custom of writing X's for kisses dates from the Middle Ages, when much of the population was illiterate. On legal documents, instead of signing them, people would write an X or the sign of the cross, then kiss the X, to promise to stick to the arrangement. In time, the written X came to mean not the signature, but the kiss.

Y y The twenty-fifth letter of the English alphabet, functioning as a consonant or a vowel. It has the same origin as V and comes from the Semitic C letter *yodh* through the Greek *upsilon* (Y). To differentiate it from V, the lower stem was added, and in some old texts it was written with a left slant. The names of the letter in French is *i-grec* and in Spanish *i griega*, to indicate its origin. The same letter was pronounced /wi/ or /wi:/ in Middle English and then changed to /wai/ during the Great Vowel Shift.

Medieval Y was often dotted, suggesting a form of I. However, the spread of printing in the 1500s made it easy to distinguish between Y and I, although the rivalry between the two letters can be seen in words like *flyer/flier* or *tyre/tire*.

Z z The twenty-sixth letter comes from the Phoenician *Zayin* through the Greek *Zeta*. In Hebrew, *Zayin* looks like an **axe**, as used in the Bible, and *Zayin* means "*weapon.*" In British English, this letter is pronounced /zed/ because it came from the Greek *Zeta*, through the French "zede." In the United States, first recorded in 1677, /zee/ was adopted to be in line with the other letters: "bee," "cee,", "dee," etc.

The "z" sound suggests sleep, bees, or high-flying planes. Although it is distinct from "s" the sound "z" has been awarded the letter "s" in words like *rose, raise,* or *ties.*

(Compiled and adapted from *Websters's Universal Dictionary of the English Language*, 1937, Florian Coulmas, *Writing Systems*, 1999, and David Sacks, *Language Visible*, 2003)

> "It is said that the Holy Roman Emperor Charles V, King of Spain, Archduke of Austria, who was fluent in many languages, spoke 'Spanish to God, Italian to women, and German to my horse.' "
>
> (Quoted by Deutscher, 2010, in his introduction to *Through the Language Glass*)

Language and Culture

Tips

1. Language grows out of culture and represents that culture.
2. Culture is learned and not inherited.
3. A language can easily be explained if we relate it to its culture.

For the ESL classroom, here are some ideas to explain **how culture influences and shapes language:**

1. People in this country like to look into **the future**, plan for it, and if possible, control it. The best example to support this idea is that, unlike many other cultures, we have multiple ways to express the Future Tense:

   Will, Going to, To be to, To be about to, Simple Present, Present Continuous, etc.

   > I *will get back* to you as soon as I can.
   > *Are you going to buy* that car?
   > The President *is to address* the Senate tomorrow.
   > I *leave* for New York tonight.
   > We *are having* the finals two weeks from now.
   > I *am about to leave* right now.

2. Since we are talking about an **active** society, this is reflected in how people use the **passive voice**. There are cases when the native

speakers instinctively avoid the passive voice and replace it with something else:

> This book *is selling* like hot cakes.
> Your car needs *washing.*

3. If we compare cultures, we can safely say that **American English prefers plurals** when other cultures would use a singular form.

Computers *are* useful tools.	American English
A computer *is* a useful tool.	Other cultures

4. Why plurals? Please remember *e pluribus unum.* In other words, *one is many.*

5. The **instinct of possession** gives us forms like "*my* lawyer' or "*my* bank" when in fact other cultures would use completely different structures.

6. Vocabulary – idioms

Business: *a ballpark figure – back to the drawing board – to corner the market, etc.*

Sports: *right off the bat - the ball is in your court now – drop the ball, etc.*

DISCOVER: Ask the students to compare the US values versus counterpart values from a more traditional country:

US Values	Some Other Country's Values
Personal Control over the Environment	Fate
Change	Tradition
Time and Time Control	Human Interaction
Equality	Hierarchy/Rank/Status
Individualism/Privacy	Group Welfare
Self Help	Birthright Inheritance
Competition	Cooperation
Future Orientation	Past Orientation
Action/Work Orientation	"Being" Orientation
Informality	Formality
Directness/Openness/Honesty	Indirect/Ritual/Face
Practicality/Efficiency	Idealism
Materialism/Acquisitiveness	Spiritualism/Detachment

(K. Jason & H. Posner, *Explorations in American Culture*, p. 12)

Language is a means of communication among people. Linguists have tried to decipher the various facets and symbols of language in what can be expressed "in image, idea, feeling, resonance, graphics, but also in what remains unexpressed." The first volume of *Webster*'s edition of 1937 provides a functional approach:

"Language consists of utterance of sounds which usage has made the representatives of ideas. When two or more persons customarily annex the same sounds to the same ideas, the expression of these sounds by one person communicates his ideas to another. This is the primary sense of language, the use of which is to communicate thee thoughts of one person to another through the organs of hearing. Articulate sounds are represented by letters, marks, or characters, which form words." (p. 938)

A more descriptive approach comes from Jean Chevalier and Alain Gheerbrant:

"Language is a symbol of intelligent entities, be they individuals, cities, ethnic groups or nation states. In this context, by language is meant strictly written or spoken language or dialect which is one of the countless forms of language and one of the components of intellectual or social structures. A deep reality resides in the relation between language and the individual. Together they develop and together they preserve all their common experiences. Language is the soul of cultures and societies. Thoughtless harm inflicted upon language affects society as a whole, damaging roots of its bonding and helping to sever them. Language is, in fact, an intellectual and social structure. It is the main channel of communication between one individual and another and between group and group. It is the most highly refined and subtle means o exchange and interfusion. It transmits a measure of unity to the individual and it is a socially cohesive factor. Societies break up when they abandon or weaken their language, and this is why ethnic minorities endeavor to preserve their languages as emblems of their own identity. [. . .] Knowledge of languages bonds its possessor with the individual or group. To attack a language is to attack an individual; to respect a language is to respect the person who speaks it."

(*A Dictionary of Symbols*, 1996, pp. 591-592)

According to *Encyclopedia Britannica*/Macropedia (1986), "Language interacts with every other aspect of human life in society, and it can be understood only if it is considered in relation to society. [. . .] Because each language is both a working system of communication in the period and in the community wherein it is used and also the product of its past history and the source of its future development, any account of language must consider it from both these points of view." (566) In other words, **language and culture** go hand in hand, with a historical background that verifies and validates that language grows out of culture and represents that culture. Over time, linguists have defined languages based on the knowledge that human beings use language to express themselves, to impart information, to talk about their feelings and emotions, in other words – to communicate. Encyclopedia Britannica devoted approximately 250 pages to "Language and Languages of the world." The *Macropedia* section of *Britannica* included in its content a plethora of topics, such as characteristics of language, language variants, physiological and physical basis of speech, meaning and style in language, language and culture, and last but not least, linguistic change. In the first chapter entitled *Characteristics of language*, Britannica provides a thorough background of what language is.

"Many definitions of language have been proposed. Henry Sweet, an English phonetician and language scholar, stated: 'Language is the expression of ideas by means of speech-sounds combined into words. Words are combined into sentences, this combination answering to that of ideas into thoughts.' The U.S. linguists Bernard Bloch and George L. Trager formulated the following the following definition in their *Outline of Linguistic Analysis* (1942): 'A language is a system of arbitrary vocal systems by means of which a social group cooperates.' Definitions like these and, indeed, any succinct definitions make a number of presuppositions and beg a number of questions. The first, for example, puts excessive weight on 'thought,' and the second uses 'arbitrary' in a specialized, though legitimate, way." (566)

In his book entitled *Through the Language Glass*, Guy Deutscher made a remarkable assertion in his subtitle: *Why the World Looks Different in Other Languages*. In his prologue, the author says:

"A nation's language, so we are often told, reflects its culture, psyche, and modes of thought. Peoples in tropical climes are so laid-back it's no wonder they let most of their consonants fall be the wayside. And one need only compare the mellow sounds of Portuguese with the sharpness of Spanish to understand the quintessential difference between these two neighboring cultures. [...]

Philosophers of all persuasions and nationalities have lined up to proclaim that each language reflects the qualities of the nation that speaks it. In the seventeenth century, the Englishman Francis Bacon explained that one can infer 'significant marks of the genius and manners of people and nations from their languages.' 'Everything confirms,' agreed the Frenchman Etienne de Condillac a century later, 'that each language expresses the character of the people who speak it.' His younger contemporary, the German Johann Gottfried Herder, concurred that 'the intellect and the character of every nation are stamped in its language.' Industrious nations, he said, 'have an abundance of moods in their verbs, while more refined nations have a large amount of nouns that have been exalted to abstract notions.' In short, 'the genius of a nation is nowhere better revealed than in the physiognomy of its speech.' The American Ralph Waldo Emerson summed it all up in 1844: 'We infer the spirit of the nation in great measure from the language, which is a sort of monument to which each forcible individual in a course of many hundred years has contributed a stone.' " (3)

Coming from a completely different culture, I soon found myself in an environment that made me think deeper and deeper if I was to really comprehend the new values all around me. Merriam-Webster Dictionary defines **culture** as being "the customary beliefs, social forms, and material traits of a racial, religious, or social group." www.merriam-webster.com During my teaching career I was inspired by many textbooks regarding culture, but one which stood the test of time, at least for myself, was *Explorations in American Culture (Readings for Critical Thinking, Writing, and Discussion)* by Kathrine Jason and Holly Posner. Their introduction is using E. A. Hobell's definition of culture: "the integrated system of learned behavior of the members of a society which are characteristic of those members and which are not the results of biological inheritance." What this definition implies is that **culture is learned and not inherited**. (2)

If we go online, we find lots and lots of definitions of **culture**. In 2017, Kim Ann Zimmerman, Live Science Contributor, presented her own point of view and added that the Center for Advance Research on Language Acquisition goes even further.

"Culture encompasses religion, food, what we wear, how we wear it, our language, marriage, music, what we believe is right or wrong, how we sit at the table, how we greet visitors, how we behave with loved ones, and a million other things," Christina De Rossi, an anthropologist at Barnet and Southgate College in London, said: The word 'culture' derives from a French term, which in turn derived from the Latin '*colere*,' which means *to tend to the earth and grow*, or *cultivation and nurture*. It shares its etymology with a number of other words related to actively fostering growth." www.amp.livescience.com

In 1984, L. Robert Kohls, Executive Director at the Washington International Center in Washington, D.C., came up with a list of 13 values he thought Americans live by. Kohls' interpretation is that "Americans tend to think they have been only slightly influenced by family, church or schools." The general idea is that people in this country think these values are very positive ones. As an ESL student and teacher, I found these values inspiring, and I did my best to introduce them to my students as such. These are those 13 American Values described by Robert Kohls:

1. *Personal Control over the Environment*
2. *Change*
3. *Time and Its Control*
4. *Equality and Egalitarianism*
5. *Individualism and Privacy*
6. *Self-Help Concept*
7. *Competition and Free Enterprise*
8. *Future Orientation*
9. *Action/Work Orientation*
10. *Informality*
11. *Directness, Openness and Honesty*
12. *Practicality and Efficiency*
13. *Materialism/Acquisitiveness"* (pp. 5-12)

What I did was to ask my students to tell me how they understood these concepts and, if they differed from their own culture values, make a quick comparison by using their own personal life experiences. In most cases, my students found these American Values helpful in understanding literary texts during the semester and agreed with me that we should be the ones to choose which values we want to live our own lives by. One example we discussed in detail was **Time and Its Control,** and we emphasized the idea that time, for the average American, is of utmost importance. Punctuality came to be a major issue, and we debated why it is so rude to be late for an appointment in the United States.

In 1984, Jacques Barzun published an essay entitled *What if-? English versus German and French*, in which he analyzed the similarities and differences between English and the other two languages. The whole essay is a delightful pleasure, and we only need to take a quick look at the beginning:

"I am asked what I think would have happened if our national language were German instead of English. My first impulse is to retort: 'Why, *isn't* it German?' I think of the thick layers of abstract jargon we carry on top of our heads, of the incessant urge to rename everything in roundabout phrases (Personal Armor System = the new army helmet), of the piling up of modifiers before the noun (easy-to-store safety folding ironing board), of the evil passion for agglutinating half-baked ideas into single terms (*surprizathon* = advertising goods by lottery) and I can only grudgingly concede: 'True, it isn't German, but some of it is more German than English.'

Had the Pilger Fathers brought with them the pure Platt-Deutsch of their time, all might have been well. After separation from its source and under stress of the hard frontier life, the language would have melted and clarified like butter, lost its twisted shapes and hard corners, and become a model of lucidity and force. What only the greatest German writers – Goethe, Schopenhauer, Nietzsche, and a few others – managed to do by main strength in their prose would have been done anonymously by everybody in Massachusetts and in the wagons crossing the plains. Tough characters like Thoreau, Lincoln, Mark Twain, and Ambrose Bierce would not have tolerated the stacking of clause within clause of yard-long words, uncaring whether meaning comes out at the other end. They were articulate beings and they articulated their thoughts – as we are doing less and less every day.

For on our former, flexible and clear Anglo-Latin-French, which we call American English, the uberwaltigend academic fog has descended and we grope about, our minds damp and moving in circles. Similar forms of the blight have struck the other languages of Western civilization, with the inevitable result of a growing inability to think sharp and straight about anything – whence half of our 'prahblems.'

Had the good forthright people who built this country in the last century met this verbal miasma on landing here, they would have either perished soon from suffocation or made tracks for the open air of Canada, which would now number 210 million. Make no mistake: syntax can change the course of history." (*The Oxford Book of Essays*, 1991, pp. 544-545)

Language itself is part of culture and language teachers should study the history of English to be better prepared in understanding and absorbing the development of what is now the 21st century English. The educators at the beginning of this century may know the intricacies of the English language and how to teach the basic language skills, but going back in history is going to elucidate and clarify many of the questions we might have to answer when we go into the classroom. Sometimes students may ask why certain letters are not pronounced, or why there are so many tenses in English. Grammar books have a plethora of information, and teachers only need to guide the students through the tomes presented to them. However, a good teacher should get all the ammunition possible so classroom instruction does not become embarrassing when students come up with unexpected questions. **The most difficult questions may become starting points for future lesson plans**, unless the answers can be provided right away.

Methodology

GENERAL OVERVIEW OF STUDENTS' MAJOR NEEDS

ESL students in the same class may be coming from different countries. Although the curriculum might be the same for everyone, ESL instructors should be aware that our students are separate entities, and we should treat them according to their needs. Here are some suggestions:

Asian students:

Pronunciation of /l/ vs. /r/ (for example, *light* vs. *right*)

The "l" sound has the same pronunciation at the beginning, middle, or end of a word. The tongue is up behind the top front teeth.

The "r" sound is pronounced with the tongue curled up but not touching the roof of the mouth.

Try: Make the students aware of the place of articulation.

Pronunciation of fricatives /f/ vs /v/ (for example, *fine* vs. *vine)*

Fricatives may be voiced (vocal chords vibrating during the articulation) and voiceless (vocal chords not vibrating). Besides /f/ and /v/, the English language also has /s/ as in *sitter*, /z/ as in zebra, and the /th/ sounds in words like *think* and *this.*

Try: Michael Sudlow, *Exercises in American English Pronunciation*

Pronunciation of diphthongs (two vowels in one syllable)

For example: *aisle, bear, noise, like, stone, brown, hear*, etc.

Try: M. Hewings, S. Goldstein, *Pronunciation Plus*, Cambridge University Press
www.netfind.com/ESL+Diphthongs

Missing prepositions

(for example,   *I go back Boston.*   *I got up nine o'clock.*
                 I go back to Boston.   *I got up at nine o'clock.*

Suggestion: Make the students aware and use Immediate Corrective Response

Transitive vs. Intransitive verbs

Transitive verbs are followed by an object whereas intransitive verbs are not.

For example:

>*Mike played football last weekend.* (transitive)
>*Mike played well last weekend.* (intransitive)

You will find lists in Clark, Moran and Burrows, *ESL Miscellany*, Pro Lingua

Try: This guidebook, pp. 260-261

Connotation and inference

A word may have implied meanings. *Cheap* is not only *less expensive*, but may also imply *low quality*. The implied meaning is also known as **connotation**.

We sometimes use evidence and/or logic to form an opinion; in other words, we make an **inference**: *"Mockingbirds don't do one thing but make music for us to enjoy . . . but sing their heart out for us. That's why it's a sin to kill a mockingbird."* (Harper Lee, *To Kill a Mockingbird*)

Try: Sandra Silberstein, *Reader's Choice*, Michigan University Press
   This guidebook, pp. 171-179

Parallel structures

(for example,   **Tokyo is clean and safety.*
                     Tokyo is clean and safe.
                     *I like swimming and to ski in the mountains.
                     I like swimming and skiing in the mountains.)

Try: This guide book, p. 318

Even vs. **even if** vs. **even though**

Even is used to emphasize a word or words: **Even** *a child can describe a car.*
Even can emphasize *if*: *We'll take the test **even if** you are not prepared.*
Even though is used to replace *although*:

>*I enjoyed the movie **even though** it was long.*

*My teacher got so angry, even she told me to leave the classroom.
My teacher got so angry, she even told me to leave the classroom.

>**You must answer the question even you think it's personal.*
>*You must answer the question even if you think it's personal.*
>>**Even she can't drive, she bought a car.*
>>*Even though she can't drive, she bought a car.*

Try: This guide book, p. 283

Arabic students

Spelling and basic writing skills (for example, missing vowels)
Suggestion: free writing exercises combined with imitations of sentences to develop the habit of writing.

Try: Linda Jeffries, *Reading Power* 1, 2, 3, Pearson

Double reference
(for example,   *This is the book I was talking about it.*
                 This is the book I was talking about.)

Suggestion: Use Immediate Corrective Response/Quick grammar review

Pronunciation of bilabials /p/ vs /b/ (for example, *park vs. bark*)
The voiceless /p/ and voiced /b/ sounds are pronounced using both lips.

Fricatives /f/ vs /v/ (for example, *ferry* vs *very*)
Try: A. Baker and S. Goldstein, *Pronunciation Pairs*, Cambridge U. Press

Missing BE verb:
(for example,   *He happy.*   *He coming.*
                 He is happy.   *He is coming.*)

Try: Raymond Murphy, *Grammar in Use*, Cambridge University Press

Misuse of *too*
(for example,   *He is too smart.*
                 He is very smart.)

Misuse of time phrases:
(for example,   *before two years ago*
                 two years ago)

Suggestion: Make the students aware and encourage self-correction.

Incorrect use of *Wish:*
(for example,   *I wish if I can go tonight.*
                 I wish I could go tonight.)

Try: Raymond Murphy, *Grammar in Use*, Cambridge University Press

Portuguese/Brazilian students:

L1 Interference/Language transfer
Some students apply knowledge from one language to another.

Have vs. **there is/are**
(for example,   *Have many people in this classroom.*

There are many people in this classroom.
*Have a parade today?
Is there a parade today?)

Try: Immediate corrective response/Quick grammar review Raymond
       Murphy, *Grammar in Use*, Cambridge University Press

Pronunciation of –ed in the Past and Past Participle
-ed can be pronounced /id/ in verbs ending in /t/ and/d/- *wanted, added*
                            /t/ in verbs ending in /p/, /k/, s/, /sh/, /ch/, /f/ - *asked*
                            /d/ in verbs ending in vowels, /b/, /g/, /z/ - *enjoyed*

For a more complete presentation, please check this guidebook, p. 399

Pronunciation of /r/ in frontal position: *Rosemary* becomes *Hosemary

Final /l/ **sound becomes** /w/ *Brazil* becomes *Brazew
Suggestion: Encourage the student to pronounce carefully this sentence: *The
student from Brazil left.* Point out that the /l/ in *Brazil* should sound the same
as the /l/ in *left.*

Try: Michael Sudlow, *Exercises in American English Pronunciation*

Tendency to pronounce all the letters although some are silent
Office – looked – walk - talk

Try: This guidebook p. 119

The sound /d/ is mispronounced: *divide* become *givide
Suggestion: Immediate Corrective Response/Quick grammar review

The *th* **sounds (voiced and voiceless) do not exist in Portuguese. They are
replaced by** /s/ **and** /z/ **instead.**

Try: A. Baker and S. Goldstein, *Pronunciation Pairs*, Cambridge U. Press

Chinese students

Pronunciation of diphthongs (*taste* vs. *test)* **and vowels** /a/ vs /e/
Try: Michael Sudlow, *Exercises in American English Pronunciation*

Pronunciation of /l/ vs. /r/ *surprise* vs. *supplies*
The "l" sound has the same pronunciation at the beginning, middle, or end of a
word. The tongue is up behind the top front teeth.

The "r" sound is pronounced with the tongue curled up but not touching the
roof of the mouth.

Try: Make the students aware of the place of articulation.

PA Announcement on a bus: *Please exit through the <u>rear</u> door.*
Student: *Is there a fake door?*

Pronunciation of /l/ vs. /n/ *fall* becomes **fawn,* and *fault* becomes **faunt*
Suggestion: Immediate Corrective Response

Short vs long vowels (for example, *heal* vs. *hill*)
Try: A. Baker and S. Goldstein, *Pronunciation Pairs*, Cambridge U. Press

Comparatives: (for example, **more easier vs. easier*)

Question formation
(for example,   **How to do this?*
                          How do we do this?)

Suggestion: Make the students aware and encourage self-correction.

Misuse of modal formation
(for example,   **You must to do your homework.*
                          You must do your homework.
                          *Henry should to study harder.
                          Henry should study harder.)

Beginning conversation with *Because . . .*

Fragmented sentences with *because: Because I love pizza.*
Suggestion: Immediate Corrective Response/Quick grammar review

Incorrect use of Subjunctive
(For example,   **I recommend that he does something.*
                          *I recommend that he to do something.
                          *I recommend that he has to do something.
                          I recommend he do something.)

Suggestion: Immediate Corrective Response/Quick grammar review

Comma splice
(for example,   **She is from Brazil, she is very smart.*
                          She is from Brazil and she is very smart.)

Function words/using *I* **instead of** *IT*
(for example,   **I am difficult to speak.*
                          It is difficult for me to speak.)

Suggestion: Make the students aware and encourage self-correction.

Sentence structure

(for example, **I love pizza is delicious.*
I love pizza. It is delicious.
This pizza is delicious. I love it.)

Suggestion: Make the students aware and encourage self-correction.

Incorrect use of tenses, especially Present Perfect/missing the Simple Past

Chinese verbs do not change tenses; a time expression is used instead.
Try: Betty Azar, *Fundamentals of English Grammar*, Longman

Word order

(for example, **Good student is my friend.*
My friend is a good student.)

Try: Manik Joshi, *English Sentence Exercises. Word Order in Sentences*

French students

Aspirated vs. non-aspirated consonants: *hungry* vs. *angry*
The disappearing *h* in *home* and *horse*
The glottal fricative /h/ does not exist in French.
Student A: *I am very angry now.*
Student B: *Are you angry or hungry?*
French students have problems articulating the vowel sounds in minimal pairs.

Try: A. Baker and S. Goldstein, *Pronunciation Pairs*, Cambridge U. Press

Order of adjectives

(for example, **the dress red*   **the children smart*
the red dress   *the smart children*)

Try: Phil Williams, *Word Order in English Sentences*

Pronunciation of voiced and voiceless dental fricatives /th/

(for example, *th*an or wea*th*er; *th*ink or you*th*)
Try: Michael Sudlow, *Exercises in American English Pronunciation*

Pronunciation of open vowels (*cat* vs. *cart*, *ham* vs. *harm*)
Try: Gertrude Orion, *Pronouncing American English*, Heinle

Tenses

(for example, **I have played tennis yesterday.*
I played tennis yesterday.
*We will talk when we will meet tomorrow.
We will talk when we meet tomorrow.)

Suggestion: Quick tense review with a focus on time and *if* clauses

Word order

(for example,   **I like very much to ski.*
I like to ski very much.
*Do you know what is the time?
Do you know what time it is?)

Try: Raymond Murphy, *Grammar in Use*, Cambridge University Press
Phil Williams, *Word Order in English Sentences*

Word stress   *French words are stressed on the last syllable.*
Suggestion: Make the students aware that word stress in English is not fixed.
Try: Linda Grant, *Well Said*, Heinle

German students

Pronunciation

(for example,   *coat* may sound like *caught*
bone may sound like *born*)

German speakers of English do not use the diphthong in *so* or *coat*.
The /th/ sound in *three* is pronounced /s/; /th/ in *there* is replaced by /z/.

Try: Michael Sudlow, *Exercises in American English Pronunciation*

Mispronunciation of initial /w/: *we* sounds like **ve* and *wine* sounds like **vine.*
Suggestion: Make the students aware and encourage self-correction.

To do vs. **to make**

(for example,   **I have to **make** my homework.*
*I have **to do** my homework.*)
Try: This guidebook, p. 107

Question formation

(for example,   **What means "antihistamine?"*
What does "antihistamine" mean?)
Try: Betty Azar, *Understanding and Using English Grammar*, Pearson

Prepositions

(for example,   **I work **by** Deutsche Bank.*
I work (in a building) near Deutsche Bank.
** I have lived here **since** 3 years.*
I have lived here for 3 years.)

Try: Tom Cole, *The Preposition Book*, Michigan University Press

Faux amis/false friends

(*cheff* vs. *boss*, *become* vs. *receive*, *actual* vs. *current*)
Try: *Longman Advanced Dictionary of American English*

Conditionals

(for example, **If I would make more money, I would travel more.*

If I made more money, I would travel more.)

Try: Martin Hewitt, *Advanced Grammar in Use*, Cambridge University Press

Raymond Murphy, *Grammar in Use*, Cambridge University Press

Indian students

Pronunciation of /v/ vs. /w/, /f/ vs. /v/

vet vs. *wet*, *fast* vs. *vast*

As vs. Like   *Like* = similar to   *As* = in the role of

*She is dressed **like** a princess.*   *He works **as** a teacher.*

Try: This guide book, pp. 308, 390

Some speakers confuse *she* **with** *see*

Try: Michael Sudlow, *Exercises in American English Pronunciation*

Parallel Structures

Parallelism is the use of similar structures that are grammatically the same. For example:

"In matters of principle, **stand like a roc**k; in matters of taste, **swim with the current**." Thomas Jefferson

Try: This guidebook, p. 318

Connotation and inference

A word may have implied meanings. *Cheap* is not only *less expensive*, but may also imply *low quality*. The implied meaning is also known as **connotation**.

We sometimes use evidence and/or logic to form an opinion; in other words, we make an **inference**: *"Mockingbirds don't do one thing but make music for us to enjoy . . . but sing their heart out for us. That's why it's a sin to kill a mockingbird."* (Harper Lee, *To Kill a Mockingbird*)

Report: "Mary Smith didn't get in until three last Saturday night."

Inference: "I bet she was out fooling around!"

Try: Sandra Silberstein, *Reader's Choice*, Michigan University Press

Japanese students

Pronunciation of consonant clusters /st/, /fr/, /cr/, /sk/, /sp/, /nt/, /nd/, /tl/, etc.

(for example,   **Macu Donaldu*   **boy furendo*   **bottol*

MacDonald,   *boy-friend*   *bottle*)

Try: Michael Sudlow, *Exercises in American English Pronunciation*

Pronunciation of /f/ **vs.** /h/ (for example, *childfood* vs. *childhood*)
In Japanese /h/ is pronounced the same as /f/.

Try: A. Baker and S. Goldstein, *Pronunciation Pairs*, Cambridge University Press

Michael Sudlow, *Exercises in American English Pronunciation*

Almost **vs.** *Most*
(for example,   **Almost Japanese like sushi.*
                    Most Japanese like sushi.)
Almost describes quantifiers and shows approximation, whereas *most* describes nouns and shows majority.

Try: This guidebook, p. 288

Incorrect use of endings: *-ed* **vs** *–ing*
(for example,   **I am exciting!*
                    I am excited!)

Try: Betty Azar, *Understanding and Using English Grammar*, Pearson

Missing prepositions
(for example,   **I go back Japan.*
                    I go back to Japan.)

Try: Betty Azar, *Understanding and Using English Grammar*, Pearson

Korean students

Pronunciation of word endings
(for example,   *How are you*? sounding
                    like *How~ are~ you~~,*)

Try: Anne Cook, *American Accent Training*, Barron's Educational Series

Voiced vs. Voiceless sounds (for example, *robe* vs. *rope, rude* vs. *root*)
Try: A. Baker and S. Goldstein, *Pronunciation Pairs*, Cambridge U. Press

Pronunciation of sibilants – fricative consonant sounds: /s/, /z/, /sh/, /zh/
Student A: *Do you know *Chuper Mario?*
Student B: *No, but I do know Super Mario.*
Suggestion: Immediate Corrective Response

Word order: using the object before the predicate
(for example,   **I homework did last night*
                    I did my homework last night.)

Try: Phil Williams, *Word Order in English Sentences*

Overuse of *"the"* **article for names of cities, people, and countries**

Incorrect use of *"a/an"* **articles**
Suggestion: Immediate Corrective Response/Quick grammar review

Latino students

Pronunciation of sibilants (/s/ vs /z/**) and bilabials** /p/ vs/ /b/

Try: Michael Sudlow, *Exercises in American English Pronunciation*

Missing subjects
(for example,   **I want to study English because is necessary.*
                             I want to study English because it is necessary.)

Try: Martin Hewitt, *Advanced Grammar in Use*, Cambridge Univ. Press

Overuse of commas resulting in run-on sentences
Suggestion: free writing exercises to develop the habit of writing

Present Perfect vs. Simple Past
(for example,   **I have eaten pizza last week)*
                             I ate pizza last week.)

Try: Betty Azar, *Understanding and Using English Grammar*, Pearson

Word order
(for example,   **Why you don't write this on the board?*
                             Why don't you write this on the board?)

Try: Phil Williams, *Word Order in English Sentences*

Sentence stress
"In Spanish every syllable is stressed, whereas in English only 1 or 2 syllables are stressed and everything else becomes weaker or shorter."

Try: www.pronunciationstudio.com

To do vs. **to make** – Romance languages have one word for *Do* and *Make*.
Try: This guidebook, p. 107

To remind vs. **to remember; to lose** *vs.* **to miss; to rent** vs **to loan**
Try: *Longman Advanced Dictionary of American English*

Faux amis/False friends
Library is not *Libreria*; *embarrassed* is not *embarazada*

Misuse of adverbs vs. adjectives

(for example,   *I want to speak English good.*
                   I want to speak English well.)

Suggestion: Make your students aware and encourage self-correction.

Subject + predicate agreement

(for example,   *People is leaving the room now.*
                   People are leaving the room now.)

Suggestion: Immediate Corrective Response/Quick grammar review

Russian (and other Slavic) Students

The verb TO BE – articles - tenses
There are only 3 tenses and no definite or indefinite articles in Russian.
Try: Raymond Murphy, *Grammar in Use*, Cambridge University Press

Sentence structure (for example, *Dark!* meaning *It is dark!*)
Suggestion: Immediate Corrective Response/Quick grammar review

Pronunciation of voiced and voiceless dental fricatives /*th*/

(for example, *than* or wea*th*er; *th*ink or you*th*)
Try: Michael Sudlow, *Exercises in American English Pronunciation*

Simple Present vs. Present Continuous

(for example, *I study English.* vs. *I am studying English.*)
Try: Betty Azar, *Understanding and Using English Grammar*, Pearson

Thai students

Pronunciation in general: /*ch*/ as in *church* becomes /*sh*/ or /*s*/
Try: Michael Sudlow, *Exercises in American English Pronunciation*

Pronunciation of /*l*/ vs. /*r*/   *led* vs. *red*
Try: A. Baker and S. Goldstein, *Pronunciation Pairs*, Cambridge U. Press

Pronunciation of consonant clusters /*dr*/, /*sm*/, /*kr*/, etc.

(for example, *drive* becomes *derive)*
Suggestion: Immediate Corrective Response/Quick grammar review

Like the French, Thai students tend to stress the words on the last syllable.

Try: Judy Gilbert, *Clear Speech*, Cambridge University Press
        Gertrude Orion, *Pronouncing American English*, Heinle

Turkish students

Pronunciation of voiced and voiceless dental fricatives /th/
(for example, *th*an or wea*th*er; *th*ink or you*th*)
Try: Michael Sudlow, *Exercises in American English Pronunciation*

Pronunciation of dipthongs – there are no dipthongs in Turkish
Pain is pronounced like /pah-een/
Try: Michael Sudlow, *Exercises in American English Pronunciation*

Pronunciation: Missing the *–s* **ending**
Suggestion: Immediate Corrective Response/Quick grammar review

Pronunciation of silent letters (for example, *doubt, debt*, etc.)
There are no silent letters in Turkish.
Try: This guidebook, p. 119

Pronunciation of words beginning with *w* **vs.** *v. (winery – vineyard)*

Punctuation – The use of the comma, for example.
In Turkish the comma is used in a completely different way.
Try: This guidebook, p. 341

To say vs. to tell
(for example,   **My friend said me . . .*
                 My friend told me . . . /My friend said to me . . .)
Try: This guidebook, p. 105

Incorrect use of tenses
(for example,   **We know each other since high school.*
                 We have known each other since high school.

Try: Raymond Murphy, *Grammar in Use*, Cambridge University Press

Omitting prepositions
(for example,   **John was school this morning.*
                 John was in school this morning.)

Instead of prepositions, Turkish uses suffixes added to words.
Suggestion: Immediate Corrective Response/Quick grammar review

Word stress: Words are stressed on the last syllable in Turkish.
Some names of places like *Ankara* or *Izmir* are stressed on the first syllable.
Try: Gertrude F. Orion, *Pronouncing American English: Sounds, Stress, and Intonation*, Cengage Learning

ESL students should know that there are **false friends**, or **faux amis** (first used in 1929 to mean *false friends of a translator*), also called **deceptive words, treacherous twins, belles infidels** - words in two languages that look or sound similar, when in fact they may differ considerably. For example, *chat* in French means *cat*, *bras* means *arm*, etc. *Actual* in Spanish means *real*, *lecture* might be misunderstood as *reading*. *Gift* in German means *poison* and in Norwegian it means *married*.

Most ESL students seem to have the same problems:

Incorrect wording or formulation:

*Every people	*too much people	*every days I go
*discussing about	*mention about	*in these days
*What means . . .?	*He came to here . . .	
*Vocabularies	*Just I want to know	*and etc

Incorrect word choice:

especially vs. **specially**	**affect** vs. **effect**
so vs. **too**	**too** vs. very
thing vs. **think**	**hard** vs. **hardly**
grow vs. **grow up**	

Misuse of grammar rules: Missing *-s /-es* **in the third person sg.**
(for example: *He **go** to school.
                   He **goes** to school.)

Depending on the frequency of the mistakes, teachers should be able to make the students aware of their mistakes and encourage self-correction. Avoid making too many corrections, but instead develop mini-lesson plans for the whole class later on. And it's always a good idea to encourage the other students in class to provide the necessary adjustments or revisions.

(Compiled together with Jenk Aral, John Artise, Calliopi Bertos, Peter Campisi, Maria Catamero, Jason Chase, Dr. Clyde Coreil, Danielle DeKoker, Melissa Kaufman, Laura Lee Lafortezza, Thomas Seo, Craig Stephens, David Stock, Evina Torres, and Elina Yasinov, 2018)

Immediate Corrective Feedback (ICF)

"One of most successful techniques in teaching ESL is to immediately correct a student's response right after the elocution of a word, phrase, or complete sentence."

As soon as the teacher detects the error, he/she articulates the <u>correct</u> response and leads the student to render the correct response by the use of well-timed, <u>positive</u> verbal and, sometimes, visual reinforcers such as:

a. Verbal: "yes," "very good," "correct," "excellent," "very nice," etc.

b. Visual: thumbs up, a big smile, a 2-3 second nodding of the head, etc.

IF the student is still not giving the correct response, the teacher repeats the process by guiding the student through each word of the phrase or sentence.

Here is an example:

The student is responding to questions asked by the teacher on a chapter already read by the student in a book about ancient Rome's battles with Carthage.

<u>Teacher</u>: "What did General Scipio finally do to defeat the Carthaginian army?"

<u>Student</u>: "The General *<u>carried on</u> his plans to conquer Hannibal's army."

<u>Teacher</u>: "You mean, General Scipio carried **OUT** his plans to conquer Hannibal's army. Please repeat your answer with **CARRIED OUT, not CARRIED ON.**"

<u>Student</u>: "The General **carried out** his plans to conquer Hannibal."

<u>Teacher</u>: (nodding his head a couple of times and smiling with 'thumbs up') **Excellent! Very Good!**

By using this technique, the tendency for the student to remember the correct response is greatly increased.

ICF Used in Pronunciation Correction

A difficulty for most Koreans is the English pronunciation of the **"F"** sound (fricative). They tend to pronounce the "F" as a **"P"** sound (plosive).

"***P**ill my glass, please", "I want to buy a birthday *gi**p**t for my wife."

"I am *a**p**raid to drive in the heavy rain."

Using ICF, the teacher should demonstrate the "F" sound by moving his/her front teeth and tongue in the ready position to make the fricative sound of the designated word.

'I am a**F**raid to drive in the heavy rain also. I am **F**rightened when I hear thunder also. Now, you repeat these words after me:

'**F**ederal,' 'Be**f**ore,' '**F**ill my glass with more lemonade, please .' (John Artise, 2018)

> "Experience is the best teacher."
>
> Julius Caesar

OVER THE CENTURIES, language teachers have been trying to organize their classroom activities so their students may benefit from their knowledge and learn the skills necessary to communicate and to understand each other. At the beginning of the 21ˢᵗ century, the communicative approach was the talk of the town, but other approaches have also been used and achieved excellent results. The curriculum always changes and the expectations also grow as our society has become so dependent on social media, mass media, and other forms of communication.

Alice Omaggio Hadley, in her book entitled *Teaching Language in Context* (1993), argues that before we talk about the communicative approach, we must go back in time and analyze the "traditional" methods of teaching a foreign language: The Grammar-Translation Method, The Direct Method, and the Audiolingual Methodology.

The Grammar-Translation Method: "Mental Discipline"

The author mentions that the grammar-translation approach was used to teach Latin and Greek and had the following characteristics:

1. "Students first learned the rules of grammar and bilingual lists of vocabulary pertaining to the reading and readings of the lesson. Grammar was learned deductively by means of long and elaborate explanations. All rules were learned with their exceptions and irregularities explained in grammatical terms.

2. Once rules and vocabulary were learned, prescriptions for translating the exercises that followed the grammar explanations were given.

3. Comprehension of the rules and readings was tested via translation (target language to native language and vice versa). Students had learned the language if they could translate the passages well.

4. The native and target languages were constantly compared. The goal of instruction was to convert L1 into L2 and vice versa, using a dictionary if necessary.

5. There were very few opportunities for listening and speaking practice (with the exception of reading passages and sentences aloud), since the method concentrated on reading and translation exercises. Much of the class time devoted to talking *about* the language; virtually no time was spent talking *in* the language." (90)

The Direct Method: A Rational Perspective on Language Learning

Originally developed in the 19th century by Berlitz, this method had (and we believe it still has) the following characteristics:

1. Language learning should start with the here-and-now, utilizing classroom objects and simple actions. Eventually, when students have learned enough language, lessons move on to include common situations and settings.

2. The direct method lesson often develops around specially constructed pictures depicting life in the country where the target language is spoken. These pictures enable the teacher to *avoid the use of translation,* which is strictly forbidden in the classroom. Definitions of new vocabulary are given via *paraphrases* in the target language, or by miming the action or manipulating objects to get the meaning across.

3. From the beginning of instruction, students hear complete and meaningful sentences in simple discourse, which often takes the form of question-answer exchanges.

4. Correct pronunciation is an important consideration in this approach, and emphasis is placed upon the development of accurate pronunciation from the beginning of instruction. Phonetic notation is often used to achieve this goal.

5. Grammar rules are not explicitly taught; rather, they are assumed to be learned through practice. Students are encouraged to form their own generalizations about grammar through *inductive* methods. When grammar is explicitly taught, it is taught in the target language.

6. Reading goals are also reached via the 'direct' understanding of text without the *use of dictionaries or translations."* (Based on Rivers, 1981, pp.31-35.) (92-93)

Audiolingual Methodology: An Empirical Perspective on Language Learning

The major characteristics (also known as 'empirical laws learning') of this method, according to Alice Omaggio Hadley, can be found in Lado (1964) and his *Language Teaching: A Scientific Approach*:

1. *The fundamental law of contiguity* states that when two experiences have occurred together, the return of one will recall or reinstate the other.

2. *The law of exercise* maintains that the more frequently a response is practiced, the better it is learned and the longer it is remembered.

3. *The law of intensity* states that the more intensely a response is practiced, the better it is learned and the longer it will be remembered.

4. *The law of assimilation* states that each new stimulating condition tends to elicit the same response that has been connected with similar stimulating conditions in the past.

5. *The law of effect* maintains that when a response is accompanied or followed by a satisfying state of affairs, that response is reinforced. When a response is accompanied by an annoying state of affairs, it is avoided. (Lado, 1964, p. 37) (95-96)

If we go by the same source of information, and that is Alice Omaggio Hadley, we need to go back to 1972 when Sandra Savignon published her *Communicative Competence: An Experiment in Foreign Language Teaching*. The "definition of communicative competence did incorporate linguistic competence as one of its components: 'Communicative competence may be defined as the ability to function in a truly communicative setting – that is, in a dynamic exchange in which linguistic competence must adapt itself to the total informational input, both linguistic and paralinguistic, of one or more interlocutors'" (p. 8). She went on to point out that successful communication would depend largely on the individual's willingness to take a risk and express himself in the foreign language, and on his resourcefulness in using the vocabulary and structures under his control to make himself understood. According to Savignon, the use of gestures, intonation, and facial expression also contributes to communication, but linguistic accuracy, though of some importance, should be considered as only one of the major constituents of a communicative exchange. (4)

Alice Omaggio Hadley continues by quoting Savignon again when she outlines the following characteristics:

1. "Communicative competence is a dynamic rather than a static concept that depends on the *negotiation of meaning* between two or more persons who share some knowledge of the language. 'In this sense, then, communicative competence can be said to be an *interpersonal* rather than an intrapersonal trait.' (p. 8)

2. Communicative competence should not be thought of as only an oral phenomenon. It applies to both written and spoken language.

3. Communicative competence is context specific, in that communication always takes place in a particular context or situation. The communicatively competent language user will know how to make appropriate choices in register and style to fit the particular situation in which communication occurs.

4. It is important to bear in mind the theoretical distinction between *competence* and *performance*. '*Competence* is what one knows. *Performance* is what one does. Only performance is observable, however, and it is only through performance that competence can be developed, maintained, and evaluated.'

5. Communicative competence is *relative* and depends on the cooperation of all those involved. 'It makes sense, then, to speak of *degrees* of communicative competence.'" (p. 9) (4-5)

We can now segue to what Alice Omaggio Hadley calls *Communicative Language Teaching.*

A Functional Approach: Communicative Language Teaching (CLT)

Let us remember that *Teaching Language in Context* was a product of the previous century, and therefore dealt with the information available at that time. Things have changed just a little bit over the past decade or so, and the communicative approach has gained more ground, although the other methods have also adapted to the needs of the ever growing number of ESL students and teachers. According to Alice Omaggio Hadley, the communicative language teaching approach originally came from the writings of British applied linguists such as Wilkins, Widdowson, Brumfit, Candlin and others, as well as American educators such as Savignon, whose name was already mentioned in the previous paragraphs. The relatively new concept also included the main principles of communicative competence, and its principles can be summarized as follows:

1. "Meaning is of primary importance in CLT, and contextualization is a basic principle.

2. Attempts by learners to communicate with the language are encouraged from the beginning of instruction. The new language system will be learned best by struggling to communicate one's own meaning and by negotiation of meaning through interaction with others.

3. Sequencing of materials is determined by the content, function and/or meaning that will maintain student's interest.

4. Judicious use of the native language is acceptable where feasible, and translation may be used when students find it beneficial or necessary.

5. Activities or strategies for learning are varied according to learner preferences and needs.

6. Communicative competence, with an emphasis on fluency and acceptable language use, is the goal of instruction. 'Accuracy is judged not in the abstract, but in context.'" (p. 92) (Based on Finocchiaro and Brumfit, 1983, pp. 91-93, cited in Richards and Rodgers, 1986, pp. 67-68.) (Quoted by Alice Omaggio Hadley, 1993, p. 104)

For more information, including **lesson plans**, please check the Appendix.

According to Diane Larsen-Freeman (1986), no matter what method we choose to use, there is always something that can be adapted to fit the needs the classroom activities. "After we identify the principles, we will consider the answers to ten questions. The questions are:

1. What are the goals of teachers who use the method?

2. What is the role of the teacher? What is the role of the students?

3. What are some characteristics of the teaching/learning process?

4. What is the nature of student-teacher interaction? What is the nature of student-student interaction?

5. How are the feelings of the students dealt with?

6. How is language viewed? How is culture viewed?

7. What areas of language are emphasized? What language skills are emphasized?

8. What is the role of the students' native language?

9. How is evaluation accomplished?

10. How does the teacher respond to the student errors?

The answers to these questions will add to our understanding of each method and allow us to see some salient differences between and among the methods presented here." (2-3)

No matter what methodology or approach we use, the ultimate goal remains the same, and that is to empower the students to develop the skills necessary to understand the basics of the teaching process and, eventually, to function in real life situations.

NOTES

Vocabulary Summary

The ancient Persian word *paradaiza* means "the lord's enclosure" referring both to "paradise" and to a garden, one's own paradise. Similarly, two words the Koran uses for "paradise" *firdaws* and *janna* also mean "garden."

Vocabulary

Tips TIPS for **ESL instructors** re: teaching vocabulary:

1. The English language is borrowing words from other languages.

   Why? New things, new concepts, new ideas pp. 55-58

2. The vocabulary component should be evaluated in your ESL program.
   pp. 61-63

   - Focus on high frequency words?
   - Appropriate level – low, high, academic, etc.?
   - Correct sequencing?
   - Do students have enough opportunities to practice?

3. Words have their own stories. pp. 64-78

   For example: "The Greeks gave the name 'Amazon' to strong, masculine women. It refers to the Grecian story of a nation of warlike women in Asia Minor."

4. Words have their own histories. pp. 79-83

   For example: "Milton adored inventing words. When he couldn't find the right term he just made one up: *impressive, jubilant, loquacious, unconvincing, Satanic, persona, fragrance, beleaguered, sensuous, undesirable, disregard, damp, criticize, irresponsible, lovelorn, exhilarating, sectarian, unaccountable, incidental* and *cooking*. All Milton's."

English is used as a first or native language spoken on at least four continents of the world and has become a world language. American English, as Albert H. Marckwardt sees it, is a variety of English that reflects the American tradition and American character, or in short, American culture. This is what he says in his *American English* published in 1958 and reprinted in 1966:

> "It is fairly accurate to say that in the United States there are at least six regional cultures: a New England, an Old South, a Middle West, a Rocky Mountain and Great Plains, a Southwest, and a Far West culture. In fact, even these are capable of subdivision." (6)

Compared to many other languages, English has been known as a word borrower. One of the major reasons certain cultures borrow words from other cultures is the need to talk about new things, new concepts, and new ideas. When the English came to North America, they encountered new plants, animals, fish, clothing, food, places, etc., and they had to learn new words. Following Albert H. Markwardt, we should start with the Indian influence. The list of American Indian borrowings would include approximately 50 words, grouped in separate categories. Here are some of them:

Trees, plants, fruits:	**hickory, pecan, sequoia, squash, tamarack**
Animals:	**chipmunk, moose, muskrat, opossum, raccoon, woodchuck**
Political terms:	**caucus**
Foods:	**hominy, hooch, succotash**
Amerindian culture:	**powwow, totem, squaw, moccasin, tomahawk, igloo, tepee**

French is the next language the colonists encountered when they arrived in the New World, and there were two types of French culture: a casual colonial one and a fully developed urban one. French was 'important in New England because Calvin had written in it; in the South because it constituted part of the equipment of a gentleman.' (34)

As was the case with American Indian, some of the French borrowings have disappeared over the centuries, but others remain.

Plants and animals:	**caribou, gopher, pumpkin**
Foods:	**brioche, chowder, jambalaya, praline**
Toponymics:	**bayou, chute, crevasse, levee, prairie, rapids**
Furniture and building:	**bureau, depot, shanty**

Exploration and travel:	**bateau, cache, carry-all, pirogue, toboggan, voyager**
Coinage:	**cent, dime**
Miscellaneous:	**apache, chambray, lacrosse, parlay, rotisserie, sashay**

We must add that some of the French words originally came from other languages. *Caribou*, for example, was Indian in origin. *Parlay*, in its turn, came from Italian (*parole*).

Moving southward and westward, the English encountered the Spanish colonization and culture. If we classify the word borrowings according to the new aspects of life, we come up with the following:

Plants and animals:	**alfalfa, marijuana, armadillo, bronco, barracuda**
Food and drink:	**chile con carne, enchilada, taco, tamale, tequila, tortilla**
Clothing:	**poncho, sombrero**
Ranch life:	**buckaroo, cinch, corral, hacienda, lasso, ranch, rodeo**
Building:	**adobe, cafeteria, patio, plaza, pueblo**
Mining:	**bonanza, placer**
Legal and penal:	**calaboose, desperado, incommunicado, vigilantes**
Toponymics:	**canyon, key, mesa, sierra**
Races and nationalities:	**creole, mulatto, pickaninny, quadroon**
Miscellaneous:	**fiesta, filibuster, hombre, marina, rumba, savvy, tornado**

Before dealing with the French, the colonists had to fight with the Dutch, whom they dispossessed of their territories one by one. As early as 1664, the Dutch, coming from Holland, became part of the English colonial empire, and brought with them their own words.

Food:	**cole slaw, cookie, waffle**
Transportation:	**caboose, sleigh, span (of horses)**
Farm and Building:	**hay barrack, stoop (porch), saw buck**

Social classification:	**boss, patron, Yankee**
Miscellaneous:	**dope, dumb** (stupid), **poppycock, Santa Claus, snoop**

The Germans came in three or four waves, and they represent an immigrant people, not a conquered colonial rival. The Germans came as early as 1683, when they settled in Pennsylvania. What we know now as Pennsylvania Dutch, by 1775 already had approximately 90,000 inhabitants, and they assimilated very quickly because these Germans "developed a language consisting of a compromise of their own various dialects with a strong admixture of English words and constructions." (51)

Food and drink:	**delicatessen, frankfurter, hamburger, lager beer, noodle,**
	sauerkraut, schnitzel, stollen
Educational:	**semester, seminar**
Social:	**Christmas tree, poker**
Miscellaneous:	**bum, fresh** (impudent), **hausfrau, loafer, nix, wunderkind**

British and American English have been using words of Latin origin because, according to David Crystal, Latin was the language of the church, medieval scholarship and early political administration.

"Here is a representative sample from some of the chief domains. (In several cases, such as the names of many minerals, Latin is being used as a 'relay' language, re-expressing a term which was originally found in Greek.)

Alchemy:	**dissolve, distillation, elixir, essence, ether, mercury**
Astronomy:	**ascension, comet, eccentric, equator, equinoxial, intercept**
Biology:	**asp, cicada, juniper, locust, lupin, pine**
Education:	**abacus, desk, et cetera, formal, major, minor**
Language and literacy:	**allegory, clause, index, neuter, scribe, simile**
Law:	**client, debenture, executor, gratis, legitimate, proviso**
Medicine:	**diaphragm, digit, dislocate, ligament, orbit, saliva**

Mineralogy:	**antimony, arsenic, chrysolite, garnet, lapis lazuli, mineral**
Religion:	**collect, diocese, lector, limbo, psalm, redemptor**" (156)

John Simpson, former Chief Editor of the *Oxford English Dictionary*, spent almost four decades of his life working with the words and intricacies of the English language. In 2016, he published *The Word Detective, A Life in Words from Serendipity to Selfie*, a comprehensive autobiographical narrative dealing with the history of words, how they come into the language, how they evolve and sometimes disappear. In his introduction, Simpson goes back to Samuel Johnson to analyze the word *lexicographer*, defined as "a writer of dictionaries; a harmless drudge, that busies himself in tracing the original, and detailing the signification of words." In other words, the public perception of lexicographers hasn't been more than a boring activity, but for language teachers, the same job can be a journey into the past, just as enjoyable as reading a book or a magazine. Among the many words under scrutiny, Simpson tells us the story of *deadline*:

"Times of crisis are times when new words are generated. In mid-nineteenth-century America the dangerous and yet thrilling push into the Wild West, and then the California Gold Rush, followed by the Civil War, brought a jumble of new words into the emerging variety called American English. (At the moment, Charlotte Bronte is accredited with the first recorded use of "Wild West": I don't think that will last.) Much of this new vocabulary is self-confidently adventurous, like the new country: badlands, bloviate, bodacious, bonanza, braggadacious, buckaroo (sorry: that's enough of a list).

The earliest recorded use of the term dead line comes from angling (1860). It's not a new creation in the world of words, but it takes another approach – it's a creative metaphor. A *dead line* is one that doesn't move or run while it's lying in wait for fish to bite. To get into the stream of the modern meanings of the term we need to travel to America around the end of the Civil War, where the same pairing of words produced a new and unrelated meaning. It seems that mid-nineteenth-century Americans did not hold enlightened views on prison management: they apparently used to draw lines around military prisons, and if a prisoner went beyond that line, he would be shot. The dead line. Here's what prolific American writer Benson John Lossing said, in his *Pictorial History of the Civil War in the United States of America* (vol. 3, 1868): Seventeen feet from the inner stockade was the 'dead-line,' over which no man could pass and live." Deadlines became less lethal in early twentieth-century America, when the newspapers picked up the expression to describe their time-limit for receiving copy. Make the deadline or else. Then it drifted into numerous other areas of life, including the OED's own schedule." (58-59)

Another word that attracted John Simpson's attention was *aerobics*:

"Our investigations of *aerobics* immediately took us into the chamber of nineteenth-century science, where we have previously met the German creation *epicentrum* and English *epicenter*. This time we were in debt to Louis Pasteur (1822-1895). French chemist and microbiologist extraordinaire. In 1863 Pasteur published an article in a French scientific journal in which he coined the term *aerobie*, as an adjective and noun. You might correctly guess that *aero-* relates to "air." You might be harder pressed to uncover the origin of the final *–bie*. And yet the steady hand of the OED tells us that Pasteur took these letters from the end of the word *amphibie* (as in *amphibian*, a creature able to live both in water and on land: the *–bie* derives ultimately from the Greek bios, "life"). *Aerobie* meant (of an organism) able to live in the presence of oxygen"; the opposite, *anaerobie*, meant "able to live in the absence of oxygen."

As English doesn't as a rule use words like *aerobie* as adjectives, when English scientists reported Pasteur's work in the *Lancet* in 1865, they generously gave it an English coloring, as *aerobian*. But even that didn't sound scientific enough as the word settled down in the language. After the scientists had tried to get used to *aerobian* for several years, they decided that they would prefer *aerobic* (and *anaerobic*), both of which are found in English from 1878, again in the context of Pasteur's work.

The terms were largely the preserve of microbiologists for a century, until the late 1960s, when scientists began to investigate how the body efficiently processes oxygen in physical exercise. As aerobic entered a more popular theatre of action, in the mouths of trainers and exercisers, we observed that they found it convenient to develop a new word, *aerobics* – at first in America (1968), and later in Britain and elsewhere. New joggers found that *aerobics* – in keeping with its lexical origins – referred to physical exercise that "increases the body's oxygen consumption in a sustainable manner" and "is aimed at improving cardiovascular fitness." It is noteworthy, given the centrality of British and American English on the world stage at the time, that these linguistic developments – begun when French science was perhaps the prestige language of scientific investigation in Europe – were concluded (to date) in the melting pot of English. I doubt if there are any early photographs of Louis Pasteur demonstrating his discoveries, but it is Pasteur whom we have to thank for our word today." (101-102)

When students learn new vocabulary, we find ourselves teaching words using textbooks, newspaper or magazine articles, reading passages, or movies, dictionaries or thesauruses. A good teacher will always find sources of information and will make sure there is a set of vocabulary words to teach on a daily basis. What makes **a vocabulary class successful is the combination of activities** that include context, parts of speech, pronunciation, synonyms, antonyms, and as a last resort, definition – but if done properly, the students should be the ones to use the new words in their original sentences and provide a definition. **Vocabulary is an integral part of almost any class**, from grammar to listening to reading, etc. Students also learn new words when they watch a movie, listen to a song, read new material, or get involved in a conversation where context, like reading passages, will provide a clue as to its meaning and usage.

A fresh, new perspective comes with *The New Ways on Teaching Vocabulary*, whose editor Paul Nation collected input from several ESL teachers working all over the world. The following table is an overview, based on Nation (1990):

Table 1. Evaluating the Vocabulary Component of an ESL Program

What to Look for	How to Look for It	How to Include It
Does the teacher know what the learners' vocabulary levels and needs are?	Ask the teacher.	Use the levels test (Nation, 1990). Interview the learners.
Is the program focusing on the appropriate level of vocabulary?	Look at what vocabulary or strategies are being taught.	Decide whether the focus is high, academic, or low frequency vocabulary.
Is the vocabulary helpfully sequenced?	Check that opposites, near synonyms, lexical sets are not being presented in the same lesson.	Use texts and normal use to sequence the vocabulary.
Are the skill activities designed to help vocabulary learning?	Look at the written input to the activities. Ask the teacher.	Include and monitor wanted vocabulary in the written input.
Is there a suitable proportion of opportunities to develop fluency with known vocabulary?	Look at the amount of graded reading, listening to stories, free writing and message-based speaking.	Use techniques that develop well-beaten paths and rich maps.
Does the presentation of vocabulary help learning?	Look for deliberate repetition and spacing. Rate the activities for depth of processing.	Develop teaching and revision cycles. Choose a few deep processing techniques to use often.
Are the learners excited about their progress?	Watch the learners doing tasks.	Set goals. Give feedback on progress. Keep records.

The introduction lists three reasons for which teachers need to plan the classroom activities when teaching vocabulary.

"Firstly, because different vocabulary gives greatly different returns for learning, it is important to make sure that the learners have good control of the high frequency words of the language before moving on to the less frequent vocabulary. In addition, the focus of teaching for high frequency vocabulary is different from the focus of teaching for low frequency vocabulary. A good vocabulary learning program should therefore focus on the appropriate level of vocabulary for the learners and should do this in the appropriate way.

Secondly, most language teaching courses make vocabulary learning more difficult than it should be as a result of the way vocabulary in the courses is sequenced. Grouping opposites, synonyms, and items in a lexical set together causes interference that results in confusion for the learners. It is a simple matter to avoid this problem.

Thirdly, vocabulary learning opportunities and the quality of vocabulary learning can be greatly increased through the careful design of both vocabulary and other skill activities."

New Ways in Teaching Vocabulary is divided into the following sections:

Part I: Meeting New Vocabulary for the first time
Part II: Establishing Vocabulary
Part III: Enriching activities
Part IV: Developing Vocabulary Strategies
Part V: Developing fluency with known vocabulary

The main idea of this collection of extremely useful material for classroom use is that learning vocabulary basically helps the students with many other skills, from listening to grammar, from reading to writing. From the multitude of resources provided in this book, let us take a look at a good example.

Twenty Questions (page 86)

Levels	Procedure
Any	1. Write one item from the target vocabulary group on each slip of paper. Make sure there is at least one slip of paper for each student. Items chosen will depend on the target vocabulary. Examples:
Aims Reinforce vocabulary groups, such as occupations, food, clothing, furniture, family, hobbies	Occupations: policeman, typist, cleaner, bus driver
	Furniture: bed, chair, wardrobe, chest of drawers
	2. Put the folded slips in a container, and allow each student to choose one. The other students must then ask questions. The questions can only be answered Yes or No; for instance:
Class time 20 minutes	Occupations: Do you earn a lot of money?
Resources Slips of paper	Furniture: Is it found in the kitchen?
	The class must work out the answer in 20 questions or fewer.
Contributor	Carol Griffiths is an ESOL teacher in Auckland, New Zealand.

The Story behind the Words

THERE ARE CASES when teachers should try to explain not only separate words and their meaning, but also the history or the story behind the words. Here are some suggestions:

Abacus   The device takes its name from the ancient Phoenician word *abak* meaning "dust" because the mathematician of that day used to cover tables with dust in order to draw their diagrams and figure their problems.

Abracadabra   This magic word is said to have been the name of the supreme deity of the Assyrians and was recommended by Severus Sammonicus as a charm against malaria – if written on a piece of paper and hung around the neck in this form:

A B R A C A D A B R A
A B R A C A D A B R
A B R A C A D A B
A B R A C A D A
A B R A C A D
A B R A C A
A B R A C
A B R A
A B R
A B
A

"The word derives from the Hebrew *abreg ad habra* meaning 'strike dead with thy lightning.' In Hebrew is comprises nine letters. 'Placing aleph on the left side of the triangle – and its ninefold repetition – is the magical element." (Quoted in J. Chevalier and Alain Gheerbrant , *The Penguin Dictionary of Symbols,* 1996, p. 1)

Acrobat   It is a Greek word which literally means "one who goes about on the tips of his toes and fingers."

Adam's apple   The term (meaning the voice box) is an allusion to the story of the Garden of Eden. It is said that a piece of the forbidden fruit stuck in Adam's throat and created his "Adam's apple" – but women have them, too.

Admiral   The Arabic word *amir* means "ruler" or "commander" and *bahr* means "sea." An Arabic sea commander was called an *amir al bahr* or "ruler of the sea."

Album   Originally, it was a table with a white top on which were kept the names of Roman officials and accounts of public proceedings which was prominently displayed in a public place. The word comes from the Latin *albus,* meaning "white." The British adopted the term during the Middle Ages and used it to signify a register or list of persons.

Alphabet   ABC and alphabet are exactly the same. The Greek alphabet begins with the letters *alpha* and *beta* – hence, **alphabet.**

Amazon   The Greeks gave the name "Amazon" to strong, masculine women. It refers to the Grecian story of a nation of warlike women in Asia Minor.

Ambulance   The "ambulance" once brought the hospital to the patient. The French devised the term and applied it to their early field hospitals which they called *hôpitals ambulants.* From this the name "ambulance" was applied to the vehicle.

Analyze   The word comes from Greek, literally meaning "to loosen up." The primitive method of gathering gold dust was "to loosen up" the earth and then toss it up into the air.

Apple of the Eye   The "apple of the eye," meaning a loved one, is correctly the pupil and the term "apple" is probably a corruption of "pupil" – although people originally thought the pupil of the eye was a little round ball like an apple.

April Fool's Day Until 1564, New Year's Day was March 25th. But since March 25th sometimes fell during Holy Week, the Church postponed its celebration to April 1st. Then New Year's Day was officially changed to January 1st (according to the Gregorian calendar) but many people still called out New Year's Greetings to their friends on April 1st.

Bachelor Originally a "bachelor" was a soldier not old enough or rich enough to lead into battle under his own banner. Therefore, the word means a person of inferior rank. It was applied to the college degree to differentiate it from the higher degree of "doctor."

Bacon We got the expression "bringing home the bacon" from country fairs. It was once the practice to grease a pig and let him loose among a number of blindfolded contestants. The man who successfully caught the greased pig could keep it – and so "bring home the bacon."

Ball How did a dancing party come to be called a ball? In Latin, *ballare* means "to dance" – but our "ball" has its origin in the Feast of Fools at Easter, when choir boys danced around the Dean in church. He threw a ball at them and they sang as they caught it. At early American dances, too, a ball was thrown at dancers as they danced around in sets.

Bankrupt The term comes from Italy, where money-changers placed the money they had to lend on a bench called a *banca*. If one of these money-changers was unable to continue the business, his counter was destroyed and so became a *banca rotta* – since *rotta* means broken. The term was then applied to the money-changer himself.

Barber The word comes from the Latin word *barba* which means "beard" – because at first, barbers only trimmed beards. In time, things changed, but the barber kept his name.

Beat around the Bush Sometimes hunters followed the game into the underbrush and made a lot of noise to scare the animals out. A person afraid of the animals lurking there would "beat around the bush" pretending to go in to find and kill the beast but not actually doing so.

Belladonna The plant got its name because ladies once used the extract to enlarge the pupils of their eyes, and so make themselves beautiful. *Bella donna* in Italian means "beautiful lady."

Bias A weight was once placed in a bowling ball to make it deviate from a straight line, and this was called the "bias." Similarly, anything today which tends to make a person deviate from accepted thought or behavior is called a "bias."

Black-out This expression was originally used in the theater to refer to the extinguishing of all lights on stage while the scenery was being shifted. In 1939, the British applied it to the precautionary measures they adopted to avoid revealing strategic targets for bombing to enemy German aircraft.

Blue Moon "Once in a blue moon" basically means hardly ever because a "blue moon" is never (or rarely) supposed to occur.

Boss A boss at one time had complete authority over his workers and could thrash them at will. "Boos" comes from Alt Hoch Deutsch (Old High German) *bozan* which means "to beat."

Brand New Formerly, the use of "brand new" was limited to things made of metal. "Brand" is an old Anglo-Saxon word which means "burn." So a horseshoe, plowshare, or sword just forged was said to be "brand new" – that is "fresh from the fire." The term was later applied to all new things.

Calendar It comes from the Latin word for an interest book kept by money-lenders called the *calendarium*. Interest was due on the *calends*, or first day of the month. Calends itself came from *calare* – the Latin verb meaning "to call" – because the Romans used to publicly "call out" the first day of the month.

Checkmate The word is used to describe the situation in which one player in a game of chess has so maneuvered his pieces that his opponent's king cannot move without being taken from the board. The term comes from the Arabic *shah-mat*, meaning "the king is dead."

Chow The word (meaning "food") comes from "chew" and was brought into the United States by the Chinese immigrants who came to California during the gold rush. Chinese restaurants still use the word in "*chow mein.*"

Clue	A "clue" is literally a ball of thread – and in the old fable, the only way Theseus could get out of the labyrinth was by unrolling a ball of thread as he went in.
Cock-and-Bull Story	The expression is a derisive allusion to the fables of Aesop and others in which cocks moralize and bulls debate.
Cold Feet	Cases of frozen feet were frequent among soldiers until the end of the 19th century. A man who has cold or frozen feet can't rush into battle. He proceeds slowly – and perhaps not at all.
Curfew	The word comes from the French term *couvre feu*, meaning "cover the fire." In other words, "put out the light and go to bed."
Dandelion	It comes from the jagged edges of its leaves – which were supposed to look like a lion's teeth. The French form is *dent de lion* - that is, "tooth of the lion."
Delta	All river "deltas" in the world are named after the "delta" of the Nile. This was called a "delta" because it was triangular – the same shape as the Greek letter *delta*.
Devil's Advocate	When any name is proposed for canonization in the Roman Catholic Church, two advocates are appointed. One is called "God's Advocate" and says all he can in support of the proposal. The other, the "Devil's Advocate," says all he can against it.
Dog Days	The Ancient Romans believed that the six or eight hottest days of the summer were caused by the Dog Star, Sirius, rising with the sun and adding heat to the day. They called these days *caniculares dies* – "dog days."
Dude	"Duds" are our clothes – from the Middle English word *dudde*, meaning "to dress." The Easterner who goes West dresses himself in fancy "duds" – and to the Westerner seems to pose or strike an attitude. "Dude" is "dud" plus "attitude."

Eavesdropper	In Saxon times in England, the owners of estates could not build their homes or cultivate their land right up to the property line. They had to leave a little space for the drip from the eaves (gutters). This space soon came to be called, from that fact, the "eavesdrip." An "eavesdropper" was a person who placed himself in the "eavesdrip" to overhear what was being said.
Fiasco	The making of a fine Venetian glass bottle is a difficult process – for it must be perfect. If, in blowing, the slightest flaw is detected, the glassblower turns the bottle into a common flask – called in Italian *fiasco*.
Free Lance	A medieval mercenary soldier who was free of any continuing loyalties was known as a "free companion." Sir Walter Scott in his novel, *Ivanhoe*, coined a more descriptive term for such a soldier – "freelance."
Grapevine	The term is a shortened form of "grapevine telegraph." In 1859, Colonel Bernard Bee constructed a telegraph line between Placerville and Virginia City by attaching the wire to trees. With time, the wire – no longer taut – lay on the ground in loops that looked like wild, trailing grapevine. During the Civil War, similar lines were used by the troops, and reports that came in over such "grapevine telegraph" lines more often than not had no definite source and were generally false.
Gypsy	The Gypsies claim Egypt as their original native land, and their name is derived from "Egypt." But it is more likely that they originally came from India in the Middle Ages - and merely passed through Egypt on their way into Europe.
Handkerchief	The "ker" of this word comes from the Old French *covrir*, meaning "to cover." The "chief" comes from *chef*, meaning "head." A "kerchief" was originally a "head covering," especially the bit of cloth used by women to cover their heads when entering a Catholic Church. A "handkerchief" was one carried in the hand.
Hippopotamus	The name comes directly from two Greek words - *hippos* and *potamos* – and literally means "river horse."

Horse Sense	The allusion is not to the sense of the horse, but to the shrewdness of horse traders.
Jog the Memory	"Jog" really means "shake," and when we "jog a person's memory" we shake it up.
Kangaroo	Captain James Cook, who discovered Australia, asked the tribesmen of the Endeavor River region the name of the animal. They answered, "Kangaroo." Whether that was the name of the animal itself or just an answer signifying "I don't know" is something that we don't know.
Kindergarten	This is a German word that literally means "children's garden." The term was originated by Friedrich Froebel, the German educator, who introduced the idea that a school for young children should gratify and cultivate the child's normal aptitude for exercise, play, imitation, and construction – just as playing in a garden would do.
Laconic	The word comes from "Laconia" – the general name for Spartan territory. The Spartans were noted for their brusque speech – the best example of it being their reply when Philip of Macedon wrote to their magistrates: "If I enter Laconia I will level Lacedaemon to the ground." The Spartans' reply was: "If."
Lavender	It was once the custom to place a sprig of this plant with the recently washed and cleaned laundry in order to scent it. The Italian word for washing is *lavanda*.
Learn by Heart	We say we learn things "by heart" instead of "by head" because of a mistaken analysis of anatomical functions made by the ancient Greeks, who placed the seat of thought in the heart.
Legend	The word comes from the Latin *legenda*, which in turn comes from *legere*, meaning "to read." The original "Legenda" was a book containing the lives of the saints read at convents and monasteries, but it included so much that was far-fetched that the word "legend" got its current meaning.
Limelight	At one time, calcium, or "lime" was a necessary element in making the light of a spotlight.

Lion's Share	The allusion is to one of Aesop's fables in which the "lion's share" is everything. In this fable, the lion went hunting with the fox and the ass. As they were about to divide the game, the lion spoke up and demanded one third as the share agreed upon and one third by virtue of his sovereignty. "And as for the remaining portion," said the lion, "I defy anyone to take it from me."
Loony	The loon is not a crazy bird, but his weird, loud cry sounds like the laughter of an insane person. However, the choice of the word was no doubt influenced by its similarity in sound to "lunacy."
Magazine	The term comes from *makhazan*, the Arabic word for "storehouse," and was originally applied to a place used by the Army for storing arms. "Magazine" was first used in its present sense in 1731 when it appeared in "The Gentleman's Magazine."
Make the Bed	We speak of "making" the bed instead of "fixing" it or "doing" it because beds were once created anew each night from straw thrown upon the floor.
Mentor	"Mentor" was the name of a faithful friend of Ulysses whose form Minerva assumed when she accompanied Telemachus in his search for his father. The term means a "wise counselor and guide."
Milliner	At one time, the city of Milan set the fashion throughout the world. The "Milaner" was therefore, a stylist – hence, "milliner."
Mug	The word "mug" is used to mean our *face* because a comparatively small jug used for drinking is called a "mug," and in the 18th century in England, those "mugs" were commonly made to represent a human face.
Muscle	The word comes from the Latin *musculus*, which means "little mouse." If you move the muscles of your upper arm, you will see what looks like a little mouse crawling back and forth.

Naked Truth According to an ancient legend, Truth and Falsehood once went bathing. When they came out of the water, Falsehood ran ahead dressed in Truth's clothing and sped away. Truth, unwilling to appear in Falsehood's clothing, went "naked."

Nemesis We call something that pursues a man relentlessly his "nemesis" because in Greek mythology "Nemesis" was an avenging goddess who saw to it that people were punished for their misdeeds. In Greek, *nemesis* really means "remorse."

Nick of Time In medieval times a "tally" was used to register attendance in colleges and churches. The "tally" was a stick of wood, and attendance was indicated by a "nick" or notch on it. The student or worshipper who arrived in time had his attendance "nicked" and so arrived "in the nick of time."

Ovation We got the word "ovation" as the name for "triumphant acclaim" from the Romans. But the Roman "ovation" was only a "second-class" celebration for a lesser triumph, like a battle won without bloodshed. The honored citizen did not appear in a chariot but only on a horse or on foot.

Panic Sounds heard on the mountain tops and in the deep valleys at night were once attributed to the god "Pan," who was believed to be the cause of any sudden, groundless fear, and so such fear was called "panic."

Pariah A despised social outcast is called a "pariah" because the "pariah" of India belongs to one of the lowest castes of Hindu society. He gets his name from the Timbal word for "drummer," *paraiyan,* because he plays the drums at Hindu festivals.

Pedagogue The word comes from the Romans. In Rome, a "pedagogue" was a slave who took the children to school, to the theater, and on their outings. He also taught them. The word comes from the Greek *paid*, meaning child, and *agein* meaning "to lead."

Phon(e)y We got the word "phony" as a synonym for "spurious" from the American manufacturer of cheap jewelry named Forney. He made a specialty of brass rings that looked like gold. He sold these rings to street peddlers and soon the rings came to be known as "Forney rings." The pronunciation was in time changed to "phony" and the word was extended to apply to other forms of jewelry and eventually to anything that was fraudulent.

Point Blank We got the expression "point blank" from the French. The center of a target was once a small white spot, and the French for "white" is *blanc*. The French *point* means "aim." So the term means "aim at the center of the target."

Powwow "Powwow" is an Indian word. The Indians of the New England coast first used it in referring to their medicine man; then it was transferred to their ceremonial rites; afterwards it came to mean any gathering at all.

Puppy The word comes from the French *poupee*, meaning "doll." By extension, it means any sort of a plaything, including a young dog.

Purchase "Purchase" comes from the French *pour chaser* which means "to hunt." Once upon a time, stores had no show windows and would-be purchasers had to "hunt" for what they wanted.

Quarantine In Italian, *quaranta* means "forty." In early days, a ship suspected of being infected with some contagious disease was kept outside of port for forty days - in "quarantine."

Raining Cats and Dogs The expression comes from Norse mythology in which the cat symbolizes heavy rain while the dog, an attendant of Odin, the storm god, represents great blasts of wind.

Ringleader The term comes from dancing. Many old dances began with all the participants holding hands in a ring. Then the circle was broken and one person led the rest of the "ring" through the figures of the dance.

Rival The word comes from the Latin word for "stream" – *rivus*. The original "rivals" were people who lived on opposite sides of a stream and fought bitterly over which side of the stream was the better to live on.

Rule of Thumb	Rough measurements came to be called "by rule of thumb" because that is one way to make rough measurements. The first joint of the thumb is approximately one inch long.
Salary	The word comes from the ancient Romans, and it literally means "salt money." The Roman soldier was once given an allowance of salt; then he was given an allowance of money for the purchase of salt. This was called a *salarium* – from *sal*, meaning "salt."
Sandwich	The sandwich was named after John Montague, Fourth Earl of Sandwich. Montague loved to play cards so much that he never wanted to take time to eat. So he solved the problem by placing slides of beef between two pieces of bread and munching away while he played.
School	The word is from the Greek and originally meant "leisure." In Ancient Greece, only a person with leisure could "go to school."
Scot-free	The 'scot' of the term comes from the Anglo-Saxon *sceot*, meaning "money put into a general fund" – hence a "tax." "Scot-free" first meant "tax free."
Sheriff	The term is derived from the Anglo-Saxon title – *shire reeve*. The *shire reeve* of 11th century England was an official appointed by the king to administer the local government, enforce the law, and collect the king's taxes.
Skin of His Teeth	The expression is a literal translation from the Hebrew text of the Book of Job. Since a person's teeth have no skin, for him to get by "by the skin of his teeth" is to get by with no margin at all.
Slush Fund	Aboard a sailing ship, "slush" is waste fat from the galley used to grease the masts. All extra slush used to be the cook's perquisite, and he didn't have to account for the money he made from selling it. Likewise, a "slush fund" is money that need not be accounted for.
Sour Grapes	The allusion is to the fable of the fox who tried to reach some grapes hanging upon a vine. When he was finally convinced that he could not get them, he turned away and said, "Well, they're 'sour' anyway."

Steal One's Thunder	Around the year 1700, the playwright Dennis said that he had invented a sound-effects machine that could produce "thunder" off stage and complained that his rivals had "stolen his thunder." The sound of someone's stealing thunder so tickled the fancy of people that the phrase was adopted into the language.
Stickler	The word comes from the Middle English *stightlen*, which means "to set in order." Originally "sticklers" were judges at duels who saw to it that the rules of fair play were closely observed. Today, the "stickler" still follows the rules very closely.
Supercilious	A haughty person is called 'supercilious' because in Latin *super* means "above" and *cilium* means "eyebrows." A supercilious person goes about with "raised eyebrows."
Taxi	The word originally referred to the "meter" carried by the cab. It was called a "taximeter" because it measured the fare or "tax," and cabs equipped with them boasted of the fact by painting "taximeter" on their doors. This was soon shortened to "taxi," and in time, cabs were called that.
Terrier	The Latin word for "earth" is *terra*. Therefore, the home of a fox or badger, being a hole in the earth, is a "terrier." And because of this, a dog trained to chase a fox or badger from its "terrier" is called a "terrier."
Thug	The original "thugs" were members of a professional gang of thieves and murderers in India who made a practice of strangling their victims. The word is from Hindustani *thag*, meaning a "cheat" or "swindler."
Trump Card	The word "trump" is a corruption of "triumph." A "trump" is a card that can "triumph" or win over other cards in the game by virtue of its special powers.

Tuxedo	A "tuxedo" was first worn at Tuxedo Park in Orange County, New York. But, according to legend, this coat was devised by King Edward VII of England while he was still Prince of Wales. As a young man, Edward liked to play cards and would often sit all night at the table - where, being rather stout, his full-dress coattails got in his way. So Edward had a coat made up with the tails clipped off, and that's how the tuxedo came into being.
Tycoon	The name comes from the Japanese *tai*, meaning "great" and *kun*, meaning "prince." Commodore Perry brought the word back from Japan with him in 1854.
Uncle Sam	The original "Uncle Sam" – goatee, twinkling eye, and all – was Samuel Wilson, born in West Cambridge, Massachusetts.
Upper Crust	High society is called "the upper crust" because the "crust" was long considered the best part of the bread and the "upper" or top crust the best part of all.
Utopia	The term is from the Greek *ou* and *topos* which, literally translated, means "not a place" or "nowhere." The word was devised by Thomas Moore.
Volume	Ancient books were written on sheets of paper which were fastened together lengthwise and rolled up like a window shade. "Volume" is from the Lain *volvere*, meaning "to roll up."
Wild-Goose Chase	A "wild-goose chase" was once a sort of game – a horse race in which the second and each succeeding horse had to follow the leader accurately and at a definite interval. Since the horses had to keep their positions like geese in flight, the chase was called "wild-goose chase." Since this was no race, for no one could win, we adopted the phrase to describe a person following a course that leads to no goal.
Zest	"Zest" is used to mean "enthusiasm" because, in its Greek form, "zest" meant a piece of orange or lemon peel. And the addition of a slice of orange or lemon peel adds "zest" to a drink or dish and makes us more enthusiastic about it.

(Selected and compiled from *Why Do We Say It? The Stories behind the Words, Expressions and Clichés We Use,* Castle, Twelfth Printing, 1991)

Cities all over the world have their own stories:

Chicago	'Place of the Bad Smell' – Shika Konk in *Ojibwa*
Copenhagen	'Merchant Harbor'
London	'Place by an unfordable river'
Manhattan	'The Place of the great drunkenness' or 'The Place where we all got drunk'
Pasadena	'Strolling Place'
Sofia	'Wisdom'
Reykjavik	'Smoky bay'
Dublin	'Black pool'
Tripoli	'Three cities'
Cairo	'Victorious'
Addis Ababa	'New flower'
Nairobi	'The place of cool waters'
Khartoum	'End of an elephant's trunk'
Kuala Lumpur	'Muddy confluence'
Tehran	'Modern'
Riyadh	'Garden'
Ankara	'Anchor'
Abu Dhabi	'Father of a gazelle'
Buenos Aires	'Good winds'
Montevideo	'I saw a mountain'
La Paz	'Peace'
Vladivostok	'Lord of the East'
Ottawa	'Traders'

NOTES

And here are some **country etymologies**:

Argentina	(Spanish)	'The silver republic'
Barbados	(Spanish)	From *barbudos* meaning 'bearded,' referring to the vines hanging from the trees
Cameroon	(Portuguese)	From *Camarao* meaning 'shrimp'
Canaries	(Latin)	'Dogs'
Chile	(Araucanian)	'End of the land'
Cyprus	(Greek)	'Copper'
El Salvador	(Spanish)	'The Savior"
Ethiopia	(Greek)	'Burning face'
Honduras	(Spanish)	From *las Honduras* meaning 'The Depths'
Hong Kong	(Chinese)	'Fragrant Streams' or 'Smelly Streams'
Jamaica	(Carib)	'Well-watered'
Japan	(Chinese)	From *Ji-pen* meaning 'Sun-root' (the sun rose over Japan)
Jordan	(Arabic)	'The Coming-down' (of rivers)
Mexico	(Aztec)	'War God, Mextli'
Pakistan	(an acronym)	P(unjab) + A(fghan tribes) + K(ashmir) + (Baluch)istan
Panama	(Guarani)	'Place of many fish'
Puerto Rico	(Spanish)	'Rich port'
Singapore	(Chinese)	'Lion City' (from the many statues of the British Lion)
Taiwan	(Chinese)	'Terrace Bay'
Thailand	(Thai)	'Land of the free'
Trinidad	(Spanish)	'The Trinity'
Venezuela	(Spanish)	'Little Venice'

The History behind the Words

I F WE WANT to synthesize the wealth of information available today, and if we want to trace our contemporary vocabulary to its origins, we absolutely need to go back in time. Famous authors and literary figures made great contributions to the ever-growing heritage of words and their usage. Here is just one example to get us started:

"Milton adored inventing words. When he couldn't find the right term he just made one up: *impressive, jubilant, loquacious, unconvincing, Satanic, persona, fragrance, beleaguered, sensuous, undesirable, disregard, damp, criticize, irresponsible, lovelorn, exhilarating, sectarian, unaccountable, incidental* and *cooking*. All Milton's. When it came to inventing wording, Milton actually invented the word *wording*.

Awe-struck? He invented that one, too, along with *stunning* and *terrific*. And, because he was a Puritan, he invented words for all the fun things of which he disapproved. Without dear old Milton, we would have no *debauchery*, no *depravity*, no *extravagance*; in fact, nothing *enjoyable* at all.

Poor preachers! People always take their condemnations as suggestions. One man's abomination is another's good idea. This is the law of unintended consequences, and yes, Milton invented the word *unintended*. (. . .)

Whether you're all ears or obliviously tripping in the light fantastic, you are still quoting Milton." (Mark Forsyth, *The Etymologicon*, Icon Books, 2011, p. 14)

What an amazing phenomenon was Shakespeare and the legacy he left!

". . . Shakespeare, with his exquisite feeling for femininity, was the creator of the beauty of character in women; a beauty which had never been seen before, even in a dream, until he called into radiant life those radiant beings, Portia, Beatrice, Perdita, Desdemona, Imogen, Hermione, and so many others." (Logan Pearsall Smith, *On Reading Shakespeare*, Harcourt, Brace and Company, New York, p. 9)

"Every word," as Thomas Gray said of him, "is a picture"; and these pictures often flash from the length of a line or phrase with the quickness of lightning flashes. This unparalleled wealth of imagery shows itself, above all, in that royal use of metaphor, which is the most distinguishing quality of his style, and which Aristotle described as the surest mark of genius.' (78)

Let us read again the familiar passage from Macbeth:

Tomorrow, and tomorrow, and tomorrow,
Creeps in this petty pace from day to day,
To the last syllable of recorded time;
And all our yesterdays have lighted fools
The way to dusty death. Out, out, brief candle!
Life's but a walking shadow, a poor player,
That struts and frets his hour upon the stage.
And then is heard no more; it is a tale
Told by an idiot, full of sound and fury,
Signifying nothing.

"We cannot but see how such images in this supremely imaginative passages, whether visual, - 'lighted,' and 'brief candle'; or audible, - 'syllable,' 'heard no more,' 'sound and fury'; or other motor images, - 'creeps,' 'walking shadow,' 'struts and frets' – are no mere decorations; and in general we may say that the great Shakespearean characters, like primitive man, create what they express by clothing their ideas in images."

(Logan Pearsall Smith, *On Reading Shakespeare*, 1933, p. 80)

Many of Shakespeare's phrases, with some modifications, have become part of General English idiomatic expressions. Some of them may have been used previously, but now that they were used by Shakespeare, they have become easily accessed by the general public.

your lord and master (*All's Well that Ends Well*)
It beggared all description. (*Antony and Cleopatra*)
We have seen better days. (*As You Like It*)
neither rhyme nor reason (*As You Like It*)
Can one desire too much of a good thing? (*As You Like It*)
The game is up. (*Cymbeline*)
I have not slept one wink. (*Cymbeline*)
in my mind's eye (*Hamlet*)
more in sorrow than in anger (*Hamlet*)
I doubt some foul play. (*Hamlet*)
Brevity is the soul of wit. (*Hamlet*)
Hold the mirror up to nature. (*Hamlet*)
I must be cruel only to be kind. (*Hamlet*)
I'll send him packing. (*Henry IV Part I*)
Tell truth and shame the devil. (*Henry IV Part I*)
Set my teeth on edge. (*Henry IV Part I*)
Thy wish was father to my thought. (*Henry IV Part II*)
Give the devil his due. (*Henry V*)
knit his brows (*Henry VI Part 2*)
dead as a door-nail (*Henry IV Part 2*)
Be it as it may. (*Henry IV Part 3*)
It was Greek to me. (*Julius Caesar*)
Play fast and loose. (*King John*)
more sinned against than sinning (*King Lear*)
the be-all and the end-all (*Macbeth*)
stretch out to the edge of doom (*Macbeth*)
all our yesterdays (*Macbeth*)
with bated breath (*The Merchant of Venice*)
mine own flesh and blood (*The Merchant of Venice*)
Love is blind. (*The Merchant of Venice*)
green-eyed jealousy (*The Merchant of Venice*)
Let us not be the laughing stocks. (*The Merry Wives of Windsor*)
what the dickens (*The Merry Wives of Windsor*)
as good luck would have it (*The Merry Wives of Windsor*)
pomp and circumstance (*Othello*)
a foregone conclusion (*Othello*)

a tower of strength (*Richard III*)
I'll not budge an inch. (*The Taming of the Shrew*)
melted into thin air (*The Tempest*)
I've been in such a pickle. (*The Tempest*)
the incarnate devil (*Titus Andronicus*)
a good riddance (*Troilus and Cressida*)
'tis but early days (*Troilus and Cressida*)
'tis fair play (*Troilus and Cressida*)
You will laugh yourselves into stitches. (*Twelfth Night*)
Make a virtue of necessity. (*The Two Gentlemen of Verona*)
with bag and baggage (*The Winter's Tale*)
(Quoted in David Crystal, *The Stories of English*, 2004, pp.330-331)

Shakespeare gave us 1,685 words that are still in use today. Here are some of them: *critical, monumental, majestic, dwindle, frugal, summit, radiance, countless, hint, excellent,* etc.

A very important moment was the publication in 1755 of what we now know as *Dr. Johnson's Dictionary*. It is considered one of the most influential dictionaries in the history of the English language, but it was not the first one. There was an earlier work by Nathan Bailey, who published his *Dictionarium Britannicum* in 1730, but that was surpassed by Samuel Johnson.

"Following the traditional practice of Greek and Latin lexicographers, he included, for his 42,000 words, 116,000 illustrative quotations, from the greatest English writers of the past. He also divided his words into carefully shaded definitions. The word 'set,' for example, as verb and noun, had ninety-nine different meanings. His method was also innovative. Though he was half blind, Johnson began by reading books and searching for the appropriate words instead of starting with a list of words that had to be defined. He occasionally used Chaucer, but extracted most of his words from books published in the two centuries between the birth of Sir Philip Sidney (1554-1586) and the death of Alexander Pope (1688-1744), who was Johnson's contemporary for thirty-five years."

(J. Meyers, *Samuel Johnson. The Struggle*, 2008, p. 161)

"Johnson enlivened his scholarly work with many playful, idiosyncratic and revealing definitions, which expressed his personal prejudices:

Dedication: A servile address to a patron

Dull: Not exhilarating; not delightful; as, *to make dictionaries is* **dull** *work*.

Enthusiasm: A vain belief of private revelation; a vain confidence of divine favour or communication.

Oats: A grain, which in England is generally given to horses, but in Scotland supports the people."

(Quoted in Jeffrey Meyers, *Samuel Johnson. The Struggle*, 2008, p. 163)

> Almost all the polysyllabic words in English are of French-Latin origin, while most one-syllable words come from Anglo-Saxon.

ANGLO-SAXON ROOTS

BEFORE THE NORMAN Invasion of 1066, the people on the British Isles spoke Celtic. Then the Anglo-Saxons came with their own language, which remained pure and unchanged for about six centuries. That was the time when the English tongue "grew" its own words from the roots. In 1066, though, when the Norman-French came, they brought thousands of new words that mixed with the local language. When a new word was needed, the local population resorted to the Norman words. However, before the Normans came, there were lots of English or Anglo-Saxon roots. Here is a list of the most important ones:

Aecer, a field — *acre, acorn*

Bacan, to bake — *bake, batch, baxter* (bacster=female baker)

Beatan, to beat — *beat*

Bed, a prayer — *bead, bead-roll, beadsman*

Belg, a bag — *bag, bagpipe, bellows, bulge*

Bellan, to bellow — *bell, bellow, bull*

Beodan, to bid or proclaim — *bid, bidding, forbid, beadle*

Beorgan, to protect — *borough, burgh, burgher, borrow, burrow*

Bindan, to fasten — *bind, woodbine, band, bond, bundle*

Bitan, to bite — *bite, bit, bitter, bait, beetle*

Blowan, to blossom — *blow, blossom, blood*

Brecan, to break — *break, breach, breakers, breakfast*

Breowan, to brew — *brew, broth, Brewster* (female brewer)

Bugan, to bend — *bow* (to bend), *bow* (a weapon)

Byrnan, to burn — *burn, brand, brimstone*

Ceap, market — *cheap, chapman, chaffer*

Ceowan, to chew	*chew, jaw*
Cleofan, to split	*cleave, cleaver, cleft*
Corn, grain	*corn, kernel*
Cunna, to know	*cunning, can, could, uncouth, con*
Cwic, living	*quick, quicksilver, quicksand*
Cyn, a tribe	*kin, kinsman, kindred, King*
Daeg, day	*day, holiday, daisy, dawn*
Dael, a share	*deal* (a quantity), *deal* (to distribute), *dealer, dole, dale, dell*
Deor, a wild animal	*deer* (Shakespeare calls mice "small deer")
Deore, precious	*dear, darling*
Dic, a ditch	*dike, ditch, dig*
Dom, judgment	*doom, kingdom, deem*
Don, to do	*do, ado, don* (=do on)
Dragan, to pull	*drag, draggle, draw, draught-board, draughtsman, draft, drawl, dray*
Drifan, to drive	*drive, drift, adrift, drove, drover*
Drincan, to drink	*drink, drunkard, drench, drown*
Eage, eye	*eye, daisy* (=day's eye)
Eal, all	*all, altogether, always, also, alone*
Eald, old	*old, elder, alderman*
Faran, to go	*fare, farewell, welfare, thoroughfare, ferry, ford*
Feower, four	*four, fourteen, forty*
Fleogan, to fly	*fly, flight*
Fleotan, to float	*fleet* (swift), *fleet* (of ships), *float, flutter*
Foda, food	food, fodder, foster, feed, feeder
Ful, foul	*foul, filth, defile*
Gangan, contr. **Gan**, to go	*gang, gangway, go*
Geard, an enclosure	*yard, vineyard, orchard* (wort-yard)
God, God	*God, godfather, godly, gospel* (=God's spell or story), *good-bye* (=God be with ye)
Grafan, to dig	*grave* (to carve), *grave* (for the dead), *graver, engrave, groove*
Gripan, to seize	*gripe, grip, grope, grasp*
Gyrdan, to enclose	*gird, girdle, girth*
Habban, to have	*have, behave, haft*
Hal, whole; **halig**, holy	*heal, health, whole, wholesale, wholesome, hallow, holy, holiday*

Hand, hand	*hand, handle, handsome, handy, handicraft, handiwork*
Hangian, to hang	*hang, hanger, hanker*
Hebban, to raise up	*heave, heavy, heaven*
Hwa, who	*who, what, which, when, where, whether, why*
Lad, a path	*lead* (verb), *lode, lodestar, lodestone*
Licgan, to lie down	*lie, lay, lair, layer*
Mawan, to mow	*mow, mead, meadow, aftermath*
Neah, nigh	*nigh, neighbor, near, next*
Nosu, the nose	*nose, nostril, nozzle* (= a little nose)
Raed, advice, counsel	*read, riddle*
Sceapan, to form	*landscape, shape, friendship, worship*
Sceotan, to shoot	*scot-free* (without payment or contribution), *shoot, shot, shut, shuttle*
Sceran, to cut	*shear, shears, share, shire, shore, short*
Sittan, to sit	*sit, set, settee, settle*
Spinnan, to spin	*spin, spindle, spinster*
Stede, a place	*stead, steadfast, steady, instead*
Stician, to stick	*stick* (verb), *stick* (noun), *sticky, stitch, stake, stoke, stockade*
Stigan, to rise, climb	*sty* (in the eye), *sty* (for pigs), *steward* (=sty-ward), *stile, stair*
Stow, a place	*stow, stowage, bestow*
Strang, strong	*strong, stronghold, strength, string*
Talu, a member, a tale	*tale, tell, tell-tale*
Thyrlian, to pierce	*thrill, nostril*
Tredan, to tread	*tread, treadle, trade* (a way of life)
Treowe, true	*true, truth, troth, betroth*
Twa, two	*two, twain, twelve, twenty, twice, twin, twine, twilight, twist, between*
Waer, cautious	*wary, aware, beware*
Weork, work	*work, wrought, wright*
Witan, to know	*wit, witness, witch*
Wrecan, to wreak	*wreak, wreck, wrack, wretch, wretched*
Writhan, to twist	*writhe, wreath, wrath, wrist, wrest, wrestle*

(Adapted from J.M.D. Meiklejohn, *A Short Grammar of the English Tongue with Three Hundred and Thirty Exercises*, 1905, pp. 107-109)

> "All recipients of honorary degrees should know that those rolled-up scrolls they are handed are not real diplomas, not in any proper etymological sense. The word DIPLOMA comes, simply and by definition, from *duo*, "two"; a diploma was a sheet of paper folded double."
>
> Lewis Thomas, *ET CAETERA, ET CAETERA*, 1990, p. 92

LATIN ROOTS

L ATIN NOUNS HAVE two forms, for example: *datum, data* which are the equivalent of singular and plural. Verbs have four forms: *ago, agere, egi, actum* which correspond to First Person Singular, Infinitive, Simple Past, and Past Participle. Latin adjectives have one form: *bene*. It's a good idea to **check all the four forms because English words may come from one of them.**

The English language of today contains words that come from one of these forms, and once students recognize one, they can make the connection and recognize others. Recognition may also lead to remembering the words.

LATIN: *Ago, agere, egi, actum* = to act
ENGLISH: **Agent, agile, agitate, act, actual, active**

Each word developed its own derivations:

Agent, agents   **agile, agility,**
agitate, agitated, agitating, agitator   **act, acts**
actual, actuality, actually   **active, actively**

Annus, anni = year
Annual, annually, biennial, anniversary, annals

Audio, audire, audivi, auditum = to hear
Audio, audible, audience, audit, auditory, auditorium

Bene = good, well
Beneficiary, benevolent, benefit, benefactor

Cado, cadere, cecidi, casum = to fall
Case, casual, cadence, decadence, case

*Caedo, caedere, caecidi, caes*um = to cut, to kill
Decide, suicide, excise, concise, precision

Cano, canere, cecini, cantum = to sing
Cantor, cant, descant, canto, enchant

Capio, capere, cepi, captum = to take, to catch
Capable, capacity, receive, captive, capture, except

Caput, capitis = head
Capital, captain, chapter, decapitate

Cedo, cedere, cessi, cessum = to go, to withdraw, to yield
Cede, precede, exceed, proceed, excess, process, procession, secede, succeed

Circus, circi = ring, circle
Circle, circular, circulate, circumference, circuit

Corpus, corporis = body
Corps, corpse, corporal, corporation, incorporate, corporeal

Credo, credere, credidi, creditum = to believe
Creed, credible, credit, credulous, discredit

Curro, currere, cucuri, cursum = to run
Current, occur, occurrence, incur, course, cursory, excursion, concur

Dico, dicere, dixi, dictum = to say
Dictionary, dictate, diction, predict, contradict, indict

Facio, facere, feci, factum = to do, to make
Manufacture, fact, factual, effect, counterfeit

Ferro, ferre, tuli, latum = to carry
Confer, refer, prefer, translate, infer, transfer, relate

Jacio, jacere, jeci, jactum = to throw, to cast, to utter
Reject, subject, adjective, project, projectile, jet

Lego, legere, legi, lectum = to read
Legend, legible, diligent, lecture, intellect, select, elector

Magnus = great
Magnate, to magnify, magnificent, magnanimous

Moveo, movere, movi, motum = to move
Move, mobile, motion, motive, motivate, promote

Pando, pandere, pandi, pansum = to stretch
Expand, expanse, pass, passage, trespass

Pello, pellere, pepuli, pulsum = to beat, to hit, to slap
Repellent, expel, pulse, repulse, expulsion

Scribo, scribere, scripsi, scriptum = to write
Scribe, describe, prescribe, transcribe, subscribe, script

Sentio, sentire, sensi, sensum = to perceive, to feel, to think
Sense, sensibility, sensitive, sentiment, sentence

Tango, tangere, tetigi, tactum = to touch
Tangent, tangible, tango, tact, contact

Tendo, tendere, tetendi, tensum = to stretch, to aim, to strive
Tend, pretend, attend, attendant, tent, contention, tense, tension

Teneo, tenere, tenui, tentum = to hold
Tenant, tenable, contain, continent, content

Traho, trahere, traxi, tractum = to draw
Tract, contract, trait, treat, treatise

Venio, venire, veni, ventum = to come
Convene, convenient, adventure, prevent, invention

Video, videre, visi, visum = to see
Video, provide, evident, vision, visible

Vinco, vincere, vici, victum = to win, to conquer
Convince, invincible, convict, victory

Vivo, vivere, vixi, victum = to live
Vivid, revive, vivacious, convivial

Volo, velle, volui = to wish, to want
Voluntary, volunteer, benevolent

Vox, vocis = voice
Vocal, voice, vociferous, advocate, provoke

DISCOVER Provide dictionaries and let the students discover new English words using the same Latin roots. For each new word, they should be able to challenge each other, change the parts of speech, and produce original sentences.

For example:

New word:	*To attend*	Can you make it a **noun**?
	Victory	Can you make it an **adjective**?
	Vision	Can you change it into a **verb**?

Read and Discover: Read the following passage and discover at least 3 or 4 words with Anglo-Saxon roots and at least 5 or 6 with Latin roots.

The SILK ROAD

"The Silk Road was an ancient network of trade routes, formally established during the Han Dynasty, which linked the regions of the ancient world in commerce between 130 BCE – 1453 CE. As the Silk Road was not a single thoroughfare from east to west, the term 'Silk Routes' has become increasingly favored by historians, though 'Silk Road' is the more common and recognized name. The European explorer Marco Polo (1254-1324) . . . traveled on these routes and described them in depth in his famous work but he is not credited with naming them. Both terms for this network of roads were coined by the German geographer and traveler, Ferdinand von Richthofen, in 1877, who designated them 'Seidenstrasse' (silk road) or 'Seidenstrassen' (silk routes). Polo, and later von Richthofen, make mention of the goods which were transported back and forth on the Silk Road. From West to East these goods included:

- Horses
- Saddles and Riding Tack
- The grapevine and grapes
- Dogs and other animals both exotic and domestic
- Animal furs and skins
- Honey
- Fruits
- Glassware
- Woolen blankets, rugs, carpets

- Textiles (such as curtains)
- Gold and silver
- Camels
- Slaves
- Weapons and armor

From East to West the goods included:

- Silk
- Tea
- Precious stones
- China (plates, bowls, cups, vases)
- Porcelain
- Spices (such as cinnamon and ginger)
- Bronze and gold artifacts
- Medicine
- Perfumes
- Ivory
- Rice
- Paper
- Gunpowder" (*Ancient History Encyclopedia*, www.ancient.eu)

> "The mediocre teacher tells. The good teacher explains. The superior teacher demonstrates. The great teacher inspires."
>
> William A. Ward

Teaching Vocabulary

TIPS for ESL students re: Vocabulary

Students must **make a mental effort** to understand, analyze, and then use the new vocabulary they are learning every day. How can we help them and what do we need to do?

Looking at the whole story from a student's perspective, teachers should start the vocabulary classes with a **quick conversation** about the words to be learned in the classroom that specific day. Suggested points to be discussed:

- What part of speech is the word? Can you change it into other parts of speech?
- How is the word spelled? Can you pronounce it?
- Can you combine it with other words? (Create a collocation?)
- If possible, can you separate it into prefix, root, and suffix?
- Can you guess its meaning by looking at the context?
- What other word or synonym/antonym comes to mind?
- If you change its stress, does it change its meaning?
- Can you use this word in an idiom?
- Last but not least: definition

Let's take for example the word "center"

concentrate on (vb.)
They concentrated on their work.

central (adj.)
central air conditioning

centrally (adv.)
centrally located

centrality (n.)
the centrality of religion in their lives

decentralize (vb.)
We decentralized our operations and opened several regional offices.

center (noun)
The center of the room/The center of attention

center (verb)
Their whole life centers on the children.

Epicenter (n.)
The patient was the epicenter of concern.

Centered (vb.)
Community centered actions

Centering (vb.)
The search was centering in the desert beyond Verdant Valley.

Centers (n. pl.)
New York is one of the major banking centers.

Centric (adj.)
Euro-centric

Concentric (adj.)
Concentric circles

Collocations:

International center	A center of government power
Financial center	Commercial center
World Trade Center	A center of excellence

The first thing a reader looks at is **the word in context**, and this might be good enough to provide its meaning. The words around the new word, the sentence itself, or the whole passage, all contain clues that will definitely help, if only the student can analyze what lies in front of his eyes. John Langan, in his *Ten Steps to Improving College Reading Skills* (1997), comes up with four common types of context clues:

Examples
    Synonyms
        Antonyms
            General Sense of the Sentence or Passage

"**Examples** within the passage would be the first clue and if we look carefully to identify other signal words (*such as, for example, including* etc.), we can guess the meaning of an unfamiliar word. For example:

Nocturnal creatures, such as **bats and owls**, have highly developed senses that enable them to function in the dark.

Nocturnal means:

a. Feathery   b. Living   c. Active at night

The example of nocturnal creatures – bats and owls – may help us to guess that they are active at night because they only come out at night." (10-11)

Synonyms are the most common types of clues and may appear anywhere in the passage. They may help the reader to identify the meaning of the new word.

1.   Are you *averse* to exercise? You would not be so **opposed** to it if you had a partner to work out with you.

2.   If we *assess* ourselves favorably, our self-esteem will be high, but if we **judge** ourselves negatively, it will suffer. (12)

"**Antonyms** – a word that has the opposite meaning – may also be a useful context clue. And again, look for signal words that can help you (*however, but, yet, on the contrary, in contrast*, etc.).

1.   Religions in America are not *static*, but *changing*, especially in this period of shifting values.

     Static means:

     a. unchanging   b. unknown   c. shifting

2. Many people have pointed out the harmful effects that a working mother may have on the family, yet there are many *salutary* effects as well.

    Salutary means:

    a. well-known   b. beneficial   c. hurtful" (14)

General Sense of the Sentence or Passage - CONTEXT

Besides examples, synonyms, and antonyms, there is another way to guess the meaning in context, but that means the reader has to consider the information presented and then draw conclusions based on what is found in the sentence or passage.

"Each of the sentences below is followed by a question. Think about each question; then circle the letter of the answer you think is the correct meaning of the italicized word.

1. A former employee, *irate* over having been fired, broke into the plant and deliberately wrecked several machines.

    Irate means

    a. relieved   b. very angry   c. undecided

2. Despite the *proximity* of Ron's house to his sister's, he rarely sees her.

    Proximity means

    a. similarity   b. nearness   c. superiority

3. The car wash we organized to raise funds was a *fiasco* – it rained all day.

    Fiasco means

    a. great financial success   b. welcome surprisec. complete disaster" (16)

Review Test

"Use context clues to figure out the meaning of the italicized words in the following textbook passages, and write your definition in the space provided.

1. When people are broke, they find that many things that seem *indispensable* are not so necessary after all.

    Indispensable means _____

2. It's amazing that my neighbors always appear *immaculate*, yet their apartment is often quite dirty.

    Immaculate means _____

Although mysteries and science fiction may seem like different kinds of writing, the two forms share some basic similarities. First of all, both are action-directed, emphasizing plot at the expense of character development. Possibly for this reason, both types of literature have been *scorned* by critics as being merely 'entertainment' rather than 'literature.' But this attack is unjustified, for both mysteries and science fiction share a concern with moral issues. Science fiction often raises the question of whether or not scientific advances are of benefit to humanity. And a mystery story rarely ends without the *culpable* person being brought to justice.

Scorned means _____
Culpable means _____   (21)"

According to John Morgan and Mario Rinvolucri, there are lots of lesson plans with workable passages attached to each section. In Unit 5, *Using corpora and concordances*, the authors are showing how corpora and their associated software can help language learners and teachers. The example they give is using reciprocal verb phrases.

Procedure "Give the students copies of the Worksheet. Tell them to complete the worksheet in groups of four, using dictionaries and other reference material they have. Tell them to call you over when they need further help. As the students work, go round helping to clarify meaning, offering (. . .) contexts for the phrases." (66)

Worksheet			
1. Look through this phase list:			
battle it out	*chew the fat*	*compare notes*	*cross words*
bury the hatchet	*do battle*	*do business*	*fall in love*
change places	*go hand in hand*	*shake hands*	*go to war*
have it off	*have it out*	*settle accounts*	*have words*
hit it off	*hold hands*	*join forces*	*link arms*
lock horns	*lose contact*	*lose touch*	*make contact*
make friends	*make love*	*make peace*	*mend fences*
part company	*pass the time of day*	*see eye to eye*	
2. Write down all the phrases you do NOT know the meaning of.			
3. Write down all the phrases that have to do with repairing relationships.			
4. Write down all the phrases which involve negative feeling between two individuals.			

5.   Write down all the phrases that basically mean to talk with, to chat with.
6.   Look at these examples:
We made contact. I made contact with him.
They lost touch.   He lost touch with her.
All the phrases above can be used in these two patterns. Choose ten of them and make your own example sentences for each, adding context and details, for example:
After she moved to London, Peter lost touch with her.

Words can be interpreted in many ways, depending on **context** or depending on **what the speaker intends to say, intonation, stress,** or **what s/he implies.**

"In Lewis Carroll's book *Through the Looking Glass, and What Alice Found There* (often erroneously referred to as *Alice through the Looking Glass*), Humpty Dumpty tells Alice: 'There's glory for you.'

'I don't know what you mean by *glory*,' Alice said.

Humpty Dumpty smiled contemptuously. 'Of course you don't – till I tell you. I meant *there's a nice knock-down argument for you*! '

'But *glory* does not mean *a nice knock-down argument*, 'Alice objected.

'When I use a word,' Humpty Dumpty said, in rather a scornful tone, 'it means what I choose it to mean – neither more nor less.'

'The question is,' Alice said, 'whether you can make words mean so many different things.' "

(quoted in Forsyth, The Etymologicon, 2011, p. 235)

In *Vocabulary,* Second Edition, Oxford University Press, 2004, John Morgan and Mario Rinvolucri focus mainly on recent developments in the field, including collocations and the mother tongue.

They also mention that "one of the principles that underpins this book is the realization that learning words is a relational process. You could describe the process as making friends with the words of the target language. We do not subscribe to the view that a word is merely a 'signifier' that acts as a label for a 'signified' in the real world. It is much more than that. If a word is simply a label, why will second language learners pick up and remember one word apparently effortlessly, while another word, met at the same time and place, will be refused a place in their mind? Just as a look, a movement, a chance remark, a tone of voice, or something in the setting can influence our first impressions of a person, so our perception of a word can be affected by, for example:

- Its sound
- The kinetic sensation of the lungs, throat, mouth, tongue, and nose when saying the word
- Its tune
- Its pitch
- Its speed of enunciation
- The other word company it keeps (collocating ability and breadth)
- Its spelling
- Its shape on the page or screen
- Conventional associations: semantic and syntactic categories to which the word appears to belong
- Literary associations
- The associations the word has for the individual learner
- The circumstances of meeting the word

All these factors play a part in 'learning' a word. If you take them into account, then meeting a word is a process of befriending, of coming to terms with a complex, self-standing reality." (6-7)

In my experience, teaching vocabulary has been one of the most satisfying and rewarding experiences. After perusing textbooks and teaching manuals, every teacher arrives at the destination following a separate or individual pathway. For the beginning of each class, students usually expect a short introduction and a couple of guidelines before tackling the main topic. They also need to make a mental effort along the way, and this should be done keeping in mind their previous knowledge, their proficiency level, and their goal.

> "That which we call a rose by any other name would smell as sweet."
>
> William Shakespeare

SYNONYMS

FROM ANCIENT GREEK, *syn* ("with") and *onoma* ("name"), via Latin and then Middle English, we now have **synonyms**, words that are similar or exactly the same as other words. Among the first significant works in the field of synonyms was *The British Synonymy* compiled by Hester Lynch Piozzi (1741-1821), better known as Mrs. Thrale, a close friend of Dr. Johnson. Here is how the author presented her work:

"... I have before me the definition of *fondness*, given into my hands many years ago by a most eminent logician. 'Fondness,' says the Definer, 'is the hasty and injudicious determination of the will towards promoting the present gratification of some particular object.' 'Fondness,' in the opinion of Dr. Johnson, 'is rather the hasty and injudicious attribution of excellence, somewhat beyond the power of attainment, to the object of our affection.' Both these definitions may possibly be included in *fondness*; my own idea of the whole may be found in the following example:

Amintor and Aspasia are models of true *love*: 'tis now seven years since their mutual *passion* was sanctified by marriage; and so little is the lady's *affection* diminished, that she sat up nine nights successively last winter by her husband's bed-side, when he had a malignant fever that frightened relations, friends, servants, all away. Nor can anyone allege that her *tenderness* is all repaid, while we see him gaze upon her features with that *fondness* which is capable of creating charms for itself to admire, and listen to her talk with a fervour of admiration scarce due to the most brilliant genius.

For the rest, 'tis my opinion that men love for the most part with warmer *passion* than women do – at least than English women, and with more transitory *fondness* mingled with that passion . . ."

(*Webster's Dictionary of Synonyms*, 1951, p. viii)

When it comes to finding the right words in concrete cases, the Piozzi method explains:

"TO ABANDON, FORSAKE, RELINQUISH, GIVE UP, DESERT, QUIT, LEAVE...though at first sight apparently synonymous, conversing does certainly better show the peculiar appropriation than books, however learned; for...familiar talk tells us in half an hour – that a man *forsakes* his mistress, *abandons* all hope of regaining her lost esteem, relinquishes his pretensions in favour of another.[...]We say that reports are *confirmed*, treaties *ratified*, and affairs *settled*. A hard question *puzzles* a man, and a variety of choice *perplexes* him: one is *confounded* by a loud and sudden dissonance of sound and voices in a still night; *embarrassed* by a weight of clothes or valuables, if making escape from fire, thieves, or pursuit...The gentleman who discharges a gaming debt in preference to that of a tradesman, apparently prefers *honour* to another virtue, *justice.* "(p. viii)

David Crystal (2005) makes a relevant remark, to caution us, when he says:

"The search for synonyms is a well-established classroom exercise, but it is as well to remember that lexemes rarely (if ever) have exactly the same meaning. There are usually stylistic, regional, emotional, or other differences to consider. [...] And context must always be taken into account. Two lexemes might be synonymous in one sentence but different in another: *range* and *selection* are synonymous in *What a nice _ of furnishings*, but not in *There's the mountain - .*" (195-196)

 TIPS for our ESL teachers and students re: synonyms:

1. In the classroom, we need to use **very easy and very simple explanations:**

    We may be dealing with exact or perfect synonyms, like BEGIN and START, or with partial synonyms, like DELAY and POSTPONE. Partial synonyms are words that may be used, in certain cases but not in all cases, to replace each other.

    We may generally say: *Don't delay or postpone paying your bills.*

    However, when we find more specific uses, the situation changes:

    I was delayed by traffic. (not postponed)
    We are going to postpone our meeting for next week. (not delay)

2. The best suggestion for our ESL students would be to encourage them to learn how to use **a thesaurus**. Simple exercises should include:

    Avoid repeating the same word several times when you speak or when you write. Use a synonym instead.

3. Challenge the students to find alternatives and enrich their vocabulary when dealing with simple words, and they will extrapolate and do the same with other, more sophisticated words.

    How many synonyms can you find for the following words:

AND	also, besides, ...
BUT	however, on the contrary, . . .
SO	therefore, . . .
BIG	great, enormous, . . .
FUNNY	hilarious, humorous, . . .

PRACTICE USING A THESAURUS:

Challenge the students to work in pairs or small groups and discover the meaning of the following synonyms and then produce their own original sentences.:

ATTRACTIVE – CHARMING – FASCINATING – ENCHANTING - CAPTIVATING

GIVE – PRESENT – DONATE – BESTOW - CONFER

TO CLOSE - TO END - TO CONCLUDE - TO FINISH - TO TERMINATE

EASY – SIMPLE – LIGHT – EFFORTLESS – FACILE - SMOOTH

TO HAVE - TO HOLD - TO OWN - TO POSSESS

HAZE – MIST - FOG

The 5th edition of the *Longman Dictionary of American English* will give you some very good examples:

TO COOK

Bake - to cook food such as bread in the over

Fry - to cook food in oil on the top part of an oven

Roast - to cook meals or vegetables in an oven

Broil – to cook food by placing it near to strong heat from above

Grill - to cook food over strong heat, especially over flames

Saute – to fry vegetables for a short time in a small amount of oil

Boil – to cook vegetables in very hot water on the top part of the oven

Steam – to cook vegetables by placing them in a container over very hot water, so that the steam from the hot water cooks them

Deep fry – to fry food in a pan containing a lot of hot oil (p. 247)

GOAL

Aim – something that you want to achieve when you do something:

His aim was to grow enough food to feed his family.

Objective – something that you are working hard to achieve, especially in business or politics:

The major objectives been achieved.

Target – the number or amount that you want to achieve:

The charity has set itself the target of raising over $1 million for cancer research.

Mission - the things that a person or organization wants to achieve, which is the main purpose for all their activities:

The company says its mission is to organize the world's information and make it available to everyone.   (p. 485)

HAPPY

Glad – pleased about a situation or something that has happened

I'm so glad you were able to come.

Pleased – happy and satisfied with something that has happened

Her parents were pleased that she had done so well.

Content – happy and satisfied

We are usually content to stay at home and read or watch TV.

Delighted/thrilled/overjoyed – extremely happy because something good has happened

We were delighted when she had a baby girl.

Ecstatic – extremely happy and excited

When he heard he'd gotten the job, he was ecstatic.

Jubilant *formal* – extremely happy and pleased because you have been successful

After the game, a jubilant crowd celebrated the win.

Elated *formal* – extremely happy and excited

Ron was elated to hear that his wife was pregnant.   (p. 515)

> "To tell" once meant *to count*. This meaning died out but is preserved in the expression *bank teller*, which appeared in Middle English around 1475.
>
> Lewis Thomas, *ET CETERA, ET CETERA*, 1990, p. 41

TO SAY vs. TO TELL

To say and *To tell* are used in different ways in reported speech. With the verb TO SAY, we are trying to use more or less the exact words someone said. The other verb, TO TELL, is used to render the content or message of what someone said.

SAY can be followed by a preposition. TELL cannot.
SAY can be used at the end of the sentence. TELL cannot.
SAY can be followed by a that-clause.
SAY is preferred before or after direct quotations. TELL is preferred in indirect quotations.
SAY focuses on utterance or pronunciation. TELL implies a narration of some kind.

Suggestion: Ask your students to write the correct form of *say* or *tell* in each blank space. Help them to study the use of *say* and *tell* in the first four examples.

1. Mr. Brown *said* that he had been too busy to leave his office.

2. Mr. Brown *said* to his wife, "I have to go to that meeting."

3. Mr. Brown *told* his wife that he had to leave right away.

4. "I will return in an hour or two," Mr. Brown *said*.

5. My friend _____ me that he was planning to leave right away.

6. John _____ to me, "I will meet you at the train station."

7. "I think we should choose a better place to meet," I _____.

8. Bill _____ his friend had _____ him about the announcement.

9. Did you _____ everyone what his friend had _____ about it?

10. Bill's friend _____ us that his friend would _____ everyone else.

11. We couldn't _____ the man exactly what Bill's friend had _____.

12. Yesterday we _____ that Alice shouldn't have _____ them anything.

13. "I really should have _____ the truth," Alice _____ later.

14. "Alice _____ a lie about that matter last week," Fred _____.

15. Don't _____ anything about what Fred has just _____ you.

16. I _____ them that I hadn't _____ a word about it to anyone.

17. I _____ quickly, "Don't worry. I haven't _____ anything at all."

18. "I'll _____ you a secret about that," Fred _____ to his friends.

19. "Fred _____ you that, didn't he?" Alice _____ with a smile.

20. "_____ something in English," Betty _____ to Pierre.

(Grant Taylor, *Mastering American English*, 1956, p.142)

Use the following collocations in original sentences:

tell a lie	*tell a story*	*tell a secret*
tell time	*tell apart*	*a telling detail*
say something	*say yes*	*say goodbye*
say it with flowers	*say what you will*	*that is to say*

TO DO vs. TO MAKE

FOR MANY ESL students, these two verbs may be difficult to use mainly because in other languages there is only one word instead of two.

TO DO is used to express the idea of **ACTION**
> *What are you doing?*   *I am cooking.*

TO MAKE focuses on **ACTION with a RESULT**
> *What are you making?*   *A chocolate cake.*

Use the following collocations with the verb TO DO in **your own questions**:

To do a favor	*Can you do me a favor?*
To do homework	_____
To do the laundry	_____
To do what's needed	_____
To do the shopping	_____
To do away with	_____
To do over	_____
To do rounds	_____

Use the following collocations with the verb TO MAKE in original sentences:

To make sense	*That doesn't make any sense.*
To make progress	_____
To make do	_____
To make an appointment	_____
To make friends	_____
To make an attempt	_____
To make up one's mind	_____
To make a decision	_____
Ask a question with MAKE	_____
Answer using the verb DO	_____

> "In the crazy English language, the blackbird hen is brown, blackboards can be blue or green, and blackberries are green and then red before they are ripe. [. . .] To add to the insanity, there is no butter in buttermilk, no egg in eggplant, neither worms nor wood in wormwood, neither pine nor apple in pineapple, and no ham in hamburger. To make matters worse, English muffins were not invented in England, french fries in France, or Danish pastries in Denmark. And we discover even more culinary madness in the revelations that sweetmeat is made from fruit, while sweetbread, which isn't sweet, is made from meat."
>
> Richard Lederer, *Crazy English*, 1989

HOMONYMS

IF WE TAKE a quick look at the word HOMONYM, the first thing that we should notice is that it contains two parts, the first one meaning "the same," and the second one meaning "name." That being said, we should also remember that the English language got this word, according to dictionaries, from Greek via Latin, sometime in the 17th century.

Homonyms can be divided into two groups:

Homophones - words having the same pronunciation, but different meanings.

Homographs - words that are spelled the same but not necessarily pronounced the same and having different meanings.

In the late 1980s, James B. Hobbs worked on a project to help a seven-year-old friend win his class challenge of generating the largest number of homophones. The result was his 1986 book entitled *Homophones and Homographs*, containing 3,625 homophones and 602 homographs. In the Overview (page 1), the author delineated very clearly what these words are:

> "Briefly, a homophone is a word that is pronounced the same as another (a 'sound-alike') but which differs in spelling and meaning, such as cite, sight, and site. On the other hand, a homograph is a word that is spelled the same as another (a 'look-alike') but which differs in sound and meaning, such as *tear* (to separate or pull apart) and *tear* (a secretion from the eye)."

HOMOPHONES

A HOMOPHONE IS A word having the same pronunciation as another, but differing in origin, meaning, and often in spelling. Here are some examples:

Aisle - a lateral subdivision of a church, theater, airplane, or train
- a passage between shelves of goods in a supermarket or other building

I'll contraction of I will or I shall

Isle a small island

Bale/bail	Beach/beech	Berth/birth
Brake/break	Cede/seed	Cell/sell
Cent/sent/scent	Chord/cord	Coarse/course
Creak/creek	Dire/dyer	Forth/fourth
Foul/fowl	Freeze/frieze	Grate/great
Hoard/horse	Knead/need	Lain/lane
Lean/lien	Maize/maze	Mean/mien
Plain/plane	Pleas/please	Praise/prays/preys
Rain/reign/rein	Rapped/rapt/wrapped	Real/reel
Rest/wrest	Right/rite/wright/write	Rung/wrung
Serf/surf	Shear/sheer	Sight/site/cite
Slay/sleigh	Soar/sore	Sole/soul
Stake/steak	Stile/style	Straight/strait
Suite/sweet	Their/there/they're	Threw/through
Waist/waste	Waive/wave	

DISCOVER: Challenge the students to see if they can match the following:

Aid	_____	a. an assistant
Aide	_____	b. to help; to further

Air	_____	a. before
Ere	_____	b. contraction of ever
E'er	_____	c. one who inherits
Heir	_____	d. invisible mixture of gases

Band	_____	a. something that ties things together
Banned	_____	b. cursed; denounced; condemned
Board	_____	a. to be weary
Bored	_____	b. piece of sawed lumber
Climb	_____	a. to ascend or rise
Clime	_____	b. climate
Feat	_____	a. plural of foot
Feet	_____	b. an act or a deed
Gait	_____	a. manner of walking
Gate	_____	b. an opening
Groan	_____	a. to utter a moaning sound
Grown	_____	b. to have increased
Heal	_____	a. the hind part of the human foot
Heel	_____	b. to cure
Hole	_____	a. an opening
Whole	_____	b. not broken; undamaged; intact
Leased	_____	a. to have granted by lease
Least	_____	b. used as superlative of little
Loan	_____	a. without company
Lone	_____	b. act of lending
Main	_____	a. the chief part; the essential part
Mane	_____	b. long, heavy hair
Pain	_____	a. a distressing feeling due to disease
Pane	_____	b. a single plate of glass
Peace	_____	a. a fragment
Piece	_____	b. a pact or agreement to end hostilities
Peer	_____	a. to look narrowly, curiously
Pier	_____	b. an intermediate support
Stair	_____	a. to gaze or look fixedly
Stare	_____	b. a step

Steal	_____	a. to take or carry away feloniously
Steel	_____	b. a commercial form of iron
Ware	_____	a. collectively, articles of merchandise
Wear	_____	b. to use by wearing

> "The true scholar learns from the known to unfold the unknown."
> Goethe, _Wilhelm Meister's Apprenticeship_

Suggestion:

More advanced students should be challenged to take a look at the following words and find their equivalent homophones:

Arrange the students in three groups and provide handouts with 6 or 7 words per group. With the help of a dictionary, they should be able to discover new vocabulary and then come up with examples in original sentences.

In each group, students should be able to ask each other questions (for example, What is an _inn_?) and then find the right definitions for the new words.

If time allows, let the students present their own questions about words that sound similar.

_In_	_____	_hoarse_	_____	_lead_	_____
knight	_____	_meet_	_____	_pair_	_____
peel	_____	_dual_	_____	_sleigh_	_____
born	_____	_chute_	_____	_gilt_	_____
pale	_____	_heard_	_____	_tear_	_____
raise	_____	_pole_	_____	_vale_	_____

NOTES

_____

_____

_____

_____

_____

HOMOGRAPHS

A HOMOGRAPH IS A word identical to another in spelling but differing from it in meaning, derivation, and often pronunciation.

Lead   verb: "to conduct"
                noun: "a kind of metal"

DISCOVER   Students can be encouraged to work in pairs or small groups, use an English-English dictionary of their choice, and discover **the so-called mysteries of homographs:**

For example:

ally	verb:	*They allied with their best friends.*
	noun:	*France is our closest ally.*
alternate	adjective:	_____
	verb:	_____
	noun:	_____
bow	verb:	_____
	noun:	_____
close	adjective:	_____
	verb:	_____
conduct	verb:	_____
	noun:	_____
conflict	verb:	_____
	noun:	_____
content	adjective:	_____
	noun:	_____
contrast	verb:	_____
	noun:	_____

convict   verb: _____
              noun: _____

desert   verb: _____
              noun: _____

excuse   verb: _____
              noun: _____

export   verb: _____
              noun: _____

extract   verb: _____
              noun: _____

frequent   verb: _____
              adjective: _____

import   verb: _____
              noun: _____

invalid   noun: _____
              adjective: _____

object   verb: _____
              noun: _____

perfect   verb: _____
              adjective: _____

permit   verb: _____
              noun: _____

present   verb: _____
              adjective: _____

produce   verb: _____
              noun: _____

progress   verb: _____
              noun: _____

project   verb: _____
              noun: _____

protest   verb: _____
              noun: _____

rebel   verb: _____
              noun: _____

refuse   verb: _____
              noun: _____

resume   verb: _____
             noun: _____

subject verb: _____
             noun: _____

suspect verb: _____
             noun: _____

DISCOVER   Prepare slips of paper with the following words, distribute them to the students, and challenge them to find out the various meanings of all these words. When they are done, students should present the results to the whole class.

Bass   **Bat**   **Digest**   **Fine**   **Fair**   **Minute**   **Second**

NOTES

_____
_____
_____
_____
_____

Similar Sounding Words
Commonly Misused Words

ENGLISH HAS A lot of words that sound similar but are completely different in spelling, pronunciation, or meaning. Sometimes they belong to different parts of speech.

Accept/except
accept my apologies   *everybody except John*

Access/excess
access to email   *a life of excess*

Adapt/adept/adopt
adapt to a new environment   *adept in several languages*
adopt a pet

Addition/edition
a good addition to our staff   *the new edition of the book*

Adverse/averse
adverse conditions   *averse to borrowing money*

Advice/advise
a piece of advice   *please advise*

Affect/effect
this can affect your health   *the effect of climate change*

Command/commend
a good command of English   *you're commended for your courage*

Complement/compliment
the hat complements the suit   *that was a nice compliment*

Consul/council/counsel
The US Consul   the city council   *to counsel the students*

Core/corps/corpse
common core   Marine Corps   *the corpse was found in the park*

Costume/custom
Halloween costume   *traditional customs*

Critic/critique
a harsh critic   *an interesting critique of the book*

Decent/descent/dissent
decent proposal   *of Irish descent*   *only one member dissented*

Device/devise
the thermostat is a useful device   *we need to devise a new plan*

Eligible/legible
eligible for extra benefits
nobody could read the message – it was not legible

Emigrant/immigrant
many emigrants leave their native country
immigrants crowd the border

Envelop/envelope
enveloped by smoke   *The envelope, please!*

Factitious/fictitious
factitious gems   *fictitious story*

Farther/further
the farther side of the mountain   *any further questions?*

Formally/formerly
we have not been introduced formally
the manager was formerly the secretary

Human/humane
human error   *the treatment was not humane*

Liable/libel
liable for someone's actions   *The Supreme Court's definition of libel*

Monetary/monitory
monetary compensations   *a monitory letter*

Personal/personnel
personal loans   *Human Resources personnel*

Principal/principle
school principal   *a matter of principles*

Weather/whether
the weather report   *whether you like it or not*

REVIEW OF HOMONYMS AND COMMONLY MISUSED WORDS

DISCOVER: Select the correct word in parentheses to complete the meaning of the sentence:

1. Although my parents rarely eat (**desert/dessert**), I sometimes prefer something sweet.

2. (**Who's/whose**) supposed to bring the refreshments for our weekend party?

3. Lily had to (**quit/quite/quiet**) drinking soda following her doctor's advice.

4. It seems (**their/there/they're**) not interested because they haven't answered our invitation.

5. In the United States, it is a (**custom/costume**) to eat turkey on Thanksgiving.

6. If you need to appear in the court of law, make sure you wear (**descent/decent**) clothes.

7. Students need to (**sight/site/cite**) several references in their research papers.

8. My grandpa still uses monogrammed (**stationary/stationery**) when he sends us his New Year's Greetings.

9. Teddy was the (**principle/principal**) speaker at the ceremony.

10. I tried to read my friend's notes, but they were not (**eligible/ legible**).

11. Please be careful how you approach your neighbors because they are very (**sensible/sensitive**) to outside suggestions.

12. Your remarks can really (**affect/effect**) their decision.

13. We all liked Jackie's essay because it was quite (**imaginative/ imaginary**).

14. She took my remark as a (**compliment/complement**).

15. (**Special/especially**) attention must be paid in selecting the right ingredients.

16. Albert Einstein formulated the (**principal/principle**) of relativity.

17. Never (**lose/loose**) your concentration when you take difficult tests.

18. We all liked the decoration of (**fictitious/factitious**) flowers.

19. Now that the plan changed, we had to (**devise/device**) a new strategy.

20. They were both (**commanded/commended**) for their outstanding performances.

21. Our mayor was (**formally/formerly**) a Congressman.

22. (**Piece/peace**) was restored in the community after a week of rioting.

23. Today's weather is better (**than/then**) yesterday's.

24. We are (**all ready/already**) to start our well-deserved vacation.

25. Everyone is going to the convention (**accept/except**) Hillary, who is studying for her final tests.

26. We had so much work to do after our vacation that we (**hard/ hardly**) knew where to begin.

27. The United States is a melting pot, a land of (**emigrants/ immigrants**).

Silent letters

Tips

TIPS: How do we present the silent letters to our ESL students?

One source comes up with wonderful examples and extremely useful information. According to this website, silent letters help English learners in many ways:

1. "Silent letters can distinguish between homophones, e.g. *in/inn*, *be/bee*, *lent*/leant. This is an aid to readers already familiar with both words.

2. Silent letters may give an insight into the meaning or origin of a word, e.g. *vineyard* suggests *vines* more than the phonetic *vineyard* would.

3. Silent letters help to show long vowels e.g. *rid/ride*.

4. Silent letters help to show 'hard' consonants e.g. *guest/gest*

5. They can help to connect different forms of the same word e.g. *resign/resignation*." www.languagelearningbase.com

B is silent after **m** in the same syllable:
  Bo**mb**, co**mb**, plu**mb**er
B is silent before **t:**
  De**bt**, dou**bt**, su**bt**le
C is silent before **t:**
  Indi**ct**, vi**ct**uals
C is silent after **s:**
  Mu**sc**le, **sc**ene, de**sc**ent, ab**sc**ess
Ch is silent in ya**ch**t, s**ch**ism, fu**ch**sia
D is silent in We**d**nesday, han**d**some, han**d**kerchief
G is silent before **m** or **n** as in diaphra**gm**, si**gn**, beni**gn**, forei**gn**
G is silent before **n** at the beginning of a word:
  Gnat, **gn**aw, **gn**arl
Gh is silent in bou**gh**t, ei**gh**t, bou**gh**
H is silent in some words that came from Old French:
  Honor, **h**onest, **h**eir, **h**our

H is silent in unaccented syllables:
    Shep**h**erd, ve**h**ement, ve**h**icle
K is silent before **n**:
    Knight, **kn**eel, **kn**ow, **kn**ot, **kn**it, **kn**owledge
L is silent before **m**:
    Sa**l**mon, ca**l**m, pa**l**m
L is silent in half, calf, talk, folk
N is silent after **m**:
    Hy**mn**, sole**mn**
P is silent in raspberry, cupboard, receipt, cou**p**
P is silent in words of Greek origin:
    Pneumonia, **pn**eumatic
T is silent in mortgage, christen, chasten, listen, castle, glisten
    Th is silent in as**th**ma
W is silent before **r**:
    Write, **wr**ong, **wr**ing
W is silent before vowels in two cases:
    Two, who, sword
    Answer, toward

There are many other cases when certain letters are not pronounced. "Silent letters are the ghosts of pronunciation past." www.independent.co.uk

According to the same source, the English language is borrowing words from other languages, and in the process, people try to pronounce those new words the best they can. For example:

> "*Tsunami* is a Japanese word and *Psychology* is Greek. Native speakers of English don't have the initial sounds in English words and therefore drop them when they speak. Another explanation would be that certain words beginning with 'h' are of French origin and the English took over the French pronunciation; for example: *honest, hour,* etc. By the same token, students should be advised that other English words beginning with 'h' do not fall into this category because they are not of French origin; for example: *however.*" www.independent.co.uk

NOTES

_____

_____

_____

_____

_____

Onomatopoeic words

T HE WORD *ONOMATOPOEIA* comes from the combination of the Greek words, one meaning "name" and the other meaning "I make," so onomatopoeia basically means "the name (or sound) I make." In other words, the word means nothing more than the sound it makes.

DISCOVER

Suggested activities for the following 101 examples of onomatopoeia in sentences from www.ereadingworksheets.com

Cut the list into workable sheets of paper and give them out to the students. Ask them to recognize the meaning of the words written in bold without resorting to a dictionary – just by looking at context.

Next, ask the students to choose 2 or 3 onomatopoeic words and compare them with words in their native languages.

You, the teacher, may want to paraphrase or change the wording to make the examples easier to understand.

1. The sheep went, "**Baa**."

2. The best part about the music class is that you can **bang** on the drum.

3. It is not unusual for a dog **to bark** when visitors arrive.

4. Silence your cellphone so it does not **beep** during the movie.

5.   Dad released a **belch** from the pit of his stomach.

6.   The bridge collapsed, creating a tremendous **boom**.

7.   The large dog said, '**Bow-wow!**"

8.   Are you afraid of things that go **bump** in the night?

9.   My brother can **burp** the alphabet.

10.   Both bees and buzzers **buzz**.

11.   The cash register popped open with a heart-warming **ca-ching**.

12.   The bird's **chirp** filled the empty night air.

13.   Her heels **clacked** on the hardwood floor.

14.   The **clanging** pots and pans awoke the baby.

15.   If you want the red team to win, **clap** your hands right now.

16.   The cadets swelled with pride when they heard the **clash** of the cymbals at their graduation ceremony.

17.   The dish fell to the floor with a **clatter**.

18.   Nothing annoys me more than rapidly **clicking** your pen.

19.   The bride and groom were not surprised to hear the familiar sound of **clinking** glasses.

20.   The horse's hooves **clip-clopped** on the cobblestones.

21.   Those **clucking** chickens are driving me crazy!

22.   The dim-witted pigeon repulsed us with its nerve crawling **coo**.

23.   If you are going to **cough**, please cover your mouth.

24.   The prisoner was terrified to hear the **crack** of the whip.

25.   We roasted marshmallows over the **crackling** fire.

26.   The two-year old **crashed** into the cabinet.

27.   The cabinet opened with a distinct **creak**.

28.   Dissatisfied with her work, Beth **crinkled** up the paper and threw it in the trash.

29.   The swamp frogs **croaked** in unison.

30.   The teacher heard the distinct **crunch** of ruffled potato chips.

31.   Jacob could not sleep with the steady **drip-drop** of water coming from the sink.

32.   The root beer **fizzed** over the top of the mug.

33. The flag **flapped** in the wind.

34. Did you forget to **flush** the toilet?

35. Daryl **gargled** the mouthwash.

36. The wounded soldier **groaned**.

37. As Tom got closer, the dog began **growling**.

38. Juan had a hard time hearing the teacher over his **grumbling** stomach.

39. When Mom asked Tommy how his day went, Tommy just **grunted**.

40. Vince **gulped** down the Mountain Dew.

41. The patient sounded like he was **hacking** up a lung.

42. If you have the **hiccups**, you should try drinking some water.

43. The snake slithered and **hissed.**

44. If you see anyone coming, **honk** your horn.

45. The wolves **howled** at the moon.

46. The new pencil sharpener **hummed** efficiently.

47. They knew the principal was coming because they heard the **jingle** of his keys.

48. Someone is **knocking** on the door.

49. That cat will keep **meowing** until you pat it.

50. John was disturbed by the strange **moaning**.

51. The cow aggressively **mooed** at the passing freight train.

52. Janet **murmured** the answer under her breath.

53. While lounging in the slop pile, the pigs **oinked** excitedly.

54. The hail **pattered** on the tin gutter.

55. When he saw the cheese, the mouse could not help but **peep** excitedly.

56. The lunch lady **plopped** a scoop of something onto Kristen's tray.

57. Billy will cry if you **pop** his balloon.

58. After eating the knight, the dragon let out a **puff** of smoke.

59. Most cats purr if you **pat** them behind the ear.

60. The kind man shared his bread with the **quacking** ducks.

61. My favorite singers have **raspy** voices.

62. Tim would have stepped on the snake had he not heard the **rattle** of its tail.

63. The race car driver **revved** his engine.

64. Our peaceful dinner ended when the phone began **ringing**.

65. I secretly **ripped** up the birthday checks that my grandmother sent me.

66. The lion's mighty **roar** could be heard across the savanna.

67. The earthquake **rumbled** the foundations of the house.

68. When the wind blew, the leaves **rustled**.

69. He took off so quickly that his tires **screeched**.

70. When Reuben saw what he thought was a ghost, he **shrieked** like a woman.

71. I love the sound of bacon **sizzling** on a weekend.

72. You could hear the **slap** echo across the valley.

73. The thirsty dog **slurped** the dirty water from the puddle.

74. The young woman **smacked** her lips and answered rudely.

75. Frank **smashed** the can on his head.

76. After making a rude remark, Jade **snapped** her fingers and rolled her neck.

77. Having never left the city, Juan eagerly **sniffed** the country air.

78. Tommy made me laugh so hard in the lunchroom that I **snorted** milk out of my nose.

79. The paintball **splattered** against the windshield.

80. Pat did a cannonball in the pool and made a big **splash**.

81. Mr. Morton told the student to **spit** out his gum.

82. Angie **sprayed** her neighbor with the hose.

83. Mark tried to sneak into the house, but the **squeak** of his shoes woke up Mom.

84. Jenna went around the lunchroom **squeaking** like a pig.

85. When he sat down, the young boy **squished** the unfortunate critter in his pocket.

86. The musician used a coin to **strum** the guitar.

87. Shaun loved the **swish** of the basketball net.

88. Mitchel gently **tapped** the ball into the hole.

89. Time just keeps on **ticking**.

90. Bobby threw his books down with a **thud**.

91. That **thump** made us jump.

92. If you see him, **toot** your horn.

93. The rain **trickled** down the gutter.

94. Birds **tweeted** long before Twitter did.

95. The lawyer chased after the **wail** of the sirens.

96. The bullet **whizzed** by his ear.

97. Bob's big dogs **woofed** at the unfortunate mailman.

98. Beth's little dog would not stop **yapping**.

99. Spaceman Spiff **zapped** the alien with his ray-gun.

100. Ronald **zipped** up his sleeping bag.

101. The race car **zoomed** past the finish line.

www.ereadingworksheets.com

> **This is how we got the days of the week in English:**
>
> **Sunday**, the sun
>
> **Monday**, the moon
>
> **Tuesday,** Tiu, god of war and the sky
>
> **Wednesday**, Wotan, king of the gods
>
> **Thursday**, Thor, god of thunder
>
> **Friday**, Freya, goddess of peace and crops
>
> **Saturday**, Saturn, the Roman god of time and revelry

Eponyms

EVERY TIME YOU use Scotch tape or Kleenex, you are using an eponym.

An eponym is a word derived from a name, or a **name that became a word**. The word *eponym* came into use around 1833 and comes from two Greek words: *epi*, meaning "upon or after," and *onyma*, meaning "name"; in other words, "named after."

The English language of today has several eponyms used on a regular basis, and they can be nouns, verbs, or adjectives. Here are some examples:

Atlas, the common term for a book of maps, comes from the Greek figure named Atlas, who was known to hold the world on his shoulders.

To **boycott**, meaning "to refuse to do business with someone" comes from Charles C. Boycott (1832-1897), who refused to conform to land reforms.

Chauvinism, or "fanatical patriotism," comes from Nicholas Chauvin, a soldier in Napoleon's army.

The beautiful flower **dahlia** comes from the Swedish botanist named Anders Dahl.

Echo comes from Greek mythology. Echo was a nymph whose unrequited love for Narcissus caused her to pine away until nothing but her voice remained.

Colonel Sir George Everest was a British surveyor and geographer who served as Surveyor General of India from 1830 to 1843. He is best known for having **Mount Everest**, the highest mountain on Earth, named in his honor.

Graham crackers were named after Sylvester Graham, a reverend who promoted the vegetarian diet and the firm bread of coarsely-ground flour we enjoy to this day.

Jumbo, "unusually large," has an interesting history. The famous elephant named Jumbo lived in the London Zoo for 17 years and then was bought by the U.S. showman P. T. Barnum for $10,000 in 1882. Circus advertising helped the name Jumbo to become a synonym for "huge."

Leotard, or "tights worn for dancing," comes from Jules Leotard (1839-1870), French acrobatic performer.

The Mason Jar is named after John Landis Mason, a tinsmith who invented the popular jar in 1858.

Mesmerize and **mesmerism** are words named after a German physician, Franz Mesmer.

Mirandize, "to read the legal rights to a suspect arrested on a criminal charge," comes from Ernesto A. Miranda (1941-1976), a laborer whose conviction was overturned because the arresting officers had failed to inform him of his legal rights.

The name **Oscar,** "statuette awarded for excellence in film acting, directing, etc." (given by the Academy of Motion Picture Arts and Sciences) was first used in 1936. Margaret Herrick, the Academy's librarian, after she looked at the statuette remarked that "He reminds me of my uncle Oscar." Her uncle was Oscar Pierce, a wheat farmer and fruit grower.

To **pasteurize** comes from the name of the French chemist and bacteriologist Louis Pasteur (1822-1895), who developed the process of sterilizing by heating (which destroys bacteria in milk, etc.) and rapidly cooling.

Sir William Penn is the eponym of **Pennsylvania**.

Poinsettia is named after the American diplomat J. R. Poinsett (1779-1851), who brought the plant from Mexico to the United States in 1828.

Sadism, or "love of cruelty," comes from the Marquis de Sade (1740-1814), who wrote a number of novels about extreme freedom, unrestrained by morality, religion, or law.

Salmonella is a genus of bacteria discovered by Daniel E. Salmon (1850-1914), an American veterinarian and pathologist.

The **saxophone** is named after Adolphe Sax, a Belgian inventor and musician who followed the trade of his father, a well-known maker of musical instruments.

Sartorial means "of or relating to a tailor or tailored clothes." It comes from the Latin *sartor*, meaning "tailor" or "patcher of clothes" and is most frequently used regarding high-end traditional men's clothing.

The phrase **sideburns** actually comes from Ambrose Burnside (1824-1881), the commander of the Army of the Potomac, whose unique hairstyling created this new word.

The use of the term Scotch in **Scotch tape** was a pejorative meaning "stingy" in the 1920s and 1930s. The brand name Scotch came about in 1925 while Richard Drew was testing his first masking tape to determine how much adhesive he needed to add.

Wisteria, the lovely climbing shrub, takes its name from the American anatomist Casper Wistar (1761-1818).

The **watt** is the common name for a unit of electric power named after its developer, James Watt (1736-1819).

(Compiled from Charles Harrington Elster, *Word Workout*, 2014; Cyril Leslie Beeching, *A Dictionary of Eponyms*, 1989; literaryterms.net/eponyms; Britannica.com; dailywritingtips.com)

Oxymora

I WAS DRIVING FROM Manhattan to Garden City, New York, when I got stuck because of heavy traffic. I called my boss, apologized, and told him that I was definitely going to be late. He asked me where I was, and I had to tell him I was "parked" on L.I.E., also known as the Long Island Expressway. I heard him laughing, and he told me not to worry about it. "L.I.E. is an oxymoron," he added. Instead of 45 minutes, it took me close to two hours. That day I really understood the meaning of oxymora. The word itself comes from the Greek word *oxumoros*, i.e. *oxus* means "sharp" or "keen" and *moros* (the same word that gave us "moron") means "foolish."

An oxymoron is a self-contradicting word or group of words that seems to go against common sense, but at the same time, still holds true. A good example would be *"less is more." Success with Words*, published in 1983 by *Readers' Digest*, gives us the following explanation starting with a short definition: "*Oxymoron* – a combination of words that gains force and point from a seeming paradox or absurdity: 'cruel kindness.' *Oxymoron* is one of the most effective of all the figures of speech and works especially well in poetry, humorous writing and political rhetoric. [. . .] Quite a few clichés in everyday language are *oxymora*, such as the now old-fashioned genteelism *frightfully amused*." (496)

"Other languages have contributed oxymora to English, such as the Chinese concept of yin-yang. The famous black and white circular symbol that expresses yin-yang shows a drop of white in the black and side and, conversely, a small bit of black in the white side. This is meant to represent that even opposites contain a bit of each other. The yin-yang symbol is thus also a visual representation of oxymoron." www.literarydevices.com

Here are some other examples in English:

Business ethics	*Plastic silverware*	*Civil war*
Constructive criticism	*Cruel kindness*	*Freezer burn*
Working vacation	*Criminal justice*	*Loose tights*
Random order	*Student teacher*	*Mobile home*
Original copy	*Pretty ugly*	*Recorded live*

Same difference	*Death benefit*	*A small fortune*
Jumbo shrimp	*Industrial park*	*Half naked*
Loyal opposition	*Spendthrift*	*Awful good*
Open secret	*Negative growth*	*Old news*

DISCOVER   Ask the students to work in small groups and decide which of the following are good examples of oxymora:

friendly fire	*extensive briefing*	*homeless shelter*
permanent temp	*definite maybe*	*tragic comedy*
minor miracle	*smokeless cigarette*	*unemployment benefits*
science fiction	*strangely familiar*	*numb feeling*
plastic glasses	*criminal law*	*domestic tranquility*
executive secretary	*Civil War*	*fresh frozen*

Word Formation

THE BRAVE NEW world of the 21st century is also a world of new ideas, now concepts, new discoveries, and new perspectives - and that means we have to come up with **new words**.

"As the experience of existence changes from one generation to another, words change their meaning." (Pei, 1965, p. 144)

There are several types of semantic change. Words had a certain meaning in the past, and now we are using the same words, but their meanings have changed.

1. In **extension** or **generalization**, a word widens its meaning, or extends its meaning over various new areas. Here are some examples:

   Virtue originally was a male quality (*vir* in Latin for "man"), but now it applies to both sexes. (*Vi-* goes all the way back to Sanskrit)

   Office and *novice* were originally only restricted to religion.

2. The opposite is called **narrowing** or **specialization**. Hundreds of years ago, *mete* referred to food in general (like *sweetmeat*), but today it refers to only one kind of food, *meat*. The word "art" had several meanings referring to "skill"; nowadays, it simply refers to certain kinds of skill, mostly to the aesthetic one.

3. There is another change in meaning called **semantic shift**, when words change from one situation to another. For example, *noble* originally meant "knowable." A *secretary* was once a "separator" and a *secret* was what set them apart. Both words come from Latin *secretus,* the participle of *secerno* – "to separate." A *foyer* was originally a "fireplace," and an *infant* originally meant "non-speaking."

4. Sometimes words change because they lose their negative connotation. An example of **amelioration** would be *mischievous*, which lost its strong sense of "disastrous." Along the same lines, *nice* comes from the French *niais* ("silly"), which in turn goes back to the Latin word *nescius* ("stupid," "not knowing"). The opposite would be **pejoration,** where the word acquires a negative shade of meaning. For example, *notorious* originally meant "widely known." (Partly adapted from David Crystal, *How Language Works*, The Overlook Press, Woodstock & New York, 2006, pp. 227-228)

If you leaf through a daily newspaper, a weekly or monthly magazine, whether in hard copies or in electronic format, you will encounter new words almost every day. What do we do? We simply find ways to go back in history and use Latin or Greek roots to name recently discovered or re-discovered bacteria, viruses, plants, insects, etc. Sometimes we just use our current knowledge of vocabulary and coin new words.

How do we go about creating new words? There are several ways of word formation:

Compounding, Derivation, Affixation, Blending, Clipping, Acronyms, Reanalysis, Folk Etymology, Analogy, Novel Creation, Creative New Spelling, etc.

Compounding

The compound words may be spelled together, separately, or connected with a hyphen:

Mailman (mail + man) - Fire hydrant - Cup holder - Email - Pick-up truck

Derivation (changing parts of speech)
Recognize – recognition   Revolve - revolution

Affixation (subtype of derivation)
The most common type of affixation is the addition of prefixes and suffixes:
Type – typical - typically   Pleasant – unpleasant – pleasantly

Blending

Blending is one of the most beloved word formation processes in English. Such words are stitched together without any regard to how we combine the words.

1. **Glitterati**   glitter + literati   (Hollywood social set)
2. **Mockumentary**   mock + documentary   (spoof documentary)
3. **Brunch**   breakfast + lunch
4. **Smog**   smoke + fog
5. **Carjacking**   car + hijacking
6. **Electrocute**   electric + execute

DISCOVER Ask the students to explain the following words:

Camcorder   *motorcade*   *Eurasia*

Clipping

When a phrase like *mobile vulgatus* or *mobile peasants* gets shortened to *mob*, linguists call it "clipping."

Taxi Cab   Taximeter cabriolet
Fan   Fanatic
Bus   Voiture omnibus
Van   Caravan
Sleuth   Sleuthhound (a kind of sniffer dog)
Film buff   Buffalo

DISCOVER Ask the students to trace the origins of the following words:

EXAM   GYM   LAB

Acronyms

POSH meaning *elegant or luxurious* is said to come from the first letters of the phrase port out – starboard home referring to the preferred cabins (those on the north away from the sun) on the ships which transported British personnel back and forth between Great Britain and India during the days of the British Raj.

(Adapted from Charles Berlitz, *Native Tongues*, 2005, p. 279)

Acronyms are words that are formed by taking the initial letters of a phrase and making a new word out of it.

SCUBA	Self-Contained Underwater Breathing Apparatus
RADAR	Radio Detection and Ranging
SONAR	Sound Navigation and Ranging
LASER	Light Amplification by Stimulated Emission of Radiation
TASER	Thomas A. Swift's Electric Rifle
NATO	North Atlantic Treaty Organization
TIME	The International Magazine of Events

What is the difference between an abbreviation and an acronym?

An abbreviation is any **shortened form** of a word or phrase. **An acronym** is a **specific type of abbreviation** formed from the first letters and **pronounced as a new word.**

Memos, email, and text messaging are modes of communication that give rise to both clippings and acronyms, since these word formation methods are designed to abbreviate.

FYI   for your information (mid-20th century)

LOL   Laughing out loud (early 21st century) – pronounced /lol/ or /el o el/; has spawned compounds like *Lolcats.*

DISCOVER   Ask the students to find the complete words for the following acronyms:

NASA   OPEC   BENELUX   SARS   ZIP   PIN

Reanalysis

From *hamburger* (chopped and formed hamburger steaks in the Hamburg style) we just separated the word into *ham + burger.*

DISCOVER   Ask the students to find at least one more example of reanalysis.

Folk etymology

FOLK ETYMOLOGY IS a popular but mistaken account of the origin of a word of phrase.

The word *cockroach* was borrowed from Spanish *cucaracha* but was assimilated to the existing English words *cock* and *roach.*

Baloney – This word was originally the name of the Italian town of Bologna (pronounced ba**lon**ya). Either this was too hard to pronounce or too confusing to spell, so we made it like the name Maloney.

Canary Islands - Canary in the name of this archipelago was originally Latin *Canaries Insulae*, or "Islands of Dogs," and English simply adapted to words already existing.

Mistletoe - This word started as *mistiltan* in Old English, made up of *mistel* (mistletoe) + *tan* "twig". However, when *tan* vanished from the language, something had to be done about its occurrence in compounds like *mistletan*. Well, don't those waxy white berries look like a baby's toes?

Piggyback - The word began as pick pack sometime before 1564. The original concept was picking up a pack of something and putting it where people carry loads on their backs. *Pick pack* became *pick-a-pack*, then *pick-a-back* by association. In the 1930s, we began using *piggyback* since, when we ride our children on our backs, we often crawl on hands and knees, roughly imitating pigs.

Turmeric - Turmeric, the name of an anti-inflammatory curry powder, came from Latin *terra merita,* or "worthy earth." In Old French it became *terre-merrite* and was borrowed as Old English *tarmaret*. Next, the ending was replaced by the recognizable suffix *–ic.*

Woodchuck - This animal name started as an Indian word, probably Cree *otchock*. Again, English words resembling the two syllables in this word replaced the two words in the Cree word even though they make no sense together. But that is all the better for the tongue-twister: "How much wood would a woodchuck chuck if a woodchuck could chuck wood?"

(adapted from www.alphadictionary.com)

Analogy "AMBIVALENCE is an almost brand new word, invented in 1901 by the German psychiatrist Eugen Bleuler to mean holding two or more strong ideas about the same subject, on the analogy of *equivalence*." (Lewis Thomas, 1990, p. 151)

Novel creation Sometimes a speaker or a writer forms a word without starting from other sources. Some examples of such words would be *blimp*, *googol* (the mathematical term), *bling*, and possibly *slang*, which appeared in the last 200 years without any etymology.

Creative respelling Sometimes words are formed by changing the traditional spelling of a word that the speaker wants to use as a new word. Product names often involve creative spelling, such as *Mr. Kleen*. www.ruf.rice.edu

Word analysis

IF STUDENTS READ a new passage and encounter new words, there are several suggestions we can make to help them use tricks to discover the meaning and usage of the new vocabulary.

Take for example roots, prefixes, and suffixes:

-spec-   meaning "something to do with the eyes"

aspect

spectator, spectacle, spectacular

inspect, inspector, inspection   suspect, suspicious, suspicion, suspiciously

-spec-

speculate, speculation, speculative   prospect, prospector, prospective

expect, expectation   respect, respective, respectively

specter, spectrum, specimen

perspective

Add your own words: _____   _____   _____

Next, use a dictionary and for each word find the corresponding part of speech:

Suspect (n.) *suspicion suspicious suspiciously suspect* (vb.)

Then, provide an original sentence for each new part of speech:

For example:

I have a **suspicion.**   *He acted* **suspiciously.**   *We* **suspected** *that.*

Write your own examples for:

Prospect	*prospective*	etc.
Expect	*expectation*	etc.
Inspect	_____	_____
Speculate	_____	_____

Sp -   words pertaining to wetness
Spray (noun and verb)   *hair spray*   *nasal spray*
Splash   *make a splash*
Spit   *spit it out!*
Sprinkle, sprinkler   *it began to sprinkle*
Spatter   *spatter some red paint over the blue*
Splatter   *wipe up that splatter of ketchup on the carpet*
Spill   *spill the beans*
Spigot   *stainless steel or plastic spigot*

-port-   from Latin *portere* meaning "to carry"

	Import	*transport*	*airport*	*support*	*portable*	*deport*
Support (noun)	*support* (verb)	*supportive*	_____			
Transport	*transportation*	*transported*	*transporting*			
Import	*importer*	*imported*	_____			
Deport	_____	_____	_____			

Use a dictionary and add your own words:

_____ _____ _____ _____
_____ _____ _____ _____
_____ _____ _____ _____

-fer-   from Latin *ferre* meaning "to bring" or "to carry"

	Offer	*refer*	*prefer*	*confer*	*transfer*	*differ*
Offer (vb.)	*offering*	*offered*	*offer* (n.)			
Prefer	*preferred*	*preference*	*preferring*			
Confer	_____	_____	_____			
Differ	_____	_____	_____			
Refer	_____	_____	_____			
Transfer	_____	_____	_____			

Add your own words:

_____ _____ _____ _____
_____ _____ _____ _____
_____ _____ _____ _____

Sn-   meaning "Something to do with the nose"

"It's difficult to resist the speculation that, aeons ago, the *sn-* onset was a linguistic reflection of a sneeze." (David Crystal, *Words in Time and Place*, 2014, p. 24)

Sneeze	*sniff*	*snore*	*snout*	*snooze*	*snarl*	*snort*
Sneeze	*sneezer*		*sneeze gas*		*nothing to sneeze at!*	
Snore	*snort*		*snored*		*snoring*	
Sniff	*sniffed*		*sniff dogs*			
Snuff	*snuffed*		*snuffing*		*snuffs*	
Snooze	*snoozed*		*snooze button*			
Snout	*A swine has a snout.*					
Snort	*to snort with laughter*				*a snort of disgust*	
snarl	*The dog snarled in defense.*					

Add your own words:

_____ _____ _____ _____

_____ _____ _____ _____

_____ _____ _____ _____

Scribe-   from Latin *scribere* meaning "to write"

Describe	*prescribe*	*subscribe*	*script*	*transcribe*
Describe	*description*	*described*	*describing*	
Subscribe	*subscribed*	*subscribing*	*subscription*	
Prescribe	*prescribed*	*prescribing*	*prescription*	
Script	*scriptwriter*			
Transcribe	*transcription*	*transcript*	*transcribed*	
Scribble				

Add your own words:

_____ _____ _____ _____

_____ _____ _____ _____

_____ _____ _____ _____

Trans -   from Latin   *trans* meaning "through" or "across"

Transport	*transfer*	*transfuse*	*transact*	*transform*	*transit*

Transport	*transported*	_____	_____		
Transfer (vb.)	*transferred*	*transferring*	*transfer (n.)*	*transferal*
Transfuse	*transfused*	*transfusing*	*transfusion*	
Transact (vb.)	*transacted*	*transacting*	*transact(s) (noun)*	
Transform	*transformed*	*transforming*	*transformation*	
Transgender				

Add your own words:

_____   _____   _____   _____

_____   _____   _____   _____

_____   _____   _____   _____

Video   from Latin *videre* meaning "to see"

Videotape	*videocassette*	*video*	*visual*	*revise*	*review*

Visual	*visor*	*visual aid*	*visually*
Visualize	*visualized*	*visualizing*	*visualization*
Vision (n.)	*vision (vb.)*	*visionary*	
Visible	*visibility*		
Envision	*envisioned*	*envisioning*	
Revise	*revised*	*revising*	*revision*
Review (vb.)	*reviewed*	*reviewing*	*review (n.)*

Add your own words:

_____   _____   _____   _____

_____   _____   _____   _____

_____   _____   _____   _____

Fl- a sense of movement, usually rapid movement

Flicker	*The flame flickered in the wind.*	*a flicker of fear*
Flutter	*birds flutter their wings*	*a flutter of panic*
Flap	*Birds flapped weakly.*	*His robe flapped in the wind.*

Flush	*to flush the toilet*
Flee	*to flee the coop*
Flare	*The candle flared to a bright light.*
Fling	*She took of her hat, flinging it onto the grass.*
Flame	*The flame became a blaze.*
Flop	*She tipped the pan and a fish flopped out.*
Fly	*fly like a bird*
Flog	*Frequently slaves were flogged.* *He received a public flogging.*

B- the application of force

Break	*to break the news*
Bash	*The cradle swayed and bashed against the wall. He bashed into a tree.*
Bounce	*The check bounced back.*
Batter	*The ship was battered by the waves.*
Blast	*Tunnels have been blasted through bedrock beneath the city.*
Bust	*She was furious about Jack busting her double bass.*
Bruise	*I'm okay. Just a few scratches and bruises.*
Bomb	*The flash news was like a bomb.*
Bludgeon	*He was bludgeoned/battered/beaten with a heavy object.*
Brawl	*His teeth were knocked out in a terrible brawl.*
Boom	*The boom of the drum echoed along the street.*
Bolster	*We need to bolster his confidence.*
Blare	*A radio was blaring out the news.*

Sw- DISCOVER: Ask the students to find out what (meaning) these words have in common:

Swallow	*He swallowed more pills.*
Swap	*He swapped a dozen goats for a female calf.*
Swarm	*The showers brought swarms of insects.*
Sway	*He did not fall, but swayed a little. Trees swaying in the wind.*
Sweep	*I must sweep the kitchen floor.*

Swerve   *The car swerved off the road and into the river.*

Swing   *I pushed the door, and it swung open.*

Swipe   *Swipe your metro card and go through the turnstile.*

Swirl   *Dust swirled in small circles around us.*

Swish   *The curtains swished open.*   *The swish of a horse's tail*

Switch   *Electric light switches*

Swivel   *He slowly swiveled his chair around.*

Swoop   *The swallow made a dazzling swoop through the air.*

Swat   *He swatted at a fly that was bothering him.*

DISCOVER Students should work in small groups and then teach other. Change the verb tenses, make the nouns plural, or ask questions for clarification.

Find other similar words:

_____

_____

_____

_____

The prefix per- meaning "through"

DISCOVER
Ask the students to use a dictionary to check the following words for meaning and synonyms. Then, ask them to change the parts of speech and see how many new words they can find.

   To percolate

   To permeate

   To pervade

   To perambulate

Ask the students to find more words, teach each other, and then use them in original sentences.

The prefix *per-* with the function of an intensifier

Ask your students to discover how this prefix intensifies or amplifies the meaning of the verb:

To perceive	*To perforate*	*Perfect*	*To perform*	*Perfume*
To persevere	*To persecute*			

_____

_____

_____

_____

According to Pei (1965), "most verbs ending in –ash have acquired the connotation of some sort of violent action: *bash, clash, crash, dash, flash, hash, lash, mash, splash, slash, smash, thrash.*" (169)

Ask your students to use the above-mentioned words and find out how they express the idea of a violent action.

For example:

To bash   *The burglar bashed down the door to get in.*

To clash   _____

To crash   _____

To dash   _____

To flash   _____

To hash   _____

To lash   _____

The suffix –er

DISCOVER: Arrange the students in pairs/small groups, and give each team a different assignment. Everybody can use any type of dictionary they like, but the groups must work independently. They should be encouraged to find as many words as possible and produce original sentences.

1. The first group should work together and find words ending in –*er* that are **nouns (doers)**: *teacher, coroner, lawyer*, etc.

2. The second group should be assigned to find adjectives ending in –*er* that are **nouns (objects)**: *typewriter, lawnmower, nail clipper*, etc.

3. The third group should look for **adjectives with their three forms of comparison**, but mostly those with two comparatives:

| Far | - | *farther* | - | the farthest |
| | | *Further* | - | the furthest |

4. Another group should look for adjectives ending in –er:

   slender, tender, bitter, etc.

5. Another group should look for **nouns (action):**

   merger, fundraiser, no brainer, slander, etc.

6. Another group should look for **verbs (repeated action or frequency)**:

   To chatter, to shiver, to mutter, to stutter, etc.

Each group should prepare original sentences with the new words they discovered and present them to the whole class. The task is to let the other student find the definition of the new words and determine what they all have in common.

From what we know into what we need to discover

Students learn a lot when they are led to discover. In this case, we start from what they should already know, and that is that the suffix –er is used to make up new words denoting doers of an action. They should also know a little bit about adjectives and their degrees of comparison. The rest should be more or less new, but they must make the mental effort to see the word formation and the commonality.

NOTES

_____

_____

_____

_____

_____

Exercises in word analysis

Suggestion: Read the following passage and analyze the words written in bold.

"Definition of Dance: A **succession** of more or less regularly ordered steps and movements of the body, commonly guided by the rhythmical intervals of a musical **accompaniment**; any leaping or gliding movement with more or less regular steps and turnings, expressive of or designed to awaken some **emotion**. The dance is perhaps the earliest and most **spontaneous** mode of expressing emotion and dramatic feeling; it exists in a great variety of forms, and is among people connected with religious beliefs and practice, as among the Mohammedans or Hindus. Modern dances includes the jig, hornpipe, etc., step-dances executed by one person; the waltz, polka, schottische, etc., the reel, quadrille, etc., usually called square dances, danced by an even number of pairs; the country dance, in which any number of pairs may take part; and the cotillion or german, consisting of many **intricate** figures, in the execution of which the waltz-movement **predominates**." www.finedictionary.com

Succession (n.)	a series of people of things that follow one another
	Can you change it into a verb?
Accompaniment (n.)	music played to support a person who is singing or playing a musical instrument
	Can you change it into a verb?
Emotion (n.)	a strong feeling (such as love, anger, joy, hate, or fear)
	Can you change it into an adjective?
Spontaneous (adj.)	done or said in a natural and often sudden way and without a lot of thought or planning
	Can you change it into a noun?
Intricate (adj.)	having many parts
	Can you change it into an adverb?
Predominate (vb.)	to be more successful or powerful than other people or things
	Can you change it to an adverb?

DISCOVER: Check the following words, provide definition and part of speech, and write a sentence:

Expressive _____

Dramatic _____

Include _____

Word analysis in literature

Read the following poem and analyze the verbs:

IF   by Rudyard Kipling

If you can **keep your head** when all about you
    Are losing theirs and blaming it on you;

If you can trust yourself when all men doubt you,
    But **make allowance** for their doubting too;

If you can wait and not be tired by waiting,
    Or being lied about, don't **deal in lies**,

Or being hated, don't give way to hating,
    And yet **don't look too good**, nor **talk too wise**;

If you can dream – and not **make dreams your master**;
    If you can think – and not **make thoughts your aim**;

If you can **meet with triumph and disaster**
    And **treat those two impostors just the same;**

If you can bear to hear the truth you've spoken
    Twisted by knaves to make a trap for fools,

Or watch the things you gave your life **to** broken,
    And stoop and build them up with worn-out tools.

If you can **make one heap of all your winnings**
    And **risk it on one turn of pitch-and toss,**

And lose, and start again at your beginnings
    And never breathe a word about your loss;

If you can force your heart and nerve and sinew
    To serve your turn long after they are gone,

And so **hold on** when **there is nothing in you**
    Except the Will which says to them: "Hold on;"

If you can **talk with crowds** and **keep your virtue,**
    Or **walk with kings** – nor **lose the common touch;**

If neither foes nor loving friends can hurt you;
If all men count with you, but none too much;

If you can **fill the unforgiving minute**
With sixty seconds' worth of distance run –

Yours is the Earth and **everything that's in it**,
And – which is more – **you'll be a Man**, my son!

Looking at the whole sentence, explain in your words (paraphrase) the following:

Keep your head _____

Make allowance _____

Deal in lies _____

Don't look too good _____

(nor) talk too wise _____

make dreams your master _____

make thoughts your aim _____

meet with triumph and disaster _____

treat those two impostors just the same _____

make one heap of all your winnings _____

risk it on one turn of pitch and toss _____

hold on _____

nothing in you except the Will _____

talk with crowds _____

walk with kings _____

keep your virtue _____

lose the common touch _____

if all men count with you _____

fill the unforgiving minute with 60 seconds' worth of distance run

_____

Yours is the Earth _____

Everything that's in it _____

You'll be a Man _____

Choose your own words and paraphrase them:

_____

_____

_____

Dictionary work (1)

ASK THE STUDENTS to use a dictionary, work in pairs or small groups separately, and then present their findings to the whole class. Each group will produce their own original sentences, and the other students will have to find commonality.

1. The first group will check the word DOMESTIC and provide 3 (three) meanings with explanations and original sentences.

2. The second group will find as many verbs ending in –er including the **meaning of frequency or repeated action**. For example: *stutter, mutter, chatter*, etc.

3. The third group will have to find words that change their meaning (of the connotation) by changing the preposition connecting them with the rest of the sentence.

    Give them one example: *to discriminate between* and *to discriminate against* and encourage them to find other verbs. (*to give in, to give up*, etc.)

4. The fourth group will have to check at least 3 or 4 prefixes and discover similar words:

Cent- meaning "hundred"	e.g. *century*_____
Chron- meaning "time"	*chronologically*_____
Com- meaning "together"	*community*_____
Corp- meaning "body"	*corporation*_____
Cred- meaning "believe"	*credible*_____
Cur- meaning "run"	*to concur*_____
Dec- meaning "ten"	*to decimate*_____
Di- meaning "two"	*dioxide*_____
Dict- meaning "speak"	*to predict*_____

Ex- meaning "out of"	*to exhale* _____
Graph- meaning "writing"	*paragraph* _____
Hydro- meaning "water"	*to dehydrate* _____
Inter- meaning "between"	*international* _____

5. The fifth group will analyze the following homonyms to discover the difference:

STILL	adjective	**Still** waters run deep.
	noun	In the **still** of the night
	adverb	I **still** don't understand.
YET	adverb	I haven't finished **yet.**
	Conjunction	The topic was quite challenging, **yet** everybody liked it.
LIGHT	noun	The **lights** are on.
	Adjective	**light** blue
	Verb	**light** a fire

To wrap up, each group will present the results of the group work to the whole class.

Dictionary work (2)

DISCOVER   Arrange the students in four groups.

1. The differences between the following words: *economic* vs. *economical*. If time allows, they should also clarify the four usages:

Economy	*the economy of this country*
Economic	*the economic development*
Economical	*an economical car*
Economics	*Economics as a field of study*

   The difference between *classic* and *classical*:

   Classic Coke or *classic mistake*
   Classical music or *classical architecture*

2. At least six ways of expressing **negation with prefixes**:

a-	*symmetrical*
anti-	*anti-war*
in-	*inaudible*
il-	*illiterate*
im-	*impossible*
ir-	*irresponsible*
un-	*unconventional*
non-	*non-violent*

3. As many words as possible using the following roots:

   Pes, pedes (Latin meaning *foot*))   for example: <u>ped</u>estrian
   Paid, pais (Greek meaning *child*)   for example: <u>ped</u>agogue

4. The difference between

Healthy and **healthful**	*healthy person* vs. *healthful food/climate*
Imply and **infer**	*imply something **in what you say*** *infer something **from what you hear***
migrate, immigrate, emigrate	*some animals migrate people emigrate/leave immigrate/enter*
incredible and **incredulous**	*incredible story* vs. *incredulous person*

Each group works independently and then teaches the other groups.

Dictionary work (3)

Group 1: DISCOVER

1. Ask the students to continue the lists:

Seek	*mop*	*eventually*
Leek	*bat*	*sharply*
Steel	*tap*	*convincingly*
Peel	*lap*	*actually*
Kneel	*sip*	*basically*
Seep	*clip*	*seemingly*
Deed	*tip*	*barely*
Heel	*mat*	*unlikely*
_____	_____	_____
_____	_____	_____
_____	_____	_____

2. Encourage them to discover other **similar words**, change their parts of speech, and then write a story and try to put them in an original paragraph.

Group 2: RE-DISCOVER

Start by giving the students some words spelled with double letters: *Dazzle, baffle, savvy*, and then ask them to find at least one word for all the letters in the English alphabet.

Baz<u>aa</u>r	*ru<u>bb</u>le*	*a<u>cc</u>ept*	*a<u>dd</u>*	*s<u>ee</u>*	*e<u>ff</u>ect*
_____	_____	_____	_____	_____	_____
_____	_____	_____	_____	_____	_____
-gg-	*-hh-*	*-ii-*	*-kk-*	*-ll-*	*-mm-*
_____	_____	_____	_____	_____	_____
_____	_____	_____	_____	_____	_____
-nn-	*-oo-*	*-pp-*	*-rr-*	*-ss-*	*-tt-*
_____	_____	_____	_____	_____	_____
_____	_____	_____	_____	_____	_____

Dictionary Work (4)

Challenge the students to discover

1. Use the following relational prefixes

   Ante-   *antecedent*
   Inter-   *intercontinental*
   Out-   *to outnumber*
   Over-   *to overestimate*
   Pre-   *to precede*
   Post-   *postwar*
   Sub-   *subway*
   Super-   *supervise*
   Sur-   *survive*
   Under-   *undersea*

2. Divide the students into groups, provide dictionaries, and assign them tasks:

   a. Group 1 will make up sentences using at least one word for each prefix.

   b. Group 1 will find collocations for at least one word for each prefix.

3. Each group will teach the other group the words using complete sentences (group 1) and collocations (group 2).

For example:

I. Group 1: Students present their own examples, e.g. *You need **to submit** your essay by the end of the week.*

   Group 2: Must paraphrase the word in bold and use synonyms or antonyms.

II. Group 2: Students present their own collocations, e.g. *survival skills, antique shop*

   Group 1: Students provide complete sentences using the collocations.

Context clues: Meaning:

The surfer was caught in an *undercurrent*.

The joke was so good we couldn't *suppress* our laughter.

No matter what happens, you need *to overcome* your problems.

Do we really need *to postpone* our meeting?

That book is only available as an *inter-library* loan.

It's not easy *to predict* the weather in this part of the country.

The weatherman predicted *intermittent* showers for the afternoon.

Are we going *to outlive* our parents?

Collocations

IN SPOKEN OR written English, words rarely exist separately. We use words in groups of words named **collocations.** The *Cambridge Dictionary* defines a collocation as "the combination of words formed when two or more words are often used together in a way that sounds correct." They are also defined as "the use of certain words together." www.learnersdictionary.com

Basic examples would be:
Do homework　　　　*seek advice*　　　*informed decision*

"A collocation is a group of words that usually go together. For example, in English, we usually say 'heavy rain.' It's correct grammatically to say 'strong rain' or 'big rain,' but both of these sound completely strange. A native English speaker would never say 'big rain.' If you use the normal collocation ('heavy rain') your English will sound a lot better and more natural and it will be easier for native speakers to understand you. Collocations are very, very important."
www.perfect-english-grammar.com

Dr. Clyde Coreil, Professor Emeritus at New Jersey City University, is a strong supporter of a new approach to these groups of words. If you check his www.formulaics.com website, this is what you will find:

" 'Preforms' are parts of a sentence that are always the same: 'call it a day,' 'get over it' and 'I thought you'd never ask!' are examples. Although there are thousands of these, language students are generally taught very few of them. I think that they should become quite near the center of all second-language classroom activities including reading, listening, writing, and speaking. That is my main suggestion in *Formulaics.com.*"

The front page of his website lists the following examples:
It is what it is.　　　*like father, like son*　　　*safe and sound*

From a student's point of view, **collocations will provide alternative and richer ways of expression**. Learners of ESL will have to recognize them in context, in spoken or written form, and once detected, these word combinations – collocations – will be easier for our brains to remember in groups or chunks. In other words, when studying a new word, students are encouraged to acquire it together with another word. Here are some examples:

BUSINESS

business card	business partner	business meeting
to own a business	to start a business	to run a business
business as usual	let's get down to business	a businesslike attitude
a business succeeds	business suit	had no business driving
to go out of business	we mean business	to be in business
business or pleasure	Mind your own business!	None of your business!

GET

to get lost	to get fat	to get sick
to get tired	to get soft	to get well
to get nowhere	to get some sleep	to get going
to get busy	to get out of trouble	to get across
to get somewhere	to get dressed up	to get down to business
to get together	to get into a fight	to get through
to get involved	to get on	to get pregnant
to get under your skin	to get back	to get out

Your own examples

_____   _____   _____

_____   _____   _____

_____   _____   _____

GIVE

to give advice	to give directions	to give a big hand
to give permission	to give an idea	to give away/a giveaway
to give rise to	to give ground	to give the benefit of a doubt
to give way	to give time	give and take
give a damn	to give notice	to give an account of oneself
to give your best	to give in	to give off

to give a lot	*to give a whipping*	*to give up*
to give into	*to give out*	*give it to them!*

Your own examples

_____ _____ _____

_____ _____ _____

_____ _____ _____

GOOD

a good idea	*good for you!*	*as good as new*
to be in good health	*had a good time*	*a good chance*
for good	*to be up to no good*	*household goods*
good grief!	*Take a good look!*	*It's a good thing*
too good to be true	*good question!*	*No good*
good to see you!	*To be good at languages*	*good point!*
for your own good	*To deliver the goods*	*Good luck!*

Your own examples

_____ _____ _____

_____ _____ _____

_____ _____ _____

TAKE

to take advantage of	*to take a rap*	*to take dictation*
take care	*to take a crack at*	*take a seat!*
to take place	*to take under one's wing*	*to take a back seat*
to take messages	*to take a shower*	*to take after*
to take shelter	*to take it for granted*	*to take a picture*
to take a bet	*to take the blame*	*to take a tumble*
to take a nap	*to take the train*	*to take a break*

Your own examples

_____ _____ _____

_____ _____ _____

_____ _____ _____

HAVE

to have a ball	*to have a good time*	*Have a seat!*
to have a headache	*to have the will*	*to have an idea*
to have a job	*to have a drink*	*to have a reason*
to have an excuse	*to have time*	*to have an interest in*
to have lots to do	*had enough*	*to have a heart*
to have an understanding	*to have good weather*	*to have nothing against*

Your own examples

_____   _____   _____

_____   _____   _____

_____   _____   _____

TIME

to tell time	*all the time*	*it takes time*
to spend/waste time	*the first/last time*	*the whole time*
at the same time	*it's about time*	*half the time*
for the time being	*time's up*	*time and a half*
in no time	*ahead of time*	*from time to time*
time and again	*behind the times*	*the right time*
time-keeper	*time limit*	*take your time*

Your own examples

_____   _____   _____

_____   _____   _____

_____   _____   _____

According to Dr. Clyde Coreil, students should be encouraged to learn/ memorize approximately 10 of these collocations every day, and then bring them back to the classroom next day, where together with the other students, they should create complete sentences or situations where these set-phrases can be used.

Exercises in identifying collocations

DISCOVER Read the following passages and try to **find as many collocations** as possible. Underline them and then try to use them in your own sentences.

"When we speak of a 'close friend,' we usually mean an intimate friend, not a friend who is standing close by. However, according to researchers who study human behavior, there are in fact four 'distance zones' in human interaction. Intimate distance is the closest zone, eighteen inches or less. This is the zone of making love, for instance, and also of physical confrontations ('in your face!'). Second is personal distance, eighteen inches to four feet, which is used for everyday conversations with friends. Then there is social distance, four to seven feet, which we use for most interactions with strangers, such as buying something in a store. The fourth zone is public distance, twelve feet or more. A public speaker or a singer at a concert is usually at least twelve feet from the nearest audience members." (Langan, 1999, pp. 73-74)

From this passage let's select the following collocations and then use it in an original sentence:

Example	*Write an Original sentence*
Close friend	John is a close friend.
Audience members	_____
Human behavior	_____
Personal distance	_____
Your own examples	
_____	_____

"Weber says that there are three types of authority from which governments gain their right to command. One type of authority is based on tradition. Kings, queens, feudal lords, and tribal chiefs did not need written rules in order to govern. Their authority was based on long-standing customs and was handed down through generations from parent to child. People may also submit to authority because of charisma, the exceptional personal quality of an individual. Napoleon, Gandhi, and Mao Zedong all illustrate authority that derives its legitimacy from charismatic personalities. The political systems of industrial states are based largely on a third type of authority: legal authority. These systems derive legitimacy from a set of explicit rules and procedures that spell out the ruler's rights and duties. Typically, the rules and procedures are put in writing. The people grant their obedience to 'the law.' It specifies procedures by which certain individuals had offices of power, such as governor or president or prime minister. But the authority is vested in those offices, not in the individuals who temporarily hold the offices." (90)

Long-standing customs   _____

Collocations with collective nouns

Common collective nouns are words that describe groups of animals, people, birds, or things. These words are used interchangeably and sometimes become idiomatic. For example, we can say *a swarm of bees*, but we can also use the same word (swarm) to refer to a group of people. Here is a short list of such words . . .

Herd, audience, pack, flock, swarm, family, assembly, council, faculty, group, crowd, gang, mob, staff, crew, choir, orchestra, panel, board, troupe, bunch, pile, heap, set, stack, class, etc.

Common collective nouns used for animals:

An army of ants
An ambush of tigers
An audience of squid
A ballet of swans
A barrel of monkeys
A bloom of jellyfish
A bouquet of pheasants
A caravan of camels
A colony of penguins
A culture of bacteria
A descent of woodpeckers
A drove of cattle
An earth of foxes
An exaltation of larks
A flock of birds/sheep
A gaggle of geese
A gang of elk
A herd of deer
A hide of tigers
A hive of bees/ a swarm of bees
A kettle of hawks
A litter of puppies
A murder of crows
An ostentation of peacocks
A pack of hounds/rats/wolves
A parade of elephants
A parliament of owls
A pod of whales
A pride of lions

A school of fish
A squabble of seagulls
A tower of giraffes
A trip of goats
A troop of baboons/monkeys/kangaroos
A warren of rabbits
A watch of nightingales

Similar expressions:

A pack of lies	*a speck of dust*
A bunch of grapes	*a touch of frost*
A bundle of nerves	*a loaf of bread*
A bouquet of flowers	*a pile of snow*
A fistful of dollars	*a pile of rubble*
A stack of books	*a piece of advice*
A collection of old stamps	*a glimmer of hope*
A band of musicians	*a breath of fresh air*
A gang of thieves	*a heap of ash*

EXERCISES IN COLLECTIVE NOUNS:

DISCOVER: Ask the students to use the following collocations in original sentences:

Armies of peacekeepers . . . ..

Herds of buffalo . . . ..

Crews of airline pilots . . . .

Swarms of bees . . . .

Our basketball team . . .

Firms of lawyers . . .

Clouds of butterflies . . .

Crowds of fans ...

Convoys of trucks . . .

Bunches of tulips . . .

The flute ensemble . . .

Your example: _____

> "The teacher who is indeed wise does not bid you to enter the house of his wisdom but rather leads you to the threshold of your mind."
>
> Khalil Gibran, Lebanese-American writer (1883-1931)

IDIOMS

TEACHING VOCABULARY ALSO involves teaching set phrases, or idiomatic expressions. A word of caution: Some ESL students take the literal meaning as the first and the only meaning of a word. When words become idiomatic, special attention must be paid as to how we introduce idioms in our classroom.

One of my colleagues once told me what happened in his class when he was teaching the idiomatic expression *to play hooky*. After writing an example on the board, the teacher also went back to the days when he was a student and did not go to class, or found a very good excuse not to attend a school activity. Students were then asked to use the same idiom in sentences of their own, or to tell personal stories about playing hooky. One student, who may have missed the point, said: "I prefer soccer."

Idiomatic expressions with colors

RED
It makes some people *see red* when they hear about animal cruelty.
There are lots of examples of government *red tape* that cripple the local economy.
When money came into the conversation, we all saw *the red light*.
The bank robber was *caught red-handed*.
Other examples: *red in the face, red carpet, in the red, to be on red alert*, etc.

BLUE
Such things only happen *once in a blue moon*.
The whole story came *out of the blue*.

That song always makes me *feel blue.*
I am going to congratulate my sister for winning *the blue ribbon.*
Other examples: *blue in the face with cold, blue pencil, blue collar, blue blood,*
etc.

BLACK

You need to put that down *in black and white.*
He was forced to pay a lot of money by *blackmail.*
John is *the black sheep of the family.*
The rescuers managed to recover the airplane *black box.*
Other examples: *black market, to black out, blacklist, pitch black,* etc.

WHITE

We all like *to tell a white lie* once in a while.
The whole project was an absolute *white elephant.*
When the army officers saw the danger coming, they waved *a white flag.*
She could not say a word because she was *as white as a ghost.*
Other examples: *white as snow, white wine, white collar, whiter than white,* etc.

GREEN

Grass is always *greener* on the other side.
We are waiting for the manager *to give us the green light.*
A hedge between *keeps the friendship green.*
New Jersey is *a green state.*
Other examples: *green with envy, green as grass, to have a green thumb, to be*
green, etc.

> There are **four seasons** in Alabama: **shrimp, crab, oyster**, and **fish**.

IDIOMS WITH ANIMALS

Throughout history, animals have been a part of everyday life. People raised
animals for food or to help with their physical work. Some animals are still used
for hunting or fishing, and others have been domesticated only because we need
them to be with us.

American English is full of idiomatic expressions because we like to
color our conversation with special words to express our feelings about an
action, a person, or simply because idioms make the language richer and the
communication more colorful.

Animals have become so popular, we see them everywhere: on TV, in the parks, at exhibitions, in movies and documentaries. We have adopted them to be our pets, and our culture reflects this in the way people talk. We use idioms to express our feelings regarding our actions and in time, idiomatic phrases with animals have become so widespread we use these phrases like second nature. Idiomatic expressions may even be considered figurative language because there is no relation between the idioms and the words in the phrases. For example, **a bull in a china shop** is a clumsy person, not a bull. When we mean to say that somebody works very hard, we might say **he works like a horse**. Using such idioms adds a special touch and makes our conversation much more interesting. Instead of using the words with their literal meaning, isn't it more colorful if we say, for example, "I think you pulled the wool over my eyes!" when in fact what we mean is "I think you tricked me!"

IDIOMS WITH DOGS

It's raining cats and dogs.	It's raining hard.
Dog eat dog world	Our society can be cruel.
Dog days of summer	hot days of summer
Let sleeping dogs lie.	Leave things as they are.
Bite the hand that feeds you	to be ungrateful
His bark is worse than his bite.	He's all talk and no action.
You are barking up the wrong tree.	You misunderstood the whole situation.

DISCOVER   Ask the students to work in groups and discover the meaning of the following expressions. Students may also try to compare English idioms with similar structures in their own native languages.

Can you guess what they mean?

Love me, love my dog.   _____

Every dog has its day.   _____

Lazy as a dog   _____

Like a dog with two tails   _____

Three dog night   _____

IDIOMS WITH CATS

To let the cat out of the bag	You say something you shouldn't say.
When the cat's away the mice will play.	When unsupervised, people do as they wish.

A cool cat	a fashionable person
A cat nap	a short nap
To play cat and mouse	trick somebody into making a mistake so you have an advantage over them
Curiosity killed the cat.	Curiosity can lead into dangerous situations.
A copycat	somebody who imitates the action of another

GUESS

Has the cat got your tongue?   _____

Like a cat on a hot tin roof   _____

Look what the cat dragged in!   _____

A cat has nine lives.   _____

IDIOMS WITH BIRDS

1. **A night owl** — somebody who stays up late or is active at night

2. **Swan song** — an artist's last performance before retirement

3. **Lovely weather for ducks** — rainy weather

4. **Goose bumps** — a sudden feeling of excitement

5. **Pecking order** — a hierarchy system of social organization

6. **Wild goose chase** — a useless pursuit or search

7. **To kill two birds with one stone** — accomplish two things with one action

GUESS:

The early bird catches the worm.   _____

A bird's eye view   _____

As free as a bird   _____

Bird brain   _____

A bird in the hand is worth two in the bush _____

Birds of a feather flock together   _____

IDIOMS WITH ANIMALS

Students might be able to understand the following idiomatic expressions by **guessing** or by **comparing** them with similar set phrases used in their native languages:

Hold your horses!   _____

You got ants in your pants.   _____

Like a fish out of water   _____

To quit cold turkey   _____

To open a can of worms   _____

Busy as a bee   _____

Pig-headed   _____

The elephant in the room   _____

The lion's share   _____

You can't teach an old dog new tricks _____

Strictly for the birds   _____

EXERCISE

Students should walk around the room and find somebody who might fit the expression:

Somebody who has butterflies in the stomach

Somebody who can tell a cock and bull story

Somebody who stopped smoking cold turkey

Somebody who could eat like a horse

Somebody who is dog tired

Somebody who has a dog-eared book

Somebody who eats like a bird

Somebody who was used as a guinea-pig

IDIOMATIC EXPRESSIONS WITH PLANTS AND TREES

ASK THE STUDENTS to read the passage below silently and try to understand the meaning of the whole story. Make sure the students understand the literal meaning of all the vocabulary words, and then ask them to select those expressions that might have a metaphorical meaning. You should write on the board everything they say plus some of the following:

To have roots	*the root of the problem*	*was flowering*	*blossomed*
bear fruit	*is blooming*	*the seeds of an idea*	*greenhouse*

1a. You are going to read a story that has the title 'A Horticultural Love Story.' What do you think the story is about? Make two predictions.

1b. Read the story. Were either of your predictions correct?

A Horticultural Love Story

Greenside Park is a large park in the middle of a town in the north of England. Three years ago, two junior gardeners started to work there. One was Vincent, the other Maya. Vincent had roots in the Caribbean. One branch of his family still lives there. Maya grew up in Kenya, but had put down roots in England. Both of them still desperately missed the brightly-colored tropical plants of their childhoods. This was something they talked about when they first met. On winter days, Maya felt depressed and she was sure that the root of the problem was the cold, grey weather. Vincent understood how she felt, and slowly the seeds of an idea started to grow in him.

In the park was an old Victorian greenhouse. It was a lovely old building, designed and built at the time when the architecture of greenhouses was flowering in England. It had not been used for many years and Vincent suggested to Maya that they try to get money to restore the missing panes of glass in its roof. They also needed to mend the heating, and to clean it up inside.

Together, they wrote many letters to local branches of the big chain stores, asking them to sponsor the restoration of the greenhouse. Finally, a branch of a large supermarket agreed to do so. Together with local schools and some local groups, Vincent and Maya organized three weekend sales in the park. People made cakes and crafts which they sold to raise money for the greenhouse. The fruit of all this effort was that Vincent and Maya had enough money for some tropical plants to grow in the greenhouse. Also, their friendship blossomed, and they realized how much they enjoyed each other's company.

At last, after two years, all their hard work bore fruit when the greenhouse was officially opened by the town's mayor. It is now filled with beautiful, brightly-colored plants from the Caribbean and Kenya. And Maya is blooming – happy to know that she and Vincent will be married in a few weeks.

1c. Read the story again, and underline any words or phrases connected with trees or plants. What do you think these words or phrases mean?" (Lazar, 2003, p.41)

SUGGESTION:

The following expressions should be written on the board:

Barking up the wrong tree

Beat around the bush

To clutch at straws

Turn over a new leaf

Knock on wood

Make hay while the sun shines.

Look for a needle in a hay stack

Nip it in the bud

Can't see the wood for the trees

As fresh as a daisy

Create individual situations, and ask the students to guess the meaning in context.

For example:

We can't wait. We'd better *nip it in the bud* now.

You should come to the point. Don't *beat around the bush*.

We can't get too involved. We can't *see the wood for the trees*.

I met Ashley just the other day. She looked *as fresh as a daisy*.

Ask the students to compare idiomatic expressions in English with similar phrases in their native language:

cream of the crop   *I heard it through the grapevine*

garden variety   *a thorn in your side*

out on a limb   *in a nutshell*

bed of roses   *a slow bloomer*

CLICHÉS

A CLICHÉ IS A group of words, a phrase, or an expression that has been used so often that today it is no longer interesting or original.

Betty Kirkpatrick (1996) in her book, *Cliches,* introduces the readers to the history of defining such expressions and finds an early explanation in John Ayto (1992) and his *Bloomsbury Dictionary of Word Origins*: "Originally, French *clicher* meant literally 'stereotype' – that is 'print from a plate made by making a type-metal cast from a mold of a printing surface.' He goes on, 'Hence a word or phrase that was a cliché had literally been repeated time and time again in identical form from a single printing plate.' In non-literal terms a cliché came to describe an expression that was repeated so often that it lost its freshness . . ." (v)

Kirkpatrick also cautions us in her *Introduction* that we have to be careful:

"It is common in English for quotations to be misquoted. If such misquotations become common enough, they become clichés. [. . .] These include **a little knowledge is a dangerous thing**, a misquotation of 'a little learning is a dangerous thing' from Alexander Pope's *An Essay on Criticism* (1709), **fresh fields and pastures new**, a misquotation of 'fresh woods and pastures new' from Milton's *Lycidas*, and **money is the root of all evil**, a misquotation of the 'love of money is the root of all evil,' a Biblical quotation from 1 Timothy (6:10)." (xi)

Examples of clichés:

Doublet clichés:

> **bag and baggage, bits and pieces, leaps and bounds, safe and sound**, etc.

Allusion clichés:

the best laid schemes – from Robert Burns' *To a Mouse*

the Midas touch – a reference to a legendary Greek king

forbidden fruit – a reference to the Biblical story of Adam and Eve

manna from heaven – also a Biblical reference

Euphemism clichés:

Kick the bucket, powder one's nose, spend more time with one's family, etc.

Metaphor clichés:

The light at the end of the tunnel

Make waves

On the warpath

Par for the course

Catchphrase clichés:

Don't call us, we'll call you.

A man's gotta do what a man's gotta do.

You can't take it with you.

Denotation, Connotation, and Inference

WORDS IN A dictionary have definitions explaining their meaning, which is what linguists call **denotation** – the literal or primary meaning of a word, in contrast to the feelings or ideas that the word suggests. Ilan Stavans (2005), owner of hundreds of dictionaries, also wrote a book about them, *Dictionary Days*. In a very attractive and enticing approach, the author chose one definition of the word DICTIONARY from *The Compact Edition of the Oxford English* Dictionary:

> "A book dealing with the individual words of a language (or certain specified classes of them), so as to set forth their orthography, pronunciation, signification, and use, their synonyms, derivation, and history, or at least some of these facts: for convenience of reference, the words are arranged in some stated order, now, ion most languages, alphabetical; and in larger dictionaries the information given is illustrated by quotations from literature; a word-book, vocabulary, or lexicon." (11)

Our ESL students should be encouraged to use English-English dictionaries, but they might need a lot of guidance in doing so, and here comes the instructor's gift of using any methods or techniques possible to make our learners aware of the benefits of a good dictionary. Teaching vocabulary using denotation is not a problem, but when words have associated meanings, we get into **connotation**.

According to James E. Coomber and Howard Peet (2000), we make use of denotation and connotation on a daily basis to express different points of view regarding a situation or condition.

> "Here's some food for thought. List as many words as you can that mean 'things to eat.' *Chow, grub, nourishment, edibles, sustenance, victuals* and *rations* are a few that might come to mind. All these words have the literal, or **denotative** meaning 'food,' and can be substituted for the word *food* in a sentence. However, each word carries extra baggage, its social, emotional, and personal associations. These associated, or

connotative meanings, determine which synonym is appropriate for a particular situation.

For example, you probably would use the word *nourishment* if you wanted to talk about food that specifically provides energy necessary for life and growth. This word has a somewhat formal connotation, so it's not likely that you would use it in discussing a lunch menu with your friends. However, you might use *nourishment* in just such a situation to create an ironic effect. You would be making ironic use of a connotative meaning if, instead of asking your junk-food-loving friend what she brought for lunch, you asked, 'What's the *nourishment* for the day?' In contrast, *chow* and *grub* are slang words used to refer to any type of meal. It would not be accurate to use *chow* or *grub* interchangeably with *nourishment*." (138)

Another point of view, this time a little bit more detailed and obviously more comprehensive, comes from an encyclopedia:

"The term 'connotation' is employed in semantics as part of a typology of meaning. Two broad uses may be distinguished. In the first place, it was established as a technical term by John Stuart Mill, opposed to 'denotation': for Mill, an adjective such as *white* denotes the class of white things, but connotes, or implies, the attribute of whiteness which they share. [...] In linguistics, 'connotation' is usually applied more narrowly, much as in everyday language, to various aspects of the communicative value of linguistic units seen as lying outside their core, descriptive meaning. [...]

First, the term is used with reference to *expressive* components of meaning, most obviously in the case of terms which care 'favorable' or 'unfavorable' connotations. Many lexical units serve to express the attitudes or feelings of the speaker toward what they describe, as in Bertrand Russell's well known 'paradigm' *I am firm, you are obstinate, he is pig-headed*. Here the adjectives may be seen as sharing a common core of descriptive meaning but express different value-judgments – favorable in the case of *firm*, unfavorable in the case of *obstinate* and *pig-headed*. Expressive connotations vary in strength: pig-headed expresses stronger disapproval than obstinate. They also vary in the type of emotive involvement expressed: for example, diminutive expressions (*doggie, Katie* etc.) express affection. [...]

Connotations may also reflect *social* or *situational* circumstances of use. Lexical units may function as markers of particular speech varieties, either in terms of the social affiliations of their typical users (such as regional provenance, class, occupation, sex, or age) or in terms of features of the situation in which they are typically used – such as the social relationship of participants, social setting, or genre of communication. Thus technical terms connote the specialist occupational roles of their users, and are also characteristic of ingroup communication. Expressive terms illustrated above may also be situationally restricted: *pig-headed* is more colloquial than *obstinate*, and *doggie* is characteristic of baby talk. [...]

Consideration of such areas of meaning highlights a third type of connotation, which derives from general *cultural associations* of what is denoted by the lexical unit. Such associations are often highlighted by cross-linguistic comparison of translation equivalents. For example, English *octopus* and Japanese *tako* denote the same species of animal, but the cultural associations are quite different: weird, sinister *octopus* vs. endearing, edible *tako*." (*International Encyclopedia of Linguistics*, William J. Frawley, Editor in Chief, Oxford University Press, 2003, p. 9)

For the ESL teacher, this information is necessary if we want to understand the minutiae and the **semantic implications regarding connotation**. We process this information, and if we go into the classroom, we can identify simple words and discuss them with our students in a way that they, in their turn, see the difference between denotation and connotation. One example is the word *cheap*. A basic explanation in a dictionary would give us this definition: "low in price," or "inexpensive." But if we look carefully, we might be able to detect the underlying negative connotation: "of inferior quality or worth." If the students see the difference, they should be asked to analyze and discuss the difference between *terrible* and *terrific*. The teacher can also find similar examples in a quick conversation, or may recommend an article in a daily newspaper. In New York, we used to give students copies of *AM New York* or *The Metro*, which always provide interesting articles about mundane topics that students might enjoy reading and talking about.

For ESL students, anything that goes beyond the literal meaning may create problems, and the first step would be to take a quick look at **inference**.

Hayakawa (1990) prefers to talk about the difference between **reports** and **inferences**.

"The reports should be about firsthand experience – scenes the reader has witnessed, meetings and social events he has taken part in, people he knows well. The reports should be of such a nature that they can be verified and agreed upon. [...] An inference, as we shall use the term, is a statement about the unknown based on the known. (24) In short, inferences are extremely important. We may infer from the material and cut of a woman's clothes the nature of her wealth or social position; we may infer from the character of the ruins the origin of the fire that destroyed the building; [. . .] we may infer from the shape of land the path of a prehistoric glacier; we may infer from a halo on an unexposed photographic plate that it has been in the vicinity of radioactive materials.

Inferences may be carefully or carelessly made. They may be made on the basis of a broad background of previous experience with the subject matter or with no experience at all. For example, the inferences a good mechanic can make about the condition of an engine by listening to it are often startling accurate, while the inferences made by an amateur may be entirely wrong.

In any case, the common characteristic of inferences is that they are statements about matters that are not directly known, made on the basis of what has been observed. Generally speaking, the quality of inference is directly related to the quality of the report or observations from which it stems and to the abilities of the one making the inference."(25)

Report: "Mary Smith didn't get in until three last Saturday night."

Inference: "I bet she was out fooling around!" (118)

The above mentioned quotations come from a book written by S. I. Hayakawa while he was teaching at the University of Wisconsin at Madison. The textbook was written for his students and has two sections: Book One: *The Functions of Language* and Book Two: *Language and Thought*. In his preface to this book translated into eight languages right after publication, the author explains the purpose of writing such a book:

"To learn to think more clearly, to speak and write more effectively, and to listening and read with greater understanding – these have been the goals of language study from the medieval trivium to the present-day English class." (vii)

That was written in the previous century and was addressed to students in English. We know ESL is only an offspring of English, but the instructors should have the ammunition and the general knowledge of the English language so the classroom instruction can be delivered with a feeling of unbiased and unabated confidence.

Nowadays, the reader will find several sources of information online and here is such an example:

"An inference is an idea or conclusion that's drawn from evidence and reasoning. An inference is an educated guess. We learn about some things by experiencing them first-hand, but we gain other knowledge by inference – the process of inferring things based on what is already known. When you make an inference, you're reading between the lines or just looking carefully at the facts and coming to conclusions. You can also make faulty inferences. If you hear a person's weight is 250 pounds, you might make the inference that they're overweight. But what if they're seven feet tall?" www.vocabulary.com

When we read between the lines, we try to decipher ideas that are not stated directly, and sometimes these ideas are crucial if we want to fully understand what other people mean to say or write. John Langan in his *Ten Steps to Improving College Reading Skills* (1997) devotes a whole section to the subject of Inferences. Here is what he says in Chapter 8:

"Consider first how often you make inferences in everyday life. For example, suppose you are sitting in a coffee shop at lunchtime. A woman sits down at the next table. Here is what you observe:

- She is wearing an expensive-looking suit, a silk blouse, gold jewelry, and a gold band on the third finger of her left hand.
- The woman opens a briefcase and takes out some manila folders; she begins to study them.
- You notice that she also has a child's crayon drawing in the briefcase.

As you sit in the coffee shop, you may make several inferences about this woman:

- She's on her lunch break.
- She works in an office, perhaps as a lawyer or an executive.
- She is married and has a young child.

How did you arrive at these inferences? First of all, you used your experience and general knowledge of people. Secondly, you made informed guesses based on the facts you observed. Of course, your inferences might not all prove true." (253)

Now you can try to make your own inferences using John Langan's example:

A high school has uniformed security guards patrolling the halls.

What you infer: _____

After talking about inferences in reading, the author quotes scholar S. I. Hayakawa, who says that inferences are "statements about the unknown made on the basis of the known." He also introduces us to his guidelines for inferences in reading:

1. **"Never lose sight of the available information**. As much as possible, base your inferences on facts.

2. **Use your background information and experience to help you in making inferences.** [. . .] The more background information people have, the more accurate their inferences are likely to be. So keep in mind that if your background information in a particular matter is weak, your inferences may be shaky. A doctor's inferences about your rash and fever are likely to be more helpful than those of your car mechanic.

3. **Consider the alternatives.** Considering alternative interpretations of the fact is one way to zero in on a likely interpretation. Don't simply accept the first inference that comes to mind. Instead, consider all the facts of a case and all the possible explanations. For example, the doctor analyzing your rash and fever may first think of then eliminate several possible diagnoses before seriously testing for one or two of the more likely ones." (257-258)

Practice exercises for understanding how to deal with inferences include the following:

"Read the following textbook passages. The put a check by the **three** inferences that are most logically based on the given facts in each passage:

The Chicago Tribune once wrote that Henry Ford, the founder of the Ford Motor Company, was an ignorant man. Ford sued, challenging the paper to "prove it." During the trial, Ford was asked dozens of simple, general information questions: "When was the Civil War?" "Name the presidents of the United States." And so on. Ford, who had very little formal education, could answer very few. Finally, exasperated, he said, "I don't know the answers to those questions, but I could find a man in five minutes who does. I use my brains to think, not store up a lot of useless facts."

__x__ 1. Henry Ford was probably angered by the article in the *Chicago Tribune*.

_____ 2. Ford frequently sued people.

_____ 3. The *Tribune* won the case in court.

__x__ 4. Ford believed that knowing where to find a fact is good enough.

_____ 5. Ford would have been even more successful in his career had he had a formal education.

__x__ 6. Ford believed that knowing how to think is more important than knowing facts. (262)

Most organizations and their managers realize the importance of maintaining good human relations. A climate of openness and trust can encourage performance and foster loyalty. According to one author, everyone at Walt Disney Productions – including the president – wears a name tag with first name only, and at IBM the chairman of the board personally answers employee complaints. This kind of atmosphere can only have a positive effect of human relations.

While many managers get a lift from knowing they're treating their workers right, there are practical benefits as well. When workers are satisfied with the interpersonal aspect of their jobs, they are usually more productive.

__x__ 1. The size of the paycheck is not the only thing that determines employee satisfaction.

_____ 2. At Walt Disney Productions, employees don't have complaints.

__x__ 3. Using first names on the job makes a company seem like a friendlier, more caring place.

_____ 4. IBM is more productive than all its competitors.

__x__ 5. Workers who feel their employers do not care about them tend to be less productive.

_____ 6. Walt Disney Productions was the first company to encourage employees and executives to use one another's first names. (263-264)

DISCOVER:
"Read the following textbook passage. The check the **five** statements which are most logically supported by the information given.

People interrupt for various reasons. One is believing that what they have to say is more important than what the other person is saying. Another reason people interrupt is that they believe they know what the other person is going to say and want the person to know that they already know. People may also interrupt when they are not paying close attention. The interruption communicates a lack of sensitivity, a superior attitude, or both. People need to be able to verbalize their ideas and feelings fully; inappropriate interruptions are bound to damage their self-concepts or make them hostile – and possibly both. Simply stated, whatever you have to say is seldom so important that it requires you to interrupt a person. When you do interrupt, you should realize that you may be perceived as putting a person down and are increasing the chances of a defensive reaction. The more frequent the interruptions, the greater the potential harm.

__x__ 1. People feel good if others listen carefully to their ideas.

_____ 2. The author suggests that people who interrupt don't mind being interrupted themselves.

__x__ 3. One reason people who are not paying close attention may interrupt is that they don't realize that the speaker is in the middle of a point.

_____ 4. The author feels it is okay to interrupt others if you feel you are superior.

_____ 5. The author suggests that if you never interrupt others, you will never be interrupted.

__x__ 6. Interruptions can make people feel that their ideas are not worth listening to.

__x__ 7. We can conclude the author would say that a boss will gain more cooperation by not interrupting others.

_____ 8. We can conclude the author would say it is okay for a parent to interrupt a child.

__x__ 9. People who interrupt don't always realize how the other person will view the interruption.

_____ 10. The author could consider anger to be an unlikely reaction to being interrupted." (288)

There are several resources that will give you an idea about inference, its definition and examples to practice with the students. For me the best choice would be *Reader's Choice* by S. Silberstein, B. K. Dobson, and M. A. Clarke. Here are a couple of suggestions:

"Mystery stories, like most other texts, require readers to note important facts and draw inferences based on these. To solve the following mysteries, you must become a detective, drawing inferences from the clues provided. Each mystery below has been solved by the fictional Professor Fordney, a master detective – the expert the police call for their most puzzling cases. Your job is to match wits with the great professor. Your teacher may want you to work with your classmates to answer the question following each mystery. Be prepared to defend your solution with details from the passage.

Mystery 1: Class Day (page 140)

"I shall tell," Fordney said to his class some years ago, of an exploit of the famed scientist, Sir Joshua Beckwith, Professor of Egyptology in London.

"He had uncovered an ancient tomb in Egypt and, through his undisputed knowledge and ability to read hieroglyphics, had definitely established the date of the birth and the reign of a great Pharaoh whose mummy he had discovered. A man of volatile temper, and emphatic scientific views which he did not hesitate to express in exposing charlatanism, he had many enemies.

"The British Museum soon received a message, signed by Sir Joshua Beckwith, which in part read as follows: 'Have discovered the tomb of an important Pharaoh who reigned from 1410 to 1438 B.C. and who died at the age of 42 years, leaving two sons and two daughters. Great wealth found in sarcophagus. One of his sons dies shortly after his reign began, etc. . . .'

"The Museum officials at first were astonished," continued Fordney, "but examination of the communication quickly told them it was either a very stupid fake or an attempt at a 'practical joke!' They were right in their belief that the message did not come from Sir Joshua Beckwith. He did make a most important discovery – but how did the Museum authorities know the communication was not authentic?"

How did they know? _____

Please refer to Appendices for extra exercises in inference.

Figurative Meaning

WAITING FOR THE bus at the Port Authority Bus Terminal in New York City on a late afternoon, I overheard two commuters, who were talking to each other at the end of a busy day and having (more or less) the following conversation:

"What are you taking? The local or the express?" said the first one.

"I am taking the express. The other one stops at every tree," replied the other one.

Was that a good example of figurative language? There are times when we want to add color or a special touch to our conversations or to our writing. We then change from the literal meaning of our vocabulary to what linguists call **figurative language**. Rosa & Eschholz (2015) devote a whole section in Chapter 12 of their classy textbook entitled *Models for Writers*. After a quick introduction to the topic, the authors assert that "figurative language brings freshness and color to writing and also helps clarify ideas. For example, when asked by his teacher to explain the concept of brainstorming, one student replied, 'Well, brainstorming is like having a tornado in your head.' This figurative language helps others imagine the whirl of ideas in this young writer's head as he brainstorms a topic for writing." (320)

In 2003, Gillian Lazar published a book of activities to practice figurative language entitled *Meanings and Metaphors* with 34 sections of photo-copiable materials that can be used in the ESL classroom. Starting with Metaphors and Similes, then going through – for example – Fabulous fables, Opening doors, Marketing your metaphors, Selling with similes, Infectious laughter, Food for thought, Keeping your cool, and ending with Metaphors in rhetoric, this book is a gem that will please the teachers as well as the ESL students. In her introduction, the author asks several questions, to which she provides ample supporting ideas.

"What is figurative language?

Figurative or metaphorical language takes many forms. There are, for example, expressions such as *to be at a crossroads* and *to shake like a leaf*. There are also many words which can have both literal and metaphorical meanings: verbs such as *to blossom, to trickle*, and *to wound*; adjectives such as *healthy, half-baked* and *burning*; nouns such as *headache, recipe* and *roots*. There are proverbs which by their very nature can only be understood metaphorically. e.g. *Birds of a feather flock together*. While these are now sometimes considered rather clichéd, they still form part of the natural repertoire of most native speakers of English." (1)

"Why teach figurative language?

It is useful for learners of English to increase their knowledge of figurative language for many reasons. Firstly, introducing figurative language in the classroom can be an effective way of expanding student vocabulary. Once students learn the literal meaning of particular words, their vocabulary can be greatly extended if they are then able to use these words figuratively (e.g. words such as *to bloom* or *to blossom* which have both literal and metaphorical meanings.) . . .

Secondly, figurative language provides a handy and memorable way of organizing new vocabulary to be learned. Most teachers and students are familiar with the notion of a lexical set, where vocabulary is grouped according to topic area. But particular lexical areas can also be extended to create 'metaphorical sets.' . . .

Focusing on figurative language in the classroom provides a way of exposing students to useful idioms (e.g. *to lend a hand*) and common collocations (e.g. *a hail of bullets*). . . .

Finally, activities incorporating figurative language can provide a useful springboard for integrated skills work. (1)

"Aren't there cultural problems with figurative language?

Figurative meanings are often culturally determined, and this can be a problem for the classroom teacher. The figurative language we use stems from the underlying values and assumptions of our culture or society, so that a common metaphor in one culture may not be understood by people from other cultures. For example, figurative meanings and associations for colors can differ widely cross-culturally. There is a wide range of connotations held by different nationalities for the word *red*. In order to understand the expression to see red, students of English need to be aware of the cultural associations activated for a native speaker in this context, i.e. red is often connected with a anger in English, and so to see red means to become angry. As teachers we need to sensitize our students to the cultural meanings inherent in many examples of figurative language in English, while encouraging them to compare these associations with those in their mother tongue.

An additional problem is that by exposing student to conventional uses of metaphorical language we may be encouraging them to accept certain cultural stereotypes. There are many words in English connected with animals that are used to describe people. [. . .] By presenting these uncritically to students, there is the danger that we will be reinforcing the stereotypical beliefs about men and women that go along with these words. "(2)

EUPHEMISMS

We may or may not be aware of the power of words. We use them on a regular basis intentionally or unintentionally, but the results can be pleasant, amazing, and comforting if we choose them carefully. However, if we just throw them into a discussion, words can have unexpected consequences, and it might be too late to apologize or retract them.

What do we do? We need to play with the words or word phrases in a more careful way to convey our messages. This can be done in our dialogues, in our conversations, or when we need to communicate and inform our audience in writing. Euphemisms are those words that people use to avoid unpleasant or offensive remarks.

According to the 1983 edition of *Success with Words* published by *Reader's Digest*, "This word comes from the Greek *euphemismos* = 'fair-speech,' a technical term in rhetoric for the substitution of a palatable expression for a bluntly accurate but offensive one." [. . .]

The avoidance of straightforward language for reasons short of taboo is also called euphemism. It ranges from tactful and convenient usage to plain lying. Sensitively chosen euphemisms can serve to smooth conversation and help to keep controversy rational and polite. 'I'm afraid we've got to let you go' is a polite alternative to the brutally direct 'You're fired.' [. . .]

How far to go is a matter of taste or ethics, not of usage. Some of may be annoyed rather than mollified to hear radio and TV commercials called *messages*, or to see pornography called adult books. The giant Japanese spider crab was virtually unsalable in the United States; renamed the Alaska king crab, it was immediately recognized as a delicacy." (215)

Some of our ESL textbooks may also include short presentations of such figurative language mostly because our students first go with the literal meaning and may find themselves scratching their heads when they see one of these euphemisms. Here some examples:

> "A euphemism is defined as 'the substitution of an agreeable or in offensive expression for one that may offend or suggest something unpleasant.' We often use euphemisms when our intentions are good. For instance, it is difficult to accept that someone we love has died, so

people use all kinds of euphemisms for death, such as 'She passed away,' 'He's gone to meet his maker,' or 'She is no longer with us.' To defend against the pain of such a reality some use the humorous euphemism, 'He's kicked the bucket.' To make certain jobs sound less unappealing, people use euphemisms. A janitor is now a 'custodial worker' or 'maintenance person.' A trash man may be called a 'sanitation engineer.' Such euphemisms are not harmful, but sometimes euphemisms can be used to camouflage potentially controversial or objectionable actions. For example, instead of saying we need to raise taxes, a politician might say we need 'revenue enhancement measures.' When psychologists kill an animal they have experimented with, they prefer to use the term 'sacrifice' the animal. Doctors prefer 'terminate a pregnancy' to 'abort the fetus.' (Smalley and Ruetten, 1995, p. 170)

Mario Pei (1967) in his exhaustive revised edition of *The Story of the English Language* enumerates euphemisms like *Congressional liaison officer* (for lobbyist), *spiritual advisor* (for fortune-teller), *custodian* (for janitor), *archivist* (for library attendant).

"*Intoxicated* for *drunk* is a characteristic Anglo-Saxon euphemism (the word etymologically means "poisoned," and no other language uses it to describe one under the influence of liquor). It is, however, a fact that Benjamin Franklin collected as many as 228 euphemisms for *drunk* current in his day. Among them are many that survive to the present time (*mellow, tipsy*), but also many that have gone down the drain (*cherry-merry, been to Barbados, nimtopsical, seeing two moons, in his altitudes, half-seas over*). [...]

One of the sweetest euphemisms reported comes from Japan, but could be recommended for American use. If a student has failed his college exams, the telegram he receives from the university office reads: 'The cherry blossoms are falling.' " (147)

Another approach, along the same lines, comes from Hans Guth (1972), who introduces his assessment of euphemisms between the short chapter on *Directness* and a longer one about *Jargon*.

"Euphemisms are 'beautiful words' – words more beautiful than what they stand for. Often they are required by politeness or tact. When referring to people you respect, you will prefer *stout* to *fat*, *intoxicated* to *drunk*, *indolent* to *lazy*, and *remains* to *corpse*. More often, however, euphemisms mislead or even deliberately deceive. Waitresses become 'hostesses,' [...] file clerks 'research consultants,' undertakers 'funeral directors,' door-to-door salesmen 'customer-contact personnel,' and fortune tellers 'clairvoyant readers.' Many readers are annoyed by such evasive tactics; they will be grateful when you call a spade a spade.

Euphemism	Blunt
Immoderate use of intoxicants	*heavy drinking*
Deteriorating residential section	*slum*

NOTE: The use of euphemisms to avoid repetition of more unpretentious words is called **elegant variation**. "(110-111)

ESL students usually understand a new concept better if they are presented with a good example. Let's take a look at Huck Finn, Mark Twain's character:

"Every night I used to slip ashore toward ten o'clock at some little village, and buy ten or fifteen cents' worth of meal or other stuff to eat. [. . .]

Mornings before daylight I slipped into cornfields and borrowed a watermelon, or a mushmelon, or a punkin, or some new corn, or things of that kind. Pap always said it warn't no harm to borrow things if you was meaning to pay them back some time; but *the widow said it warn't anything but a soft name for stealing*, and no decent boy would do it. Jim said he reckoned the widow was partly right; so the best way would be for us to pick out two or three things from the list and say we wouldn't borrow them anymore – then he reckoned it wouldn't be no harm to borrow the others. So we talked it over all night, drifting along down the river, trying to make up our minds whether to drop the watermelons, or the cantelopes, or the mushmelons, or what. But toward daylight we got all settled satisfactory, and concluded to drop crabapples and p'simmons. We warn't feeling just right before that, but it was all comfortable now. I was glad the way it come out, too, because crabapples ain't ever good, and the p'simmons wouldn't be ripe for two or three months yet." (Quoted in Judith Oster, *From Reading to Writing*, p. 242)

To clarify what Mark Twain was saying, the author poses the following questions:
"What is the moral dilemma? What does 'borrow' mean? Is the widow right? Why? What does the word *borrow* do for Huck and Jim?" (242) Instead of answering all these questions, Judith Oster continues the conversation about euphemisms:

"Euphemisms can help us deliver bad news and soothe the feelings of an angry or grieving person. But as in the Huck Finn example, euphemisms can also distort our view of reality. They can make stealing seem like borrowing; they can make the horrifying seem not so bad. When euphemisms obscure the realities and moral issues that we need to know in order to make judgments and take action, we need to be careful – to 'tell it like it is' and to hear it as it really is." (242)

DISCOVER: Together with the students, discuss the following words and expressions and see if they qualify as euphemisms and what they imply:

A little tipsy	_____
Downsizing	_____
Mentally challenged	_____
Special child	_____
Before I go	_____

METAPHORS

Students usually respond to new material by asking questions about terminology. Instead of starting with a scholarly approach regarding metaphors, let us try and provide examples first, and the examples will speak for themselves.

"In Antonio Skarmeta's *Burning Patience* (the novel on which the film *Il Postino* was based), the Chilean poet Pablo Neruda tries to explain to the young postman Mario what poetry is all about:

'Metaphors, I said!'

'What's that?'

The poet placed his hand on the boy's shoulder.

'To be more or less imprecise, we could say that it is a way of describing something by comparing it to something else.'

'Give me an example.'

Neruda looked at his watch and sighed.

'Well, when you say the sky is weeping, what do you mean?'

'That's easy – that it's raining.'

'So, you see, that's a metaphor.'

Mario desperately wants to become a poet himself, but he fails to come up with any metaphors of his own. So Neruda tried to give him a helping hand:

'You are now going to walk along the beach to the bay and as you observe the movement of the sea, you are going to invent metaphors.'

'Give me an example!'

'Listen to this poem: "Here on the island, the sea, so much sea. It spills over from time to time. It says, yes, then no, then no. It says yes, in blue, in foam, in a gallop. It says no, then no. It cannot be still. My name is sea, it repeats, striking a stone but convincing it. Then with the seven green tongues, of seven green tigers, over seven green seas, it caresses it, kisses it, wets it, and pounds on its chest, repeating its own name."

He paused with an air of satisfaction. 'What do you think?'

'It's weird.'

'Weird? You certainly are a severe critic.'

'No, Sir. The poem wasn't weird. What was weird was the way I felt when you recited it . . . How can I explain it to you? When you recited that poem, the words went from over there to over here.'

'Like the sea, then!'

'Yes, they moved just like the sea.'

'That's the rhythm.'

'And I felt weird because with all the movement, I got dizzy.'

'You got dizzy?'

'Of course, I was like a boat tossing upon your words.'

The poet's eyelids rose slowly.

'Like a boat tossing upon my words.'

'Uh-huh.'

'You know that you just did, Mario?'

'No, what?'

'You invented a metaphor.' "

(Quoted in Guy Deutscher's *The Unfolding of Language*, 2005, pp. 115-116)

Even in a daily conversation, we can hardly say a couple of words without using a metaphor. *"Meta-phora* is Greek for 'carry across,' or to use the Latin equivalent, *meta-phor* just means *trans-fer*." (117)

SIMILES

We use similes **when we speak** to add something special, to create an artistic image, or to give a nuance to our thoughts and ideas.

As happy as a clam	*As black as coal*
As light as feather	*As busy as a bee*
As easy as pie	*As solid as a rock*
As bold as brass	*As bright as a button*
As cold as ice	*As good as gold*
As large as life	*As cool as a cucumber*
As hard as nails	*As hot as hell*
As innocent as a lamb	*As tall as a giraffe*
As smooth as silk	*As free as a bird*
As gentle as a lamb	*As quick as lightning*
As clear as crystal	*As wise as an owl*
As proud as a peacock	*As straight as an arrow*
As tough as nails	*As white as a ghost*
As sweet as sugar	*As black as coal*

"Similes can make our language more descriptive and enjoyable. Writers, poets, and songwriters make use of similes often to add depth and emphasize what they are trying to convey to the reader or listener. Similes can be funny, serious, mean, or creative.

Following are some examples of similes regularly **used in writing**:

You were as brave as a lion.
They fought like cats and dogs.
He is as funny as a barrel of monkeys.
This house is as clean as a whistle.
He is as strong as an ox.
Your explanation is as clear as mud.
Watching the show was like watching grass grow.
That is as easy as shooting fish in a barrel.
This contract is as strong as the ground we stand on.
That guy is as nutty as a fruitcake.
Don't just sit there as a bump on a log.
They are as different as night and day.
She is as thin as a rake.
My love for you is as deep as the ocean.
I am so thirsty that my throat is as dry as a bone."
www.examples.yourdictionary.com

Similes using the word LIKE:

Cry like a baby.
Grow like a weed.
Run like the wind.
She smells like a flower.
He drinks like a fish.
She swims like a dolphin.
He slithers like a snake.
She runs like a cheetah.
He walks like a ninja and runs like a cat.
His eyes lit up like two headlights.
The lake is like a mirror.
My memory is like a sieve.

EXERCISE "Read the text and underline all the words or phrases connected with food:

The Cook's Tragedy   A Short Play for Ham Actors by Brian Patten

A: I once knew a cook who moved among the cream of society.
B: A good egg?
A: Unfortunately, he thought he could have his cake and eat it.
B: You mean he wanted everything on a plate?
A: Exactly. He thought life was going to be as easy as pie.
B: Obviously he never used his loaf.
A: One day, when the chips were down, he turned sour.
B: I suppose he became a fast liver?
A: He didn't give a sausage for anyone.
B: No doubt he ended up in a soup?
A: Of course. He realized his goose was cooked when he heard the police had a bone to pick with him.
B: You mean he was acting fishy and they grilled him?
A: He told them a half-baked story and they gave him a real roasting.
B: Such lives are food for thought."

(Quoted in Lazar's *Meanings and Metaphors*, 2003, p. 91)

> "We can never attain knowledge unless we retain what we hear."
>
> Dante

Mnemonics

ESL STUDENTS ACCUMULATE a lot of information in every class they take. They absorb vocabulary even when they see a new ad on the Internet; they use their listening skills every time they have a conversation with native speakers; and they practice what they learn in one class by applying the new information in another class. We, as teachers, guide them through the whole process by empowering them to **understand**, **analyze**, and eventually **practice** what they have learned. Besides the theoretical and the practical knowledge offered and acquired, students should also make a mental effort to process this information. One of the ways to retain would be the **use of memory**.

 Tips   TIPS for the power of MEMORY:

1. In the 5ᵗʰ Century B.C., Simonides invented the science of memory based on three elements:

   location – object – image   p. 189

2. According to Coulmas (1996), writing is a visual medium of communication that circumvents and transcends speech. Among the five functions of writing, **memory is the most important**. Accumulation of knowledge developed thanks to the supportive potential of writing. (p. 159)   p. 191

3. When talking about mnemonic techniques, Lorayne & Lucas (1974) mention that the basic memory rule is:

   You Can Remember Any New Piece of Information If It Is Associated to Something You Already Know or Remember. (p. 231)   p. 196

4.   You should try a self-test: Memorizing lists as stories   p. 197

5.   Good examples of mnemonic techniques for the ESL classroom:

HOMES   The Great Lakes: Huron, Ontario, Michigan, Erie, Superior

FANBOYS   The coordinating conjunctions: For, And, Nor, But, Or, Yet, So

p. 199

"Thinking is not possible without memory and memory itself, in a wide consciousness, may well depend upon reading."

Harold Bloom, *Genius,* Warner Books, 2002, p. 84.)

Defined in broad terms, a mnemonic is a device, procedure or operation that is used to improve memory.

"The historical development of mnemonics or mnemonic devices begins with a poet named Simonides of Ceos in the fifth century B.C. Simonides, as the tale has it, was hired to recite an ode at a nobleman's banquet. In the fashion of the time, the poet began with a few lines in praise of divinities – in this case Castor and Pollux – before going on to the serious business of talking about his host. The host, however, objected to this diversion of the flattery, deducted half of Simonides' fee, and told the poet that he could seek the rest from the gods he had praised. Shortly thereafter, a message was brought to the poet that two young men had come to the door of the house and wished to speak to him. When Simonides went to speak with them, there was no one there – but in his absence the banquet hall had collapsed behind him, killing the impious nobleman and all the dinner guests as well. Castor and Pollux, traditionally imaged as two young men, had indeed paid their half of the fee.

Tales of this sort were commonplace in Greek literature, but this one has an unexpected moral. When the rubble was cleared away, the victims were found to be so mangled that their own families could not identify them. Simonides, however, remembered the places they had been sitting and so was able to identify the dead. Such was the discovery of the method of loci (or locations). It became so much a part of the study of rhetoric that the most venerable of the Roman orators used the method of loci for memorizing their speeches. Their procedure was as follows: First, a series of locations (loci), such as those in a public building, were memorized. Second, some object was thought of to represent each part of the oration, such as a spear to represent the tenth topic, war. Third, the image created for each topic was combined with the image of its corresponding location. The spear might be imagined as penetrating the tenth locus, a door. While making his speech, the orator thought of each location in turn and used the image seen in his mind's eye as the prompt for the next part of his address. After a few days, the images from the speech would fade from memory, but the more highly learned loci could be used to memorize a new speech."

http://www.learninginfo.org/simonides-history-mnemonics.htm

MEMORY AND WRITING

In 1996, Florian Coulmas published the first edition of his rich, thoroughly researched, *Encyclopedia of Writing* in which he emphasized the values of "the writing systems, scripts and orthographies of the world's major languages." (xxxv) Among the many scientific fields closely related to writing, but also benefitting from it, would be, in the author's view: history, paleography, psychology, linguistics, and sociology.

One idea fervently advocated by the author is that there is a close relationship between writing and speech. He calls them communication practices and then goes on to analyze what sets them apart.

"Writing evolved as a visual medium of communication which circumvents or transcends certain limitations of speech. Five functions in particular stand out as distinguishing writing from speech: the mnemonic function, the distancing function, the reification function, the social function, and the aesthetic function.

Memory

Although members of oral societies are often said to command a memory that far surpasses that of literate people, the amount of information that can be stored by means of writing and retrieved from written records clearly transcends the capacity of individual remembrance. Accumulation of knowledge on a large scale and historical reflection – as opposed to myth and legend – developed thanks to the memory supportive potential of writing.

Distance

Communicating in speech requires the co-presence of speaker and listener. Writing, by contrast, enables communication over any spatial or temporal distance. Hence, the three essential components of linguistic communication

– speaker, listener and utterance – can be separated from each other. The same message can be received by many in different places and at different times. [...]

Reification

Reification means that in writing a linguistic message becomes an interpretable object which must be self-sufficient because the author may not be at hand for clarification. Accordingly, written messages rely much less on context and situation than spoken ones.

Social control

As in language, codified standards of correctness laid down in writing being about changes in social organization. The permanence of writing gives written documents the character of seemingly objective guidelines of human conduct independent of personal interests.

Aesthetic

Language is used for aesthetic purposes both orally and visually, but the form and appeal of verbal and written language arts clearly differ. The written medium has added to the range of artistic expression by means of language. [...] The aesthetics of writing is less immediate, for the consumption of literature is potentially a solitary experience which again is a result of the physical properties of writing as a visible language. In a wider sense the stylistic traits associated with written texts and spoken discourse are also to be subsumed under the aesthetic function." (159-160)

Memorization and Mnemonic Techniques

From Greek and Roman orators to Simonides (the father of mnemonics) to Cicero to Thomas Aquinas to Peter of Ravenna to Erasmus to Shakespeare (whose Globe Theatre was also called "the memory theatre") to Matteo Ricci, to name just a few, memorization has been a memory training technique that functioned with a great deal of success.

We know from historical reports that the Greek and the Roman orators utilized mnemonic techniques to prepare and to deliver their public speeches. Cicero wrote about the relationship of writing to memory in one of his works entitled *Partitiones Oratoriae*:

> "Memory ... is in a manner the twin sister of written speech and is completely similar to it, [though] in a dissimilar medium. For just as script consists of marks indicating letters and of the material on which

those marks are imprinted, so the structure of memory, like a wax tablet employs places and in these gathers together images like letters"

(quoted in Carruthers, *The Book of Memory, 2008,* p. 18)

St. Augustine (354 – 430), theologian and philosopher from Numidia, profoundly influenced the medieval worldview. He wrote:

"I arrive in the fields and vast mansions of memory, where are treasured innumerable images brought in there from objects of every conceivable kind perceived by the senses. There too are hidden the modified images we produce when by our thinking we magnify or diminish or in any way alter the information our senses have reported. There to is everything else that has been consigned and stored away and not yet engulfed and buried in oblivion . . . The huge repository of the memory, with its secret and unimaginable caverns, welcomes and keeps all these things, to be recalled and brought out for use when needed; and as all of them have their particular ways into it, so all are put back again in their proper places.." (xi)

Peter of Ravenna (c. 1448 – 1508) was an Italian doctor of law, trained in Italy but who in later years worked at a couple of German universities. In 1491, Peter's *Phoenix* exalted the less known qualities of memory in the world of the legal profession, although he professed the idea that mnemonic devices could be useful in many other professions.

Shortly after Thomas Aquinas died, one of his contemporaries, Bernardo Gui, said this:

"Of the subtlety and brilliance of his intellect and the soundness of his judgment, sufficient proof is his vast literary output, his many original discoveries, his deep understanding of the Scriptures. His memory was extremely rich and retentive; whatever he had once read and grasped he never forgot." (quoted in Carruthers, 2008, p. 3)

It is said that, when confused or perplexed, Aquinas would always return to his memory.

"Thomas Aquinas was a highly literate man in a highly literate group, yet his contemporaries reserved their greatest praise not for his books but for his memory, for they understood that it was memory which allowed him to weave together his astonishing books. Memory also marked his superior moral character." (Carruthers, 2008, p. 14)

Erasmus of Rotterdam (1466-1536) was a great scholar who was very happy to see the Middle Ages gone and welcomed the new era of modern humanist scholarship. Although the art of memory in the 16th century was "on the wane," for Erasmus the study of memory entered a new phase:

> "Though I do not deny that memory can be helped by places and images, yet the best memory is based on three most important things, namely study, order, and care." (quoted in Yates, 1966, p. 127)

In 2005, Lina Perkins Wilder published her exhaustive study entitled *Shakespeare's Memory Theatre: Recollection, Properties, and Character* (Cambridge University Press). Starting from the prerogative that "the materials of theatre are, for Shakespeare, the materials of memory," in Chapter I, she makes the following statement:

> "By the time that the Elizabethan theater began to place exorbitant demands on the memorization skills of players, early modern memory culture had begun to chafe at the medieval expectation that memory should be 'copious' and 'accurate.' A number of new, or relatively new, developments – among them print, challenges to the medieval university curriculum, the Protestant Reformation, human dissection, and finally the professional theatre – offer new ways of thinking about memory. The relatively new technology of printing allows treatises on the memory arts to be disseminated more widely, but printing also offers and even requires new ways of organizing knowledge. As both the number of books and the breadth of the field of knowledge increase, mechanical aids and adjuncts become both a necessary and, for some, a distrusted part of mnemonic practice." (24)

In 1577, Matteo Ricci (1552 – 1610) left Italy and went to China. He took with him the Western thought and delivered a powerful message to Ming dynasty China, where he taught the Chinese how to use memory. Jonathan Spence did not go for the conventional biographical techniques but, instead, he related Ricci's life to images brought from religion and from his book on the art of memory Ricci wrote in Chinese and circulated among the Ming Dynasty folks. Here is how he started his remarkable work based on historical facts:

> "In 1596 Matteo Ricci taught the Chinese how to build a memory palace. He told them that the size of the palace would depend on how much they wanted to remember: the most ambitious construction would consist of several hundred buildings of all shapes and sizes; 'the more there are the better it will be,' said Ricci, though he added that one did not have to build on a grandiose scale right away. One could create modest palaces, or one could build less dramatic structures such as a temple compound, a cluster of government offices, a public hostel, or a merchant's meeting

lodge. If one wished to begin on a still smaller scale, then one could erect a simple reception hall, a pavilion, or a studio. And if one wanted an intimate space one could use just the corner of the pavilion, or an altar in a temple, or even such a homely object as a wardrobe or a divan.

In summarizing this memory system, he explained that these palaces, pavilions, divans were mental structures to be kept in one's head, not solid objects to be literally constructed out of 'real' materials. Ricci suggested that there were three main options for such memory locations. First, they could be drawn from reality – that is, from buildings that one had been in or from objects that one had seen with one's own eyes and recalled in one's memory. Second, they could be totally fictive, products of the imagination conjured up in any shape or size. Or third, they could be half real and half fictive, as in the case of a building one knew well and through the back wall of which one broke an imaginary door as a short cut to new spaces, or in the middle of which one created a mental staircase that would lead up to higher floors that had not existed before.

The purpose of all these mental constructs was to provide storage spaces for the myriad concepts that make up the sum of our human knowledge. To everything that we wish to remember, wrote Ricci, we should give an image; and to every one of these images we should assign a position where it can repose peacefully until we are ready to reclaim it by an act of memory. Since this entire memory system can work only if the images stay in the assigned positions and if we can instantly remember we stored them, obviously it would seem easiest to rely on real locations which we know so well that we cannot ever forget them. But that would be a mistake, thought Ricci. For it is by expanding the number of locations and the corresponding number of images that can be stored in them that we increase and strengthen our memory. Therefore the Chinese should struggle with the difficult task of creating fictive places, or mixing the fictive with the real, fixing them permanently in their minds by constant practice and review so that at last the fictive spaces become 'as if real, and can never be erased.'

How on earth had such a system first evolved, the Chinese might have asked, and Ricci anticipated the question by summarizing the ancient Western tradition that ascribed the idea of memory training through precise placement to the Greek poet Simonides." (Spence, 1984, 1-2)

Harry Lorayne and Jerry Lucas in *The Memory Book* also mention William Stokes, philosopher and memory teacher of the 1800s, who, in his own book about the same subject, said:

"It is true ... that notwithstanding the records of the past and the achievements, triumphs, and trophies of the present, the 'educated,' the intelligent masses – the world – know not and seem not to care to know its wondrous worth. The adoption of the science by a few paltry thousands cannot be regarded as anything when we consider the countless myriads peopling the earth – when we realize the fact that it is as essential to the proper exercise and full development of our intellectual existence as proper breathing is to our physical well-being; in spite of all that has been said and done, we may say comparatively – almost absolutely – that the art is a thing unknown!" (19)

"The basic memory rule is: You Can Remember Any New Piece of Information If It Is Associated to Something You Already Know or Remember." (23)

Over three thousand years ago, this is what we find in a scroll called *Ad C. Herennium* (as mentioned in *A History of Reading*):

…" Now nature herself teaches us what to do. When we see in everyday life things that are petty, ordinary, and banal, we generally fail to remember them, because the mind is not being stirred by anything novel or marvelous. But if we see or hear something exceptionally base, dishonorable, unusual, great, unbelievable, or ridiculous, that we are likely to remember for a long time.

Accordingly, things immediate to our eye or ear we commonly forget; incidents of our childhood we often remember best. Nor could this be so for any other reason than that ordinary things easily slip from the memory while the striking and the novel stay longer in the mind." (34)

Rolo May (1991) made an interesting connection between memory and myth in *The Cry for Myth*. Before providing an example, the author resorts to literature to prove his point:

"Looking into literature – the written home of memory – we find some exciting poets describing the function of this capacity. 'This is the use of memory,' said T.S. Eliot toward the ending of *Little Gidding*:
For liberation – not less of love but expanding,
Of love beyond desire . . . and so liberation
From the future as well as the past.
Memory can liberate us from attachment, from desire or attachment to the wrong things. Memory is our internal studio, where we let out imaginations roam, where we get our new and sometimes splendid ideas, where we see a glorious future that makes us tremble. Memory and myth are inseparable a point I have never heard in any psychology courses. Memory can, according to Dante, form then past into any myth, story, any hope. […]

Memory is the mother of creativity. This is a myth worth pondering. For it is in memory that one saves and savors the significant experiences, the dazzling sights, the critical events. In memory these precious experiences form themselves together into a myth which tells us a story. We say we 'sleep on an idea,' and then we wake up we may feel we have arrived at a new insight, as though it were a gift from the gods. And who is to say it is not? Mnemosyne, or "Memory,' is the goddess who puts together our materials with which new discoveries are made and poems are written and great books and enduring paintings are inspired." (70-71)

A rich source of practical information was provided by David Gamon and Allen D. Bragdon in *Building Mental Muscle* (1998), who invited readers to discover the most recent scientific discoveries to develop skills in the six zones: executive and social, memory, language, emotional response, computation skills, and creative spatial visualization. Here is an example of mnemonic techniques the authors recommend in the *Memory* section of their book:

SELF-TEST: Memorizing lists as stories

"A typical trick for memorizing arbitrary lists is to connect the items in a meaningful way, by stringing them together into a story. For example, take the following list of apparently unrelated items:

airplane	*ball*
hyena	*grease*
cream cheese	*monument*
moon	*mailman*
volcano	*lunch*

Most people, when presented with such a list, would find its memorization to be a tedious or even daunting work. However, consider an alternative mode of presentation (based on Bower and Clark 1969; Higby 1977; and Crovitz 1979):

"The first word is airplane. Just remember that however you like. The next word is hyena, because all the passengers sitting in their seats are hyenas. The next word is cream cheese because each of the hyenas is taking bites out of a cream cheese sandwich. The next word is moon, because the moon is really made out of cream cheese. The next word is volcano, because there is volcano on the moon. The next word is ball, because the volcano on the moon erupts, it spews out balls. The next word is grease, because the balls are covered with grease. The next word is monument, because the balls have so much grease on them it flows all the way to the Washington Monument. The next word is mailman, because a group of mailmen is touring the Washington Monument. The last word is lunch, because when the mailmen finish their tour they go to have lunch.

After being presented this mini-story, most people can recall the ten words embedded in it in both forward and backward order. This sort of mnemonic method, which promotes that is nowadays known as 'elaborate' encoding of the material, can be traced back two and a half thousand years to the Greek poet Simonides. " (106)

"A mnemonic technique which does *not* work well for memorizing arbitrary lists involves what is sometimes called 'first-letter mnemonics.' For example:

hammer
slipper
peach
trunk
leopard

By taking the first letter of each word and filling in vowels where needed, you can form a word such as 'HOSPITAL.' An effective trick for coding and retrieval? No. This sort of mnemonic technique is only useful for memorizing the order of otherwise known items, as in the use of the phrase 'Richard of York Gave Battle in Vain' for memorizing the order of the colors of the rainbow." (107)

The LOCI (place) Method

"If a student is learning 5 new words (*firm, stick, king, God, grass*) they could use their house as the loci. They imagine opening the door (and imagine the door is really *firm*) and tripping over a *stick* as they walk inside. As they stand up they imagine they see a *king* sitting on a sofa talking to *God* about a game of golf they have just played. They are commenting on the brightness of the green *grass* on the fairways." www.joshesl.com

If we **take the idea into the ESL classroom**, we might find it appealing to our students because they will encounter obstacle after obstacle in acquiring the knowledge necessary to function in the target language, and some of the aforementioned suggestions might be a good start. Teachers will definitely resort to their own teaching experience when dealing with unexpected student questions regarding retaining very important information from textbooks or classroom instruction.

Examples:

HOMES   Great Lakes: **H**uron, **O**ntario, **M**ichigan, **E**rie, **S**uperior

STAB   The four voices of a quartet: **S**oprano, **T**enor, **A**lto, **B**ass

FAN BOYS   The coordinating conjunctions: **F**or, **A**nd, **N**o, **B**ut, **O**r, **Y**et, **S**o

Mount Fujiyama is **12, 365** feet high -   **12** months, **356** days in a year

> **I** before **e** except after **c**
> Or when sounding like **a**
> In *neighbor* and *weigh*

ARITHMETIC   **A R**at **I**n **T**he **H**ouse **M**ay **E**at **T**he **I**ce **C**ream

> *30 days hath September, April, June, and November.*
> *All the rest have 31*
> *Except February my dear son.*
> *It has 28 and that is fine*
> *But in Leap Year it has 29.*

> *In 1492 Columbus sailed the ocean blue.*

NOTES

_____

_____

_____

_____

_____

Reading

Tips TIPS for ESL instructors:

As soon as you start reading these words, you, the reader, will become engaged physically and mentally, and you will need the motivation to continue reading. No problem! Once you know that, you will actively take part in a discovery of what will test your reading, and at the same time, thinking skills. No worries! Your eyes will go back and forth to the next passages and maybe pages to anticipate what the following pages will have to provide for your hungry appetite. I mean knowledge at the personal level with larger implications because we are communicating with each other already.

Reading is not just another skill. Teachers in all classes, at all levels of proficiency, but especially at the beginning levels, should be aware that **people start reading for pleasure**. If that is good enough for some of us, students must understand that reading is going to help them function in many other types of subjects and will eventually make them better thinkers.

After spending 33 years teaching literacy, Lorraine Peoples (2011) finally managed to compile her book entitled *You Can Teach Someone to Read*, in which she laid out clear procedures to encourage teachers to find the ways to encourage and guide their students to get involved in the reading process. One of her major pillars in this edifice of teaching methodology is motivation (again!), which the author describes as a necessary tool both for the teacher and for the students. Section 7 of Lorraine Peoples' book is devoted to *Teaching Reading in English to Students Who Speak Another Language*, in which the author advances some basic considerations the instructor should think about:

1. "The student will progress best if he already understands what is spoken to him in English and can speak at a beginning level or more.

2. How well the learner speaks and understands English will highly correlate with the speed with which he learns to read and comprehend well in English.

3. Research tells us that teaching only in English to a learner whose first language is not English will ensure faster learning.

4. The basic reading skills for successful reading in English are the same basic skills required whether or not the student's first language is English and regardless of his age.

5. When a student is learning new reading skills in a language different than his first language, more repetition is normally required.

6. Some languages use the same letters as English, but that is not always the case. It is important for the instructor to know that the student recognizes each letter, both upper case and lower case.

7. Consonant letters in some languages have only one sound. In the English language most consonant letters have only one sound – until they are combined with a second letter. Sometimes those combinations make a totally new sound.

8. Vowel letters in some languages have only one sound. In the English language all vowels have more than one sound and have yet more when combined with certain other consonants or other vowels.

9. Word meanings and the structure of phrases and sentences can often be quite different in English than in the learner's first language." (pp. 21-24)

Skimming is one the basic concepts mentioned by linguists all over the world. "Skimming is essentially what has been called 'speed reading.' You can skim at high speed for an overview. The dictionary defines skimming 'to look at hastily...to glance through a book without reading word for word.

Scan for key words.

Skim for structure and gist.

Pre-read to understand and retain.

Deep read when every word counts.' "(Mindell, 1993, p. 12)

"Skimming is an essential filter in your in-basket strategy, and a fast, efficient way to see what's in a book or long article. And scanning and skimming together are probably sufficient to whisk you through most daily newspapers and magazines, particularly when you know that subject well or need only a glancing acquaintance with the content.

But how much of what you skim do you actually understand? One percent? Two percent? Maybe even less. Skimming tells you what's in a book, but not what the book says. It's like reading the label of a wine you haven't tasted." (25)

It is a very good idea, many researchers say, **to keep a notebook and a pen ready at hand while you read**. Even if that means interrupting the flow of thoughts following the writer's ideas, taking a couple of minutes to write your own comments will eventually help you remember what is relevant in what you read.

There are also many other ways readers can keep track of what they read. Over the centuries, people have written annotations right on the page of those books they were reading. Public and private libraries keep records of those priceless documents validating the idea of marking textbooks.

In 2001, H. J. Jackson published his *Marginalia: Readers Writing in Books*, where he supported the concept of writing marginalia, or notes in margins of a book. After giving a lot of examples of writers like Coleridge or Proust, who wrote copious notes while they were reading, this is what he said:

"But I digress from the subject of what it is that induces readers to expose themselves by writing marginalia in the first place. Using a notebook or keeping a diary might be neater, but it is a quite different procedure that increases the distance between reader and text and emphasizes the autonomy of the reader. Writing notes on the page takes less time than turning aside to a notebook and poses less of a threat to the reader's concentration. In the long term, it has potential benefits for both parties. As long as the notes are permanently attached to the text, the text stands as a reminder of the source and a corrective check on the interpretation. Annotated books also constitute a ready-made filing and retrieval system." (88)

> "Read not to contradict and confute, nor to believe and take for granted . . . but to weigh and consider."
>
> Francis Bacon

My father was the first one to teach me how to read. While reading aloud a short story or a poem (his favorite kind of lecture), he would emphasize certain words or phrases to give them ample meaning or nuance but at the same time trying to entice me to do the same. Although he was a Francophone and a Francophile, he also noticed early on that I veered toward the Anglo-Saxon culture. He came to me one day with a translation of Oscar Wilde's *Portrait of a Young Man* and confessed to me that was the book he devoured when he was a little bit more than a kid and that I should read it as a teenager. During my high school years, one of our teachers, who used to play soccer with us during the breaks, came to us one day with a copy of *The Catcher in the Rye*, which he had borrowed just to show it to us, and which he had just finished reading, but cautioned us that Salinger's book was not on the list of required summer reading. That was in the 1960s, when certain authors were on the black list and therefore not accepted anywhere in the classrooms.

One day, when a new teacher entered the room to tell us that, for some, books were an irrelevant luxury, she took out a collection of short stories and read to us Anton Chekhov's *The Chameleon*. We could not believe our eyes (and ears) when she went into a luxurious flurry of details and enacted the dialogues with a Russian flavor she had acquired while living in Moscow with her former husband.

What left an indelible impression on me, as an early apprentice (reader) of literature, was Ms. Valeria Magda, our English teacher, with her short quotes and memorable lines from Shakespeare. In no time, she combined several scenes from *Hamlet, The Taming of the Shrew, Julius Caesar* and her favorite selection of the 154 sonnets, and we found ourselves banding together and rehearsing for the end-of-year school production. Reading the Bard has never been an easy task, but it was a necessary challenge, and it proved quite fruitful in the following years.

In time, I came to realize that reading was becoming another home for me. The traveling companion, should we say? Books in my native country were not easy to come by, especially in English, and the only way to lay your hands on Hemingway, for example, was to find a good public library or the American Embassy in Belgrade, which was much closer to my hometown in Transylvania than the one in the capital city of Bucharest.

From Alberto Manguel and his well-documented book, *A History of Reading*, I discovered that I was not the only one who took refuge in books. I sporadically go back to his gem and refresh my memory or re-read certain passages, mostly because the act of reading is a universal tool that enables us to whet our appetite when it comes to exploring the unknown world of signs and images that beckon to us from manuscripts, scrolls, maps, charts, diagrams, or textbooks, be it to inform or to entertain our senses. Over the years, as a student and then as an educator, I came to realize that what we do as young readers or novices is to **read for pleasure** first, and **then to get informed** and entertained. The classroom experience re-confirms the utility of such mental activity as reading out loud or in silence. And these days, we read a lot, whether we look at the weather map, or try to read (like Carl Jung and Sigmund Freud) people's minds, whether we indulge in cook books or travel books, or whether we need to answer an email or a text message. We read food labels, road signs, food recipes, blogs, memes, text messages, movie subtitles, birthday cards, bank statements, credit card agreements (do we really?), job descriptions, magazines, journals, newspapers, textbooks, brochures, blurbs, etc. These days, reading is not confined to a library or a classroom; it can be done almost anywhere we can have access to a source of information. And we sometimes get fined because we read text messages while driving . . .

Among the many books that came from the encyclopedic mind of Harold Bloom is *How to Read and Why* (Scribner, 2000), and this is what the author said about reading:

> "There is no single way to read well, though there is a prime reason why we should read. Information is endlessly available to us; where shall wisdom be found? If you are fortunate, you encounter a particular teacher who can help, yet finally you are alone, going on without further mediation." (19)
>
> "One of the uses of reading is to prepare ourselves for change, and the final change alas is universal." (21)

According to Matthew Parfitt (2012), teachers should place a strong emphasis on reading and rereading. This will lead to taking useful and effective notes that can eventually be used when the writing process begins. *Writing in Response* has five sections, and Part One comes right after an exhaustive introduction. This chapter is entitled *Responsive Reading,* and the author asserts the value of reading in his subchapter dealing with *Reading with a Purpose*:

> "We read for many different purposes – to be informed, edified, entertained, stirred, provoked, persuaded. Much of our reading rewards us on several levels at the same time. In college, of course, the principal purpose for reading is to learn, and so the way you read *should* differ from the way you would read a book for entertainment. As you have probably already discovered, reading to learn often requires more effort than reading for pleasure, more focused concentration, and more active involvement. [. . .]
>
> Close reading (reading slowly, with careful attention to the text) is a fundamental skill required not only in the academy but also in many professions. Good academic writing presents fresh and interesting ideas that are based on solid research and sound reasoning. While research can take many forms (chemists conduct experiments in laboratories, anthropologists observe human culture in locations far and near, archeologists dig through the remains of lost civilizations, historians study documents in archives, and so on), nearly every kind of research involves reading at some point – not just casual reading but a careful analysis of arguments made by others concerning the problem under investigation." (24-25)

Another perspective comes from Axelrod, Cooper, and Warriner (2005), who argue that we also **read for meaning** when we do it "in order to understand and respond critically to what is being said." From their point of view, this approach offers complementary ways of looking at a text.

> "When you read, your primary effort is to make the characters on the page or computer screen meaningful. But as you know from your experience as a reader, a text may be more meaningful or less so depending on your familiarity with the words that are used, your knowledge of the subject, and the kind of text or genre you are reading. If you have some knowledge about an issue currently being debated, for example, then an essay arguing for a position on that issue is likely to be relatively easy to read and full of meaning to you. [. . .]
>
> Reading for meaning requires you to use your knowledge and experience to create meaning. You must bring to the text your knowledge about the subject and genre, your belief and values, your personal

experience, as well as the historical and cultural contexts you share with others. Reading with this rich context helps you to see many possibilities for meaning in a text. Therefore, you will not be surprised that what you find meaningful in a given reading may overlap to some extent with what others find meaningful in the same reading, but also retain your own unique stamp." (2-3)

Going back to Alberto Manguel, I discovered a treasure trove of historical information about reading. On page 77 of his *History of Reading*, he quotes from another source:

"Following the scholastic method, students were taught to read through orthodox commentaries that were the equivalent of our potted lecture notes. The original texts [...] were not to be apprehended directly by the student but to be reached through a series of preordained steps. First came the *lectio*, a grammatical analysis in which the syntactic elements of each sentence would be identified; this would lead to the *literra* or the literal sense of the text. Through the *littera* the student acquired the *sensus*, the meaning of the text according to different established interpretations. The process ended with an exegesis – the *sententia* – in which the opinions of approved commentators were discussed." (Jacques Le Goff, *Les Intellectuels au Moyen Age*, Paris, 1985)

For hundreds of years, students of all ages just copied passages from whatever was available at that time – mostly religious texts – not knowing how to read. They copied them automatically and would have associated the words with the sound of the memorized lines. These days, blind students go through a somewhat similar process. Alberto Manguel mentions Helen Keller, who remembered how she was educated. "I quickly learned that each printed word stood for an object, an act or a quality. I had a frame in which I could arrange the words in little sentences; but before I ever put sentences in the frame I used to make them into objects. I found the slips of paper which represented, for example, *doll, is, on, bed* and placed each name on its object; then I put my doll on the bed with the words *is, on, bed* arranged beside the doll, thus making a sentence of the words, and at the same time carrying out the idea of the sentence with the things themselves." (Helen Keller, *The Story of My Life*, London, 1903)

The Reader's Timeline   (from the dust jacket cover of Alberto Manguel's *A History of Reading.*)

c. 4000 BC   With the inscription of signs representing ten goats and sheep on a clay tablet the first reader comes into being

c. 2300 BC	The first recorded author, the high priestess Princess Endehuanna (in the Sumerian city-state of Ur), addresses for the first time a "dear reader" in her songs.
593 BC	The prophet Ezekiel has a vision in which he is ordered to open his mouth and read a book by eating it, thereby ingesting its meaning.
c. 420 BC	Socrates argues against reading. For him, books are useless tools, since they cannot explain what they say but only repeat the same words over and over again.
c. 330 BC	Standing before his troops, Alexander the Great silently reads a letter from his mother, to the bewilderment of his soldiers, who have only seen reading done aloud.
213 BC	The Chinese Emperor Shih Huang-ti decrees that history is to begin with his reign. All books published before his time must be condemned to the fire.
c. 55 BC	For his dispatches, Julius Caesar invents one of his earliest codices – pages folded into a booklet – thereby presaging the end of the scroll and the beginning of the book as we know it.
c. 230	By royal edict, every ship that passes through Alexandria must surrender any books it might be carrying so that they can be copied and kept in the city's library. When it burns to the ground, half a million titles – the greatest collection of books in the world – are irredeemably lost.
c. 540	St. Benedict of Nursia (a patron saint of Europe) sets out the rules for his monastery. Among them he includes reading out loud during mealtimes to nourish the spirit at the same time as the body.
c. 1000	To avoid parting with his collection of 117,000 books while traveling, the avid reader and Grand Vizier of Persia, Abdul Kassem Ismael, has them carried by a caravan of four hundred camels trained to walk in alphabetical order.
c. 1010	At a time when "serious" reading in Japan is exclusively restricted to men, Lady Murasaki writes the world first novel, *The Book of Genji*, to provide reading material for herself and the other women of the Heian Court.
c. 1100	The Islamic theologian Muhammed al-Ghazali establishes a series of rules for reading the Koran. Rule number six is for weeping, since certain sections of the Holy Book must be read with sorrow in one's heart.

c. 1284   Eyeglasses are invented in Venice or Florence, saving the reading lives of those with poor sight.

1333   The painter Simone Martini places a book in the hands of the Virgin in his *Annunciation*. The Catholic Church, uncertain about the intellectual capabilities of women, debates whether the Mother of God can be recognized as a reader.

1455   Gutenberg invents the printing press, offering readers more and cheaper books. For the first time, readers can be certain of possessing identical copies of the same text.

1536   The humanist William Tyndale, believing that his fellow Englishmen should be allowed to read the Bible in their own language, translates the New Testament and most of the Old into English for the first time. For his efforts, he is strangled and then burned at stake.

1559   The sacred Congregation of the Roman Inquisition publishes the first *Index of Forbidden Books*. Revised for the first time in 1948, the final printing appears in 1966, including among the banned authors Graham Greene and Colette.

1703   Saint Jean-Baptiste de la Salle, in his *Rules of Decorum in Christian Civility*, thunders against idle people who read in bed.

1740   South Carolina passes a law prohibiting the teaching of slaves to read, and several other states followed suit. A slave caught learning to read would be flogged; after a third offense, the first joint of the forefinger would be cut off. The law was in effect until 1865.

1752   Pope Benedict XIV, aware of the acquisitiveness of readers, proclaims a bull in which book thieves are punished with excommunication.

1781   Denis Diderot claims to have cured his wife, who was suffering from depression, by reading raunchy literature to her. "I have always spoken of novels as frivolous productions," he observed, "but I have finally discovered that they are good for the vapours." The new science will be called bibliotherapy.

1933   On May 10, Nazi Propaganda Minister Paul Joseph Goebbels encourages a vast crowd in Berlin to demonstrate their discrimination as readers and burn the books of "degenerate" writers: Sigmund Freud, Thomas Mann, Ernest Hemingway, Karl Marx, Emile Zola, H. G. Wells, Marcel Proust.

1953	Ray Bradbury publishes *Fahrenheit 451*, a novel set in a future where books are burned and readers must memorize the texts to preserve them, becoming walking libraries.
1970	Computer buff Ted Nelson coins the term "hypertext" to define the narrative made possible by the use of computers, which the reader can enter and move around at will.
1985	According to UNESCO, 28% of the world's population cannot read."

I remember that, as a young learner, I read and then copied short passages from various English or American writers, but for my German studies, I used a kids' magazine entitled *Freulich Sein und Singen*, which was full of short stories and a lot of pictures that illustrated the development of the narrative. On many occasions, I found myself writing two or three words as one, not knowing how to divide them into separate entities. To my surprise, my teachers told me not to worry about it because, in our history, the first written documents must have been drafted in a very similar way. Information was first written on scrolls, and after Julius Caesar, on separate pages, since he wanted to disseminate relevant information to his troops.

Whenever I run into problems with punctuation, syllabication, capital letters or low caps, I am reminded that they were all irrelevant, so long as there was no problem reading the text. I also remember that the comma was invented by the Greeks because they wanted to give the reader time to breathe. In other words, the next time you read aloud somewhere at a public meeting, when you see a comma, take a deep breath before you tackle the rest of the sentence.

Keith Houston, in *The Mysterious Origins of Punctuation* (2015) says:

"As readers and writers, we're intimately familiar with the dots, strokes and dashes that punctuate the written word. The comma, colon, semicolon and their siblings are integral parts of writing, pointing out grammatical structures and helping us transform letters into spoken words or mental images. We would be lost without them (or, at the very least, extremely confused), and yet the earliest readers and writers manage without it for thousands of years. What changed their minds?

In the 3rd Century BCE, in the Hellenic Egyptian city of Alexandria, a librarian named Aristophanes had had enough. He was chief of staff at the city most famous library, home to hundreds of thousands of scrolls, which were all frustratingly time-consuming to read. For as long as anyone could remember, the Greeks had written their texts so that their letters ran together "withnospaceorpunctuation" and without any distinction between lowercase and capitals. It was up to the reader to pick their way through this unforgiving mass of letters to discover where each word or sentence ended and the next began.

Aristophanes' breakthrough was to suggest that readers could annotate their documents, relieving the unbroken stream of text with dots of ink aligned with the middle (.), bottom (.), or top (.) of each line. His 'subordinate', 'intermediate' and full points corresponded to the pauses of increasing length that a practiced reader would habitually insert between formal units of speech called the *comma, colon* and *periods*. This was not quite punctuation as we know it – Aristophanes saw his marks as representing pauses rather than grammatical boundaries – but the seed had been planted." http://www.bbc.com/culture/story/20150902-the-mysterious-origins-of-punctuation

My first year in college was the big eye-opener, and that is an understatement. From all the courses we took, I remember the World Literature course that spanned over three years, dealing with various periods of time, beginning with the Greeks and the Romans and ending with the 20th century. The volume of information required careful note-taking, which posed questions as to the validity of what was recorded and how it was going to be retrieved. Memory was definitely a word that came to mind right away, and there is so much to remember, especially for a teacher.

We go into the classroom armed with all the knowledge from our college days to which we add the vast expanse of reading sources, but we also bring our personal life experience, our culture, our own perception of what the language learning process may entail. I also believe that teachers should exchange opinions, teach each other, ask each other questions, because this was for me at least as important as going to college and learning from our professors. Conferences, seminars, TESOL local, national and international meetings are a must for anybody who wants to accumulate, process and deliver information to their students.

Everything we learn eventually has a meaning if it is shared. We learn not only from books, classroom experience, scientific journals and magazines. We learn a lot simply from teaching. When students ask questions, when they debate issues, when they express their points of view, we automatically learn something. We as educators develop our own teaching style by interacting with other teachers, with our colleagues, and above all, we channel our flow of ideas in the presence of our students. They, the students, are the ultimate reason and the only critical judges of what we so much live for: **the spread of knowledge**.

Over the years, I have personally gone over books, magazines, journals, conference materials, and I think it is only fair to present in this book what I think helped me enormously in my profession. That is why I am asking you, the reader, to give me a chance to enumerate, list, quote, summarize, and paraphrase what I think would also help you.

Teachers never have enough time to read as much as they would like to, so this is going to give me a chance to put together from short quotes to paragraphs or even longer passages, what otherwise would take a long time to find and peruse.

Where should I start? Every day in the classroom is a fresh start, mostly at the beginning of each term. **Every new group of students represents a new beginning,** and we need to look fresh because we are the ones who organize, deliver and supervise the whole process of learning. Students of all ages and all nationalities expect the world of us. Literally and figuratively.

Teaching languages in general and ESL in particular is a unique life experience. It broadens the mind, it challenges our own persona, and it never ends. Every time we meet a new group of students, they are different because they come from various countries, bringing with them their own culture and their own questions. Books and materials don't mean too much unless we, the educators, **attach a personal touch to each and every individual.** What works for one culture is irrelevant for others. What we think is important may be useless to some of our students because our perception is not their perception. When teachers run out of ideas, the best thing to do is ask the students how they perceive a certain subject and what needs to be explained or analyzed.

NOTES

_____

_____

_____

_____

_____

> "The oldest surviving writing in Anglo-Saxon written in the Roman Alphabet comes from around the year AD 600. One of the most interesting pieces of Anglo-Saxon writing was written by King Alfred the Great himself."
>
> Essinger, 2007

Writing

Tips   TIPS for ESL instructors:

1. The way we write is not the way we speak.

    The way we write is the way we think.

2. There is a **connection between language and writing.**

    p. 215

3. Writing is a form of **magic**, "which preserves language, and enables reason, emotion, and experience." (Essinger, 2007)

    pp. 215-216

4. The **learning outcomes** are really the ones that **make teaching so rewarding.**   p. 218

5. The motto for the class should be **CLEAR and CONCISE.**

6. Students should build their writing **from sentence to paragraph.**

    To exemplify what you expect from your students, write a topic sentence on a piece of paper and then circulate it. Ask each student to add another sentence, but to continue along the same lines. When they reach a reasonable number of sentences, the students should have an idea of what a paragraph should be. **Share it with the whole class.**

7. Basic writing skills should start with:

    Scanning, skimming, paraphrasing, summarizing, and
    quoting   p. 219

8. Encourage a lot of **free writing** that does not need to be corrected.

9. Motivate your students to **share opinions** and **support each other**.

10. Our perception is **not the students' perception**. Let the students
    voice their own concerns and make changes, if necessary, to
    address those issues.

> "On the border between art and technology stands writing in its boundless
> variety: typography and calligraphy to please the eye, signs and symbols
> to satisfy the mind, games to amuse, and graffiti to provoke."
>
> Georges Jean, 1987, p. 129

The history of writing goes back approximately six thousand years from
what we know today about the Tigris and the Euphrates, from hieroglyphics
and cuneiform to the invention of printing and finally to all the tools and styles
we use these days.

Georges Jean was a professor of linguistics and semiology at the University
of Maine (France). Among the forty plus works he published during his
lifetime, he was remembered and appreciated mostly for *Le Plaisir des Mots*, for
which he was awarded the 1980 *Fondation de France* prize. The 1987 English
translation of his book entitled *Writing: The Story of Alphabets and Scripts*
brings the history of writing to the forefront with wonderful graphics including
photographs, book plates, and reproductions.

From the rich history of documented information about the humble
beginnings of writing, the author focuses on crucial moments when writing
started to look like our writing. With Phoenicians (people who inhabited what
is now Greece, Italy, North Africa, and southern Spain) at its roots, the alphabet
was invented three thousand years ago. The Phoenician alphabet contained
only consonants, and to this day some forms of Arabic and Hebrew still have
no vowels. The Phoenicians traveled and took with them the alphabet which
spread quickly to other cultures. However, in about 800 B.C., another alphabet,
very similar to that of the Phoenicians developed: Aramaic, which had a huge
impact mostly because several books of the Old Testament were written in this
language.

And now we have **another mystery: the Etruscan Mystery**. The Etruscan
civilization, Georges Jean asserts, ruled Rome until the 4th century B.C. and then

the Latins (the future Romans) came and borrowed the Etruscan alphabet to write down their language, Latin. Other historians claim that the Latin alphabet came directly from Greek, without any connection to Etruscan.

"Whatever the truth may prove to be, it is known for certain that around the 3rd century B.C. an alphabet consisting of nineteen letters evolved; X and Y were added much later, around the 1st century B.C., in Cicero's time. The Romans wrote in the same way as the Greeks, using uppercase letters for stone inscriptions and lowercase for other media, such as papyrus or wax tablets." (65-66)

The Romans left us Latin, their language, which later developed into what is now Italian, French, Spanish, Portuguese, and Romanian, also known as Romance languages. The Latin language also included writing, which almost disappeared had it not been for Charlemagne, who proclaimed Christianity the heir to Roman civilization.

"Very few lay individuals mastered the art of writing. Charlemagne, the most powerful man in Western Europe at the time, was illiterate. He signed royal commands with a cross, which he inserted into the loops of the signature prepared for him by a scribe." (74)

From Charlemagne on, monks were the ones who kept the tradition going by simply copying biblical texts on rolls of papyrus called *volumen* in Latin. However, papyrus did not last very long because only one side could be used.

"The introduction of a new medium, parchment, was to alter the art of writing completely. Parchment appears to have originated at Pergamon, in Asia Minor; the word 'parchment' comes from the Greek *pergamene*, meaning skin 'from Pergamon.' In the 2nd century B.C. Egypt had refused to supply its rival Pergamon with the papyrus essential for writing, so the scribes of Asia Minor had to resort to an alternative material: leather. If fact, it would seem that animal skin had been used at an earlier date by the Egyptians themselves." (80)
   The next stage of development in the history of writing came with Johann Gutenberg of Mainz, who basically "mechanized" printing around 1440. It seems the Chinese had been using something similar since the 11th century, but the Western culture made the quantum leap forward with Gutenberg and one of his friends, Peter Schoeffer, who "discovered a method for casting letters, especially those with asymmetrical shapes, by using an alloy of lead and antimony." (93)

Over time, **books** became what Georges Jean calls **the "accumulated memory of humankind."**

According to Essinger (2007), there are cultures even today where writing is considered **a form of magic**. He asserts that Karen Blixen, also known as Isak Dinesen, who wrote *Out of Africa*, recorded how the Kikuyu tribesmen reacted when they were exposed to writing:

> "I learned that the effect of a piece of news has many times magnified when it was imparted to writing. The messages that would have been received with doubt and scorn if they had been given by word of mouth were now taken as gospel truth." (xxv)

Today we look at what has been written over the centuries, whether on one continent or another, and we can obviously see **the connection between language and writing**. This is how we have inherited treasure troves of artifacts and therefore consider ourselves lucky we can trace the history of our culture through the scrolls and manuscripts, and later on, books.

In 1953, Ray Bradbury published his futuristic *Fahrenheit 451*, in which he describes a group of people who memorize the most important books in order to save them from destruction and oblivion. They burn the books deliberately, and that is where the title comes from: the temperature at which paper burns. Looking back at our times, one member of this society mentions that "Books were only one type of receptacle where we stored a lot of things we were afraid we might forget . . . The **magic** is in what books say, how they stitched the patches of the universe together into one garment for us." (quoted in Essinger's introduction, page xix)

> *"Be a scribe! Put it in your heart*
> *that your name should exist like theirs! . . .*
> *A man has perished; his corpse is dust,*
> *and his people have passed from the land;*
> *It is a book which makes him remembered*
> *in the mouth of a speaker.*
> *More excellent is a [papyrus] roll than a built house,*
> *than a chapel in the west."*

> From a poem, entitled by modern scholars, *Eulogy to Dead Authors*, found on a papyrus manuscript, among the papyri of the author and scribe Qenherkhepshef at the tomb-chapels near Deir el Medina, Egypt. The poem dates from the Nineteenth Dynasty (c. 1200 B.C.)

This is how James Essinger (2007) starts his introduction to his *Spellbound*, with its enticing subtitle *The Surprising origins and astonishing secrets of English spelling.* He goes on to say that writing is a form of **magic**, and his reason for doing so was that writing, "which preserves language, [. . . .] enables reason, emotion, and experience to overcome what would otherwise be the desperate and insurmountable barriers of forgetfulness and death." (p. xvii)

To prove that **writing is a form of magic**, Essinger takes the word "spell" and its origin as the best example. According to the author, "spell' comes from the Germanic word *spel*, meaning 'recital' or 'tale.'

"This word resulted in a word, also *spel*, that was part of the Old English or Anglo-Saxon language first spoken in about A.D. 500. The first and original meaning of the Old English *spel* was, following from the meaning of the ancient Germanic word, a 'narrative' or 'story.' Another meaning of 'spell,' first recorded in 1589, is still with us today; it means a special set of words, formulae, or verse possessing magical powers.

Where did the second, magical, meaning come from? We can't know for certain, but perhaps we can imagine how our ancestors, so dependent on spoken stories for their entertainment and their understanding of the world, might have started to see those who told them best stories as sages, and eventually even as magicians possessed of dark secrets. [. . .]

By about A.D. 1300 the verb 'to spell' had appeared, meaning the process of reading or writing a text letter by letter. This meaning came into English via an Old French word, *espeller*, which also originally derived from the ancient Germanic word *spel*. The idea of spelling out a text letter by letter appears quite different from the meaning of the word *spel* as a recital or tale, but in fact there was a close connection. A tale will have its most potent effect only if all its elements – its letters, that is – are in the right order. The same is true, of course, of a magical formula." (xxv-xxvi)

Without their books of spells, even wizards would lose their magical power. Essinger quotes Shakespeare's play *The Tempest*, in which Prospero the magician is willing to give up his powers in order to reconcile with his enemies:

> *But this rough magic*
> *I here abjure: and, when I have required*
> *Some heavenly music, - which even now I do, -*
> *To work mine end upon their senses, that*
> *This airy charm is for, I'll break my staff,*
> *Bury it certain fathoms in the earth,*
> *And deeper than did ever plummet sound*
> *I'll drown my book.*

"Chances are, you learned how to write – indirectly – from Aristotle. Look up the history of English grammar, composition, and rhetoric teaching; you'll find that it all started a couple of centuries ago when people first hit upon the idea of teaching English-speaking boys and girls not only Greek and Latin, but English too. Courses and textbooks came into being; naturally, what was taught was simply Greek and Latin grammar and rhetoric, applied to English. Now since all Greek and Latin grammar and rhetoric go straight back to Aristotle (as any encyclopedia will tell you) and since the principles of English teaching are still much the same as they were hundreds of years ago, what you were taught in school really comes down from Aristotle.

Take two rather striking examples, one from composition and one from grammar. In composition, probably the most important rule you were taught is the rule of unity. It is pure Aristotle - based on his famous principle that everything must have 'a beginning, a middle, and an end.' And in grammar the first thing you were taught was the parts of speech. Who first thought of parts of speech? Aristotle, again. So, whether you like it or not, you are an umptieth-generation Aristotelian."

(Rudolph Flesch, *The Art of Readable Writing*, 1949, p. 1)

Orators like Quintilian (35-100 AD) took the Aristotelian example and refined it by expanding it to include five or six parts:

1. Exordium: the introduction
2. Narratio: the statement or exposition of the case under discussion
3. Divisio: the outline of the points or steps in the argument
4. Confirmatio: the proof of the case (sometimes called *probatio*)
5. Confutatio: the refutations of the opposing arguments
6. Peroratio: the conclusion

(*The Norton Reader*, 2012, p. xxxvi)

Now that we mentioned the word **argument**, we should also remember that although argumentation has roots in the Greece and Rome, this is **a Western concept that represents the way people contribute their ideas, perspectives, and opinions to the public debate.**

The obvious inter-dependence of language and culture is also acknowledged in Deutscher (2011):

"Philosophers of all persuasions and nationalities have lined up to proclaim that each language reflects the qualities of the nation that speaks it. In the seventeenth century, the Englishman Francis Bacon explained that one can infer 'significant marks of genius and manners of people and nations from their languages.' 'Everything confirms,' agreed the Frenchman Etienne de Condillac a century later, 'that each language expresses the character of the people who speak it.' His younger contemporary, the German Johann Gottfried Herder, concurred that 'the intellect and the character of every nation are stamped in its language.' Industrious nations,' he said, 'have an abundance of moods in their verbs, while more refined nations have a large amount of nouns that have been exalted to abstract notions.' In short, 'the genius of a nation is nowhere better revealed than in the physiognomy of its speech.' The American Ralph Waldo Emerson summed it up in 1844: 'We infer the spirit of the nation in great measure from the language, which is a sort of monument to which each forcible individual in a course of many hundred years have contributed a stone.' "

(Deutscher, *Through the Language Glass*, p. 3)

I remember teaching classes in writing to ESL students at all levels of English proficiency. They gave me the best rewards. It is true that preparation for such classes might take extra time compared to teaching other skills. However, the progress throughout the session usually comes with a well-deserved result. Properly taught, writing classes require more guidance and students must make the extra effort to improve, but the **learning outcomes** are really the ones that **make teaching so rewarding.**

Suggestion: Ask the students to tell you **what is difficult** in a writing class and **why.** The best idea would be to start by talking about the basics in ESL writing for students of any level of English proficiency.

What is a sentence? A sentence is a group of words containing a subject and a predicate expressing **a complete thought.**

What is a paragraph? A paragraph is a group of sentences organized as a unit of writing and dealing with a particular **point or idea.**

What is a topic sentence? The topic sentence, **the first sentence in a paragraph**, is a group of words expressing the main idea of the paragraph.

What is a thesis statement? The thesis statement, usually at the end of introduction, **states the main idea** of a writing assignment and helps control the ideas in the paper.

What is an essay? An essay or a composition is **a piece of writing dealing with a single subject.** The essay is derived from the French "essai" meaning "experiment" or "attempt" and is usually written to support a thesis or proposition.

What is a research paper? An extended essay may become a research paper when the writer uses **research questions** and **documents his/her sources of information.**

What is a book report? A book report is an **essay written about a book,** including several types of opinion: plot summary, character analysis, and theme analysis.

What is a book review? A book review is not a summary. The focus of a book review is to analyze its contents, determine its theme, and then describe how its theme is presented and how well it is defended. The review should make it clear that the students read and understood the book, the article, the excerpt, or the essay.

What is a film review? A film review is a piece of writing presenting a personal (original) opinion about a movie without giving away too much of the plot, and should **entertain, persuade, and inform.**

The reading and writing skills are in most cases combined. We read and then we talk about the reading. We think, we analyze, and then we write. In other words, writing as a response to reading.

Scanning

On a regular basis we use scanning to find an address or a phone number. Students use scanning to look up a word in a dictionary or to pick out a website. Scanning is also a type of **fast reading.**

Skimming

If we want to read a book, a magazine or newspaper article, we first browse through. Teachers and students also look through the options given on a Google search to see what options are available. Skimming is **another type of fast reading** when you focus on the **main idea.** Some say that skimming is "to read, study, or examine superficially." www.merriam-webster.com

For most instructors, skimming and scanning are basic **Reading Comprehension Skills.**

Paraphrasing

Paraphrasing is a re-statement of a text, passage, or message in our own words to make it **shorter** and **simpler**, but also to test our own knowledge and understanding. The main idea(s) and the meaning of the original must be more or less the same, but rendered in our own words. The term itself comes via Latin from Greek, and it means "additional manner of expression."

Summarizing

If the paraphrase is a rewording of an oral or written text to clarify the content, a summary is a brief statement of the main idea(s) and should be shorter than a paraphrase. We usually **summarize only what is essential** and leave out the irrelevant.

Quoting

There are times when the original material is so important and so effective in expressing a point of view that we simply use the exact words in order to show authority and relevance. Quotations should be introduced properly so the reader is cautioned before we introduce the exact words used by somebody else. Signal words like "according to" are going to make the transitions smoother.

Paraphrases, summaries, and quotations have their own **benefits** and Purdue OWL (www.owl.english.purdue.edu) explains what purposes these skills present. ESL teachers and students use them to:

- "Provide support for claims or ad credibility to your writing
- Refer to work that leads up to the work you are doing now
- Give examples of several points of view on a subject
- Call attention to a position that you wish to agree or disagree with
- Highlight a particularly striking phrase, sentence, or passage by quoting the original
- Distance yourself from the original by quoting it in order to cue readers that the words are not your own
- Expand the breadth or depth of your writing."

"Writers frequently intertwine summaries, paraphrases, and quotations. As part of a summary of an article, a chapter, or a book, a writer might include paraphrases of various key points blended with quotations of striking or suggestive phrases as in the following example:

In his famous and influential work *The Interpretations of Dreams*, Sigmund Freud argues that dreams are the "royal road to the unconscious" (page #), expressing in coded imagery the dreamer's unfulfilled wishes through a process known as "dream-work"(page #). According to Freud, actual but unacceptable desires are censored internally and subjected to coding through layers of condensation and displacement before emerging in a kind of rebus puzzle in the dream itself (page#)." https://owl.english.purdue.edu>owlprint

Paraphrasing

On a regular basis, sometimes several times a day, we paraphrase ourselves when we speak because we need to make sure that our communication is clear and that we convey the right message to our audience. "Do you know what I am saying?" "Do you know what I mean?" or similar collocations are part of our conversations and we do it without thinking, instinctively. A good paraphrase "will go far to show how much clearer and more effective an idea can be when expressed in simple terms." (Blackstone, 1965, p. 175)

Here is another definition: A restatement of a text, passage, or work giving the meaning in another form

The teacher asked the students to write a paraphrase of the poem. www.merriam-webster.com

A much simpler definition would be "to say (something that someone else has said or written) using different words." www.learnersdictionary.com

DISCOVER Ask your students to work in pairs and analyze the following proverbs and use their own words to explain how they understand each of the following proverbs:

You can lead a horse to water, but you can't make it drink.

Once bitten, twice shy.

A stitch in time saves nine.

Too many cooks spoil the broth.

Actions speak louder than words.

Birds of a feather flock together.

Knowledge is power.

Laughter is the best medicine.

People who live in glass houses should not throw stones.

Add your own: _____

Proverbs from around the world – students should be able to explain

If you want to go fast, go alone. If you want to go far, go together. (African)

A man who uses force is afraid of reasoning. (Kenyan)

Measure a thousand times and cut once. (Turkish)

There is no shame in not knowing; the shame lies in not finding. (Russian)

Give a man a fish, and you feed him for a day. Teach a man to fish, and you feed him for a lifetime. (Chinese)

Examine what is said, not who speaks. (Arabic)

_____

The heart that loves is always young. (Greek)

_____

To be willing is only half the task. (Armenian)

_____

A teacher is better than two books. (German)

_____

Don't sail out farther than you can row back. (Danish)

_____

Still waters run deep. (Latin)

_____

Shared joy is a double joy; shared sorrow is half a sorrow. (Swedish)

_____

Add your own:

_____

SUGGESTION   Challenge the students to paraphrase the following idioms and expressions in original sentences:

Head and shoulders above the rest   _____

With open arms   _____

Bend over backwards   _____

By word of mouth   _____

Slip of the tongue   _____

Save one's breath   _____

By the skin of one's teeth   _____

All thumbs   _____

Shake a leg _____

A cold shoulder _____

Split hairs _____

Narrow-minded _____

Rub elbows with _____

Put one's foot down _____

To have a sweet tooth _____

Tongue in cheek _____

Pull one's leg _____

On all fours _____

Tooth and nail _____

Keep one's fingers crossed _____

By heart _____

Keep a straight face _____

Over one's head _____

All ears _____

Nosey _____

Brainstorm _____

NOTES

_____

_____

_____

_____

_____

Summarizing

HOW DO WE **write a summary**? A summary can be done quite easily if we know what to do before we put pen to paper. Most textbooks recommend asking the questions that reporters use: **Who? What? When? Where? Why? How?** These questions will be of great help in writing a summary.

1. Read the passage, the article, or the text **quickly, looking for main ideas**.

2. Read everything all over again, this time a little bit **more carefully** and absorb as much information as possible.

3. Sometimes the main idea is located in the introduction or first paragraph. Look for the **thesis statement** and **topic sentences**. The thesis should be at the end of introduction, and the topic sentences should start each of the body paragraphs. Pay attention because there are times when the thesis statement is implied or suggested.

4. Next, select **the major idea(s)**. In other words, what is the author trying to say or communicate?

5. Keep those **wh-** and **how** questions in the back of your mind, and use your own words.

6. Avoid expressing your own opinion and **simply relate to the main ideas** only.

7. Begin your summary with a sentence to inform your reader of the **title**, the **author**, and the **source**.

Challenge: Read the following passage and summarize it following the above-mentioned suggestions:

"A marathon is any kind of endurance contest - running, dancing, bicycling, flagpole-sitting. It is named for the narrow valley in Greece where in 490 BC the Athenians, under Miltiades, pinned down superior

Persian forces so that they could not use their cavalry, and proceeded to slaughter them. The Persians lost 6,400 men in battle; the Greeks, 192. Miltiades, fearing that Athens might surrender to a Persian attack by sea in ignorance of the victory at Marathon, dispatched Pheidippides (also known as Philippides), his fastest runner, to take home the good news. Though nearly exhausted, having already run to Sparta and back, Pheidippides raced twenty-some miles to Athens, gasped out 'Rejoice - we conquer!' and fell dead.

The modern marathon road race is exactly 26 miles and 385 yards long. It was first staged at the revival of the Olympic Games in Athens in 1896. Boston's marathon is held every year on Patriot's Day (April 19) and commemorates such Bostonian matters as Paul Revere's ride. New York City too has an annual marathon run; apparently one of the conditions is that at least one contestant be in a wheelchair."

(Willard R. Espy, *Thou Improper, Thou Uncommon Noun*, New York: Clarkson N. Potter Publishers, 1987, p. 210)

NOTES

_____

_____

_____

_____

_____

Writing Topic Sentences

THE FIRST SENTENCE in a paragraph is usually a sentence that will tell the reader what the paragraph is all about. Some linguists call it **the main idea sentence**, but generally it is known as **the topic sentence.** This should be a single sentence, and it will establish the topic of the paragraph. Each paragraph should contain such a sentence to guide the reader and provide direction for what the writer should include.

"As a general rule, make the topic sentence one of the first few sentences in the paragraph. Sometimes a paragraph has no topic sentence; occasionally the topic sentence occurs at the end of the paragraph. These exceptions are permissible, but the early topic sentence is more popular because it helps in three ways to produce an effective message:

1. It defines your job as a writer and states a manageable objective – a single topic.

2. It establishes a guide for your development of the basic idea. You must supply evidence of or support for any assertion in the topic sentence. The topic sentence is only a beginning, but it predicts a conclusion that the paragraph must reach.

3. It warns your reader what the paragraph is going to contain."

(Emery, Kierzek and Lindblom, *English Fundamentals*, 1985, p. 245)

Teachers should also be able to teach their students little secrets about writing wonderful topic sentences. One of these tips would include talking about SIGNAL WORDS. These words, if used correctly, may help in determining how the paragraph will be organized.

"Signal words are used to:

Indicate the number of items to be discussed in a paragraph:

Three basic *methods* are used in building construction in America.

Indicate reasons or prove a position:

Fire resistance, structure stability, and *design flexibility* are the reasons to use reinforced concrete as a construction method.

Indicate a method of organization to be followed in the paragraph development:

If we *compare* reinforced-concrete construction and steel-frame construction, we can see that reinforced concrete is superior.

Aquatic animals can be *classified* into two major groups: those animals which have a backbone and those which do not.

Humor can be *defined* in a number of ways depending on whom you ask for a *definition.*

Applying to graduate school is not a complicated *process.*"

(Harfiel et al., *Learning ESL Composition,* 1985, pp. 35-36)

102 Great Ideas

"The Great Ideas are the conceptions by which we think about things. They are the terms in which we state fundamental problems; they are the notions we employ in defining issues and discussing them. They represent the principal content of our thought. They are what we think as well as what we think about."

Mortimer Adler

ANGEL	INDUCTION	PLEASURE AND PAIN
ANIMAL	INFINITY	POETRY
ARISTOCRACY	JUDGMENT	PRINCIPLE
ART	JUSTICE	PROGRESS
ASTRONOMY	KNOWLEDGE	PROPHECY
BEAUTY	LABOR	PRUDENCE
BEING	LANGUAGE	PUNISHMENT
CAUSE	LAW	QUALITY
CHANCE	LIBERTY	QUANTITY
CHANGE	LIFE AND DEATH	REASONING
CITIZEN	LOGIC	RELATION
CONSTITUTION	LOVE	RELIGION
CUSTOM AND CONVENTION	MAN	REVOLUTION
DEFINITION	MATHEMATICS	RETHORIC
DEMOCRACY	MATTER	SAME AND OTHER
DESIRE	MECHANICS	SCIENCE
DIALECTIC	MEDICINE	SENSE
DUTY	MEMORY AND IMAGINATION	SIGN AND SYMBOL
EDUCATION	METAPHYSICS	SIN
ELEMENT	MIND	SLAVERY
EMOTION	MONARCHY	SOUL
ETERNITY	NATURE	SPACE
EVOLUTION	NECESSITY AND CONTINGENCY	STATE
EXPERIENCE	OLIGARCHY	TEMPERANCE
FAMILY	ONE AND MANY	THEOLOGY
FATE	OPINION	TIME
FORM	OPPOSITION	TRUTH
GOD	PHILOSOPHY	TYRANNY
GOOD AND EVIL	PHYSICS	UNIVERSAL AND PARTICULAR
GOVERNMENT		VIRTUE AND VICE
HABBIT		WAR AND PEACE
HAPPINESS		WEALTH
HISTORY		WILL
HONOR		WISDOM
HYPOTHESIS		WORLD
IDEA		
IMMORTALITY		

(Hartfiel et al. *Learning ESL Composition*, 1985, p.30)

DISCOVER   Arrange the students in small groups and ask them to work together, find **a topic they like**, and then write together a **topic sentence** for the topic of their choice.

Writing Thesis Statements

A **thesis statement**
- states the main topic
- lists the subdivisions of the topic
- may indicate the method of organization of the entire paper
- is usually the last sentence in the introductory paragraph

Analyze the following thesis statements:

    A.   Find the main topic and the subtopics in each of the following thesis statements.

    B.   Underline the subtopics.

1. Women generally live longer than men for two main reasons: they tend to take better care of their health, and they lead less stressful lives.

2. An architect should be both an artist and an engineer.

3. In choosing a major, a student has to consider various factors, such as personal interest, job opportunities, and the availability of training.

4. Capital punishment should be abolished, not only because it deprives another person of life, but also because it does not stop crime.

Complete the following statements by adding subtopics to them.

1. Living together before marriage is becoming increasingly popular for three reasons:

    _____.

2. Owning an automobile is a necessity both

    _____.

3. The life expectancy of the average person is increasing because of

   _____.

4. A teacher must have the following qualities:

   _____.

5. Foreign students have a difficult time taking notes in class due to

   _____.

6. Television commercials are insulting to the average viewer because

   _____.

7. Technology is changing our lives in three important areas:

   _____.

8. Poverty creates negative consequences for society, such as

   _____.

(Adapted from Alice Oshima and Ann Hogue,
Writing Academic English, Longman, 1991, pp. 78-82)

Writing INTRODUCTIONS

The most challenging chapter of my college days reminds me how difficult it was for me to write an introductory paragraph. No matter how hard I tried, I couldn't get it right, and my professors were aware that I needed a lot of counseling. The best piece of advice came from one of my favorite professors, who told me to write the essay or the composition and then go back and put together the introduction. Guess what? It worked!

During my best years of teaching, I always shared this anecdote, and I have a feeling my students followed my advice and liked the idea. Giving students advice is not enough; teachers have to provide examples, and sometimes the best ones come from our personal experience.

In 2000, I found a book that, more or less, explains in plain English what the process of writing introductions should involve. The book is entitled *Write Better Essays in Just 20 Minutes a Day*, and its author is Elizabeth Chesla.

"Specifically, essay writers have four tasks to accomplish within the first few paragraphs. An effective introduction should do the following four tasks.

1. **Provide the context necessary to understand your thesis**. [. . .] you may need to provide some basic background information. For

example, if you are writing about literature, you should include the titles, authors, publication dates of the texts you will be analyzing. Similarly, if you are writing about an historical event, you should name the event, the date, and the key people (or countries, or issues, and so on) involved.

2. **Clearly state the main point of the essay.** Your readers should know from the beginning what idea you will be developing throughout the essay. A clear thesis statement is a key component of an effective introduction.

3. **Set the tone for the essay.** Like the opening notes of a song give you a sense of the listening experience ahead, an introduction gives readers a sense of what they're going to experience by setting the tone of the essay. Tone is the mood or attitude conveyed through language, particularly through word choice and sentence structure. Your tone may be personal and informal, serious and formal, urgent, relaxed, grave, or humorous.

4. **Grab the reader's interest.** Consider all of the things that compete for your reader's attention. To get readers to devote time to your essay, you must grab their attention. This means you need an introduction that stands out – one that piques their interest and makes them want to learn more." (90)

To create what she calls 'eye-catching introductions,' Chesla recommends the following strategies that will 'make the introduction an invitation to read':

- "A quotation
  - A question
    - A surprising statement or fact
      - An imaginary situation or scenario
        - An anecdote
          - Interesting background information
            - A new twist on a familiar phrase" (91)

> An idea drowns in a sea of words.

Experienced teachers prefer to show their students that there are several ways of writing a good introduction. Depending on the proficiency level, or the background of the students, ESL instructors should encourage their students to make their introductory paragraphs attractive and interesting, and at the same time make the readers continue to the next paragraphs. Remember that the best writing is always **clear and concise.**

Smalley & Ruetten (1995) assert that there are four ways a student can write the most difficult paragraph, the introduction:

The Funnel approach
The Turnabout
The Dramatic Entrance
The Relevant Quotation

The Funnel technique is usually the most common type and the easiest to write. The name, according to the two authors, comes from the fact that "ideas progress from the general to the specific just as a funnel is wide at the top and narrow at the bottom." (126)

In my experience, ESL students want to see a sample first, and then they can go to work on their own. To make things even easier, the teacher can provide examples of introductory paragraphs from previous students, or they can write one that can be separated into:

General statement
More specific information
Even more specific information
Thesis statement

Sample of the **Funnel Approach**

"Traveling to a foreign country is always interesting, especially if it is a country that is and learning about different customs, some of which may seem very curious. If you were to visit my country, for instance, you would probably think that my people have some very strange customs, as these three examples will illustrate." (127)

To add diversity, or to offer a variety of possibilities, teachers can also recommend other techniques. Here are some examples from the same source:

Sample of the **Turnabout Technique**

"We live in an era where television is the national pastime. Since the invention of the television set, people have been spending more of their free time watching television than doing anything else. Many of the television addicts feel that this particular pastime is not a bad one; indeed, they argue that people can learn a great deal watching television. I am sure if you look long and hard enough, you can probably find some programs that are educationally motivating. But, for the most part, I say

that watching television is a waste of time." (Pamela Moran, quoted in
Refining Composition Skills, p. 237)

Sample of the **Dramatic Entrance**

"The rain pours down as if running from a faucet, lightning streaks
across the dark restless sky, and thunder pounds the roof and walls of
the house. All of a sudden the wind picks up. Trees sway madly back
and forth; loose objects are picked up and thrown all around. The house
creaks and moans with every gust of wind. Windows are broken by
pieces of shingle from a neighbor's roof or by loose objects picked up
by the wind. Power lines snap like thread. The unprepared house and
its occupants are in grave danger as the awesome hurricane approaches.
Had they prepared for the hurricane, they might not be in such danger.
Indeed, careful preparation before a hurricane is essential to life and
property." (Donald Landry, quoted in *Refining Composition Skills*,
p. 272)

Sample of the **Relevant Quotation**

"It took an Englishman, William Gladstone, to say what Americans have
always thought: 'The American Constitution is, so far as I can see, the
most wonderful work ever struck off at a given time by the brain and
purpose of man.' From this side of the water, however, the marvel has not
been so much the unique system of government that emerged from the
secret conclave of 1787 as the array of ordered and guaranteed freedoms
that the document presented. 'Every word of [the Constitution],' said
James Madison, the quintessential Founding Parent, 'decides a question
between power and liberty.' "

(H.B. Zobel, "How History Made the Constitution," *American Heritage*,
Mar. 1988: p. 54, quoted in *Refining Composition Skills*, p. 308)

Writing OUTLINES

Before proceeding to the first paragraph, the introduction, students should be working on pre-writing, which may take a long time, but if properly organized, these activities will definitely provide useful information for the writing of the composition, essay, book report, or even oral presentation. The pre-writing may include keeping a journal, brainstorming, clustering, freewriting, and even compiling an outline, or a list of the most important parts of the spoken or written plan.

How important is an outline? As teachers, we all know that even before we tackle the most challenging topics in the classroom, we need to put our details into **a well-thought, well-organized plan**. For the sake of our students, we should do the same when we teach out students.

> "Have you ever taken your Halloween candy and made an inventory of what you have? Once you've poured out your bag, you put all the chocolate items in one pile, all the gum in another pile, all the lollipops in another pile, and all the inedible items (like dimes and quarters) in another pile? Then maybe you broke those piles down into piles of plain chocolate (like Hershey bars), candied chocolate (like M&M's), and candy bars (like Snickers). Well, this is basically what you are doing when you make an outline. You are taking your topic and breaking it down into smaller categories. Only instead of candy, you are categorizing the information that will go into your paper.
>
> Start with your topic and break that into three main categories:
>
> • Introduction
> • Body
> • Conclusion"

(Michelle McLean, Essays & Term Papers, 2011, p. 16)

The introductory paragraph has two parts: a few sentences or general statements about your subject, going from general to more specific and even very specific, leading to the last sentence that should be the thesis statement. This thesis statement for an essay is like a topic sentence for a paragraph. The thesis names the specific topic and the controlling ideas or major subdivisions of the topic.

The body may have one or more paragraphs. The number of paragraphs depends on the number of controlling ideas or subdivisions mentioned in the thesis. The paragraphs in the body of the essay are like the main supporting points of a paragraph.

The conclusion of an essay, like the concluding sentence in a paragraph, should be a summary of the main points described in the body.

ESSAY		
I. INTRODUCTION		
General Statements		
Thesis Statement		
II. BODY		
A. Topic Sentence		
1. Support		
2. Support		
3. Support		
PARAGRAPH	(Concluding Sentence)	
Topic sentence	B. Topic Sentence	
A. Support	1. Support	
B. Support	2. Support	
C. Support	3. Support	
(Concluding Sentence)		
C. Topic Sentence		
1. Support		
2. Support		
3. Support		
(Concluding Sentence)		
III. Conclusion		
Restatement or summary of the		
main points; final comment		

Note: The body is the longest part of the essay and can contain as many paragraphs as necessary to support the controlling ideas of your thesis statement."

(Alice Oshima and Ann Hogue, *Writing Academic English*, 1991, p. 77)

WRITING AN ESSAY

Of all the academic skills, writing remains one of the most challenging. Next to developing good aural skills, or approximately the same as good speaking techniques, writing is a useful skill mostly because it helps ESL students develop and improve their thinking skills.

Rhetorical styles
The four most common rhetorical styles are:

EXPOSITION (or expository writing)
Writers **explain and analyze information** by presenting an idea and its relevant support.
This style may take one of several forms: Process/how to, Comparison/contrast, Cause/effect, Problem/solution.

ARGUMENTATION
These essays are written to **prove the validity of an idea** or point of view.
Persuasive writing is a type of argumentation that is meant to urge some form of action.
The IELTS tests are known to use this rhetorical style.

DESCRIPTION
Descriptive writing can be **objective** and straightforward, or **subjective** and deceiving.
The writer describes a place, a person, an object, an event, or action by using all five senses.

NARRATION
The purpose of this type of writing is **to tell** an interesting story or **to narrate** a series of events the author considers relevant and important to share. To add a special touch to the narrative, writers sometimes resort to descriptive writing as well.

**THESE FOUR WRITING STYLES
ARE ALSO REFERRED TO
AS MODES OF DISCOURSE.**

Our ESL learners will jump right in when it comes to writing a compare/contrast essay, for example. Other rhetorical styles, like cause and effect, process/how to, definition, classification would be relatively easy, but **argumentation** is the one that creates confusion and needs a lot of preparation for the instructor. Some of our students may not be acquainted with this concept because, in their culture, especially young people may not be allowed to argue with their parents or their teachers. By extrapolation, we may say that even adults may not argue with their supervisors, or any other human entity of higher status.

> "The way to convince another is to state your case moderately and accurately. Then scratch your head or shake it a little and say that is the way it seems to you but that of course you may be mistaken about it; which causes your listener to receive what you have to say and as like as not turn about and try to convince you of it since you are in doubt. But if you go at him in a tone of positiveness and arrogance you only make an opponent of him."
>
> Benjamin Franklin

To introduce the ESL students to **the idea of argumentation**, maybe we should start by **talking** about **persuasion**, which is a similar concept, but a little bit easier to understand and digest. A quick oral exercise asking the students to teach other about a type of food they like, or about a movie they would recommend to the class, would be a good start.

Laurie G. Kirszner and Stephen R. Mandell (2011) assert that we find arguments everywhere - on TV, in newspapers, in magazines, talking to friends and family, or discussing daily topics online. When they define argument, they also mention **quarrel, spin,** or **propaganda**, which they insist are not exactly argument. A clear distinction should also be made between **formal** (academic debates, discussions and writing) and **informal arguments** (those that we encounter in sports, politics, social issues, etc.). Their definition of argument is the following: "An argument takes a stand and presents evidence that helps to convince people to accept the writer's position." (5)

The authors go back in history and use Aristotle's idea of persuasion. Since ancient Greece was mainly an oral culture, persuasion was an effective technique when its citizens had to speak in public or before judicial bodies. "In *The Art of Rhetoric*, Aristotle examines the different means of persuasion that a speaker can use to persuade listeners (or writers):

- The appeal to logic (*logos*)
- The appeal to emotion (*pathos*)
- The appeal to authority (*ethos*)

The Appeal to Logic According to Aristotle, argument is the appeal to logic or reason (*logos*). Aristotle assumed that at their core, human beings were logical and that they would therefore respond to a well-constructed argument. Such an argument would resonate with people and convince them that the conclusion that they were hearing or reading was correct.

The Appeal to Emotion Aristotle also knew that an appeal to the emotions (*pathos*) could be very persuasive. For example, after December 7, 1941, graphic photographs of the Japanese attack on Pearl Harbor helped to convince Americans that entry into World War II was both justified and desirable. Contemporary American audiences respond in a similar way when they are shown images of planes crashing into the World Trade Center on September 11, 2001.

The Appeal to Authority Finally, Aristotle knew that the character and authority of a speaker or writer (*ethos*) could contribute to the persuasiveness of an argument. If the person making an argument is known to be honorable, truthful, knowledgeable, and trustworthy, audiences are likely to accept what he or she is saying. If, on the other hand, the person is known to be deceitful, ignorant, dishonest, uninformed, or dishonorable, audiences are likely to dismiss his or her argument – no matter how persuasive it might seem." (8)

What makes **the argumentation technique so efficient is the structure** of the essay:

INTRODUCTION
Thesis statement

BODY PARAGRAPH 1
First argument (evidence)

BODY PARAGRAPH 2
Second argument (evidence)

BODY PARAGRAPH 3
Third argument (evidence)

BODY PARAGRAPH 4
Counterargument and refutation

Conclusion

A similar approach comes from J. M. O'Neill, C. Laycock, and R.L. Scale, who published *Argumentation and Debate* in 1925:

"Argumentation is the art of influencing others, through the medium of reasoned discourse, to believe or act as we wish them to believe or act." (1)

(Quoted in Annette Rottenberg, *Elements of Argument*, 5th edition, 1997, p. 5)

Check the Appendices to see a sample of an argumentative essay.

Transitions

IN SPOKEN OR written language, **transitions are the spice of life.** They add fluency to our language, and they help us move smoothly from one idea to another. To make words glue to each other, to establish a logical connection between words, phrases, or sentences, we utilize **these magical markers**. In writing, transitions guide the reader to what we intend to say, emphasize, or simply direct our thoughts and ideas. The use of transitions will also distinguish between boring or flat speech and interesting or attractive verbiage when you write. These useful cues will make a difference if they are used efficiently.

Addition:	*and, again, too, also, furthermore, similarly, moreover, besides*
Illustration:	*for example, for instance*
Comparison:	*similarly, likewise, in like manner, by comparison*
Logical conclusion:	*so, therefore, thus, accordingly, consequently, as a result, hence*
Contrast or objection:	*but, however, nevertheless, on the other hand, conversely, on the contrary, in spite of*
Concession:	*granted that, no doubt, to be sure, it is true that*
Reiteration:	*indeed, in fact*
Time:	*afterward, later, subsequently, at the same time, simultaneously, meanwhile, currently, formerly, when, immediately, lately*
Sequence:	*first, second, third, next, finally*
Place:	*here, below, farther on, there, beyond, nearby, around*
Summary:	*in conclusion, to conclude, to summarize, in short, in brief*
Restatement:	*that is, in other words, in simpler terms, simply stated*

A good example of using, in this case **enumeration, as transition signals** is the following discussion about language:

> "There are *five simple facts* about language in general which we must grasp before we can understand a specific language or pass judgement on a particular usage . . .
>
> *In the first p*lace, language is basically speech . . .
> *In the second place,* language is personal . . .
> *The third fact* about language is that it changes . . .
> *The fourth great fact* about language . . . is that its users are, in one way or another, isolated . . .
> *The fifth great fact* about language is that it is a historical growth of a specific kind . . ."

Donald J. Lloyd, "Snobs, Slobs, and the English Language," *The American Scholar*

(Quoted in Hans Guth, *Concise English Handbook*, 1972, p. 209)

DISCOVER
Ask the students to read the following passages and **identify the transition words:**

> "I am always drawn back to places where I have lived, the houses and their neighborhoods. For instance, there is a brownstone in the East Seventies where, during the early years of the war, I had my first New York apartment. It was one room crowded with attic furniture, a sofa and fat chairs upholstered in that itchy, particular red velvet that one associates with hot days on a train. The walls were stucco, and a color rather like tobacco-spit. Everywhere, in the bathroom too, there were prints of Roman ruins freckled brown with age. The single window looked out on a fire escape. Even so, my spirits heightened whenever I felt in my pocket the key to this apartment; with all its gloom, it still was a place of my own, the first, and my books were there, and jars of pencils to sharpen, everything I needed, so I felt, to become the writer I wanted to be."

(Truman Capote, *Breakfast at Tiffany's*, New York, Random House, 1958, p. 5)

Besides transitions, monotonous writing can be made more interesting by using what some linguists call **sentence variety**. Rosa & Eschholz (2015) suggest a comparison between the following two paragraphs:

"Unvaried Sentences

Water surrounds Vancouver on three sides. The snow-crowned Coast Mountains ring the city on the northeast. Vancouver has a floating quality of natural loveliness. There is a curved beach at English Bay. This beach is in the shape of a half moon. Residential high-rises stand behind the beach. They are in pale tones of beige, blue, and ice-cream pink. Turn-of-the-century houses of painted wood frown upward at the glitter of office towers. Any urban glare is softened by folds of green lawns, flowers, fountains, and trees. Such landscaping appears to be unplanned. It links Vancouver to her ultimate treasure of greenness. That treasure is thousand-acre Stanley Park. Surrounding stretches of water dominate. They have image-evoking names like False Creek and Lost Lagoon. Sailboats and pleasure craft skim blithely across Burrard Inlet. Foreign freighters are out in English Bay. They await their turn to take on cargoes of grain.

Varied Sentences

Surrounded by water on three sides and ringed to the northeast by the snow-crowned Coast Mountains, Vancouver has a floating quality of natural loveliness. At English Bay, the half-moon curve of beach is backed by high-rises in pale tones of beige, blue, and ice-cream pink. Turn-of-the-century houses of painted wood frown upward at the glitter of office towers. Yet any urban glare is quickly softened by folds of green lawns, flowers, fountains, and trees that in a seemingly unplanned fashion link Vancouver to her ultimate treasure of greenness – thousand-acre Stanley Park. And always it is the surrounding stretches of water that dominate, with their image-evoking names like False Creek and Lost Lagoon. Sailboats and pleasure craft skim blithely across Burrard Inlet, while out in English Bay freighters await their turn to take on cargoes of grain."

(Alfred Rosa & Paul Eschholz, *Models for Writers*, 2015, pp. 218-219)

Grammar Summary

TIPS for the power of grammar

> "Language is full of irregularities. Carelessness and common usage bring statements with serious grammatical flaws into everyday speech. When they become common, we assume that they are correct. Two of these, **rest easy** and **clear-cut**, have been inspirations for numerous calls to the Hot Line. ... **Clearly cut** and **rest easily** are technically correct. However, **clear-cut** and **rest easy** are also acceptable simply because they are in common use."
>
> Michael Strumpf and Auriel Douglas, 2004, *The Grammar Bible*, p. 124

Grammar and Glamour

THERE IS **MAGIC** in studying grammar, and it starts with a puzzle. Few people know that there is a connection between the words *glamour* and *grammar*. There was a time when these two words were **one and the same**.

In his introduction to *The Glamour of Grammar*, Roy Peter Clarke (2010) invites us to look into this paradoxical correlation.

"The bridge between the words *glamour* and *grammar* is magic. According to the OED, *glamour* evolved from *grammar* through an ancient association between learning and enchantment. There was a time when grammar described not just language knowledge but all forms of learning, which in a less scientific age included things like magic, alchemy, astrology, even witchcraft.

Evan Morris, editor and publisher of *The Word Detective*, leads us through the maze:

"'Glamour' and 'grammar' are essentially the same word. In classical Greek and Latin, 'grammar' (from the Greek *grammatikos*, meaning 'of letters') covered the whole of arts and letters, i.e. high knowledge in general. In the Middle Ages, 'grammar' was generally used to mean 'learning,' which at the time included, at least in the popular imagination, a knowledge of magic. The narrowing of 'grammar' to mean 'the rules of language' was a much later development, first focusing on Latin, and only in the 17th century extended to the study of English and other languages.

Meanwhile, 'grammar' had percolated into Scottish English (as *gramarye),* where an *l* was substituted for an *r* and the word eventually became *glamour*, used to mean specifically knowledge of magic and spells. "(3)

As it was already mentioned in a previous chapter, language has been defined as the medium of communication between individuals, and this takes place as an interchange of ideas in every aspect of our everyday life. It can also be said that the success of such exchange of opinions or statements depends on the accuracy with which the language itself is used. A clear understanding of the grammatical structure of any language is an essential step towards a full grasp of the routine practice which people had acquired over the years. And this brings us to the intrinsic value of good grammar.

Mason Long (1935) begins the 500+ pages of his grammar book with a question he then proceeds to answer:

"What is grammar? - Grammar is the backbone of expression. It supports the body of rules which govern correct speaking and writing. Grammar enables a man to go to the sources of his trouble in English and thus to effect a cure. Do you wish to speak and write more accurately and effectively? Are you desirous of acquiring more of the cultural niceties of speech which distinguish men of ability and prestige? Would you like to mingle more confidently with those whose friendship and esteem you covet? John Locke, the great English philosopher of the seventeenth century, was convinced that 'to write and speak correctly gives a grace, and gains a favorable attention to what one has to say." (3)

Long goes on to say that grammar "has become a science in itself. It may be defined as that science which presents the sets of rules or principles underlying correct speaking or writing. These rules state what is known about the accurate use of words and the way in which words are related to each other. Grammar further tells you how to apply these rules correctly in speaking and writing. It even undertakes to suggest how various words ought to be grouped so as to express the precise shade of meaning which we have in mind." (4) The author ventures to defend his perspective by compounding his definition with the assertion that grammar improves self-expression and thinking and makes reading easier and more enjoyable. (7-9)

Such ideas came sometimes at the beginning of the previous century, and they were the fundamental principles for the dissemination of knowledge regarding the English language in general. Towards the end of the 20th century, when teaching ESL emerged as another approach from a different perspective, **grammar kept its strong position of importance and relevance**, but that was **counteracted by the idea that language can be acquired as an immersion experience.**

After presenting both alternatives, Marianne Celce-Murcia and Diane

Larsen-Freeman (1999) admitted that neither approach is entirely successful, and added that "the more teachers know about grammar, the more expeditiously they should be able to raise a learner's consciousness about how the language works. They should be able to focus learner attention on the distinctive features of a particular grammatical form in less time than it would take for the learner to notice them on his or her own. Teachers may accomplish this in an explicit fashion by giving student rules and exercises with the appropriate grammatical terminology, but they can also teach grammar implicitly as well. Asking students to engage in particular tasks that require the use of certain structures is an implicit means of getting students to focus on and to practice form. In addition, a teacher might highlight properties of the grammatical structures by providing negative evidence – that is, helping students to see what is not possible in English. In this way, learners are encouraged to notice the gap between what they are producing and what the target language requires. Another example of teaching with an implicit focus on grammar is when teachers choose to 'enhance the input' of their students by exposing them to language samples in which particular grammatical structures are highlighted or and are more prevalent than they might be in ordinary communication." (1-2)

The word **grammar** comes via Latin from Greek *grammatike*, meaning "*art of letters.*" The Cambridge English Dictionary defines grammar as "*the study or use of the rules about how words change their form and combine with other words to make sentences.*" (www.dictionary.cambridge.org)

If we check other sources of information, we will find more or less similar underlying rules and precepts about **grammar**. It is usually subdivided into **morphology**, or the study of words/parts of speech, and **syntax**, or the way in which words are used and arranged to form phrases, clauses, and sentences. Anthony Burgess in his *A Mouthful of Air*, William Morrow and Company, Inc., New York, 1992, calls syntax "higher-order structures." (48)

In January of 1984, after teaching in various public schools, I went for an interview at a private school in Rutherford, New Jersey. I was lucky and blessed to get the job, and I stayed with the same institution for approximately 33 years. The school changed its name several times (from *LIFE Program* to *Berlitz on Campus* and then we merged with *ELS Language Centers*), but in fact remained the same for me: the extended family of instructors and students vying for the same goal: the teaching of ESL to folks from all over the world. Very soon after I was hired, I realized the importance of grammar and how relevant it was for me to understand what was necessary to select, from the plethora of books and materials provided to us, what the students in each class needed at each level of English proficiency. Integrating grammar with other skills was one thing I learned very quickly. We take the grammar topic, we digest the information for us, the educators, and then go into the classroom and deliver the information to our audience, our students, by whatever means we consider appropriate. A quick warm-up activity or an ice-breaker might be useful, and then we tackle the issue at hand, whatever that might be: a specific tense, a preposition, a coordination conjunction or correlative conjunction, an adjective clause, an *If* clause, or any other such topic.

Grammar remains, for me, a necessary tool and one that teachers should master right away after graduation, and one that will help them enormously if they know how to resort to the textbooks as required by the curriculum. No matter what level the students are, they come expecting the school to provide a basic introduction to what the English language requires for them to communicate efficiently, not only among themselves, but also with native speakers.

Whenever I ran into unanswered questions, I went next door and approached one of my colleagues, and when they ran into similar situations, they came to me and asked me what I would do in this or that case. Not that we know the answer to all the questions, but making the mental effort to find the right answer can bring forth the most surprising answers.

Students can take you by surprise, and they can ask you quite unexpected questions, most of which you never heard in your college days. Each nationality will look into their own bags of language and culture, and then will definitely let you know they have a problem. Some will have difficulty formulating the questions: others won't understand why the word order is so important. Some will use double reference, and you will need to explain why "*My brother coming*" may be correct in some languages, but not in English. Some will automatically translate from their native language a word or a structure that makes no sense in English. Some will see no difference between "most" and "almost' because in their language there is only one and the same word. Others will use "where" and "which" interchangeably because this is what they do in their own culture. Sometimes students will ignore the verb "to be" because this verb does not exist in their native tongue. And the list goes on and on. The antidote? You guessed it: **it's good explanations, or correct grammar.**

Another very important point to make at this point is that we need to impress upon our students the basic concept that **Good Grammar** is also a combination of two things, and they cannot exist without each other:

$$\text{Grammar} \quad = \quad \text{structure} + \text{meaning}$$

A sentence such as
The cat has five legs.

may be grammatically correct, but it makes no sense and therefore it is incorrect.

By the same token, any good phrase or word combination may not be acceptable because its structure is **not correct**. For example:

That was the movie I was talking about it. (What is the problem here?)

This section of the book contains suggestions and ideas I found useful for me, and if they worked for me, I suppose they will work for anybody who embraces this wonderful job called teaching ESL.

In a nutshell, we can say that:

1. Words are made up of letters. The part of grammar that teaches us how to use letters is called **orthography**. Orthography is **the science of letters,** and its etymology comes from two Greek words which mean "correct writing." Letters are marks that tell us what sounds to make with our voice.

2. The part of grammar that teaches us how to use the words is called **morphology**. Morphology is **the science of words**, how they are formed, and their relationship to other words in the same language. It analyzes the structure of words, parts of the words, such as stems, root words, prefixes, and suffixes.

3. Words are built into sentences. The part of grammar that gives the rules for the making of sentences is called **syntax**. Syntax is the **science of sentences.** Syntax is a Greek word that means "arrange together."

4. Words have an origin and a history; they grow, and as they grow, changes are made to them. The story of this origin and the description of the changes in words are parts of grammar called **etymology**. The word **etymology** is made up of two Greek words which mean a "true account." Etymology treats the origin of words and the changes made on them.

In **morphology**, these are the eight parts of speech:

1. A **noun** is a name.

2. A **verb** is a word that tells you what the noun does.

3. An **adjective** is a word that describes a noun. An **article** is a word used to modify a noun.

4. An **adverb** is a word that modifies a verb, an adjective, or another adverb.

5. A **preposition** is a word that comes before the noun.

6. A **conjunction** is a word that combines other words or sentences.

7. A **pronoun** is a word that stands for a noun.

8. An **interjection** is a word that represents a sound.

NOTE: An **adjective describes** a noun, whereas an **article** tells us whether a **noun in a sentence is general or specific.**

In syntax, we have:

1. **Simple sentences** containing a subject and a predicate. They can be:

    a.   A statement   *He lives in New York.*
    b.   A question   *Where do you live?*
    c.   A request or command   *Open the door!*
    d.   An exclamation   *How interesting this class is!*

2. **Compound sentences** containing two or more sentences (called independent) joined together by:

    a.   Punctuation
         The storm came unexpectedly; we canceled our outdoor party.

    b.   Punctuation and a conjunctive adverb
         The storm came unexpectedly; therefore, we canceled our outdoor party.

    c.   A coordinate conjunction
         The storm came unexpectedly, so we canceled our outdoor party.

    d.   **Complex sentences** containing one or more dependent (called subordinate) clauses:

         a.   Adverb clauses
              We canceled out outdoor party because the storm came unexpectedly.

         b.   Adjective clauses
              The storm, which came unexpectedly, made us cancel our outdoor party.

         c.   Noun clauses
              I know why we had to cancel our outdoor party.

    e.   **Compound-complex sentences** containing two or more independent clauses and one or more dependent clauses:

         We had to cancel our outdoor party because we had a storm that came unexpectedly and invited our friends to join us the following weekend.

Morphology

NOUNS

There are several kinds of nouns:

1.	Proper nouns	*John, Mary, New York*
2.	Common nouns	*boy, girl, river, country*
3.	Collective nouns	*crowd, family, team, jury*
4.	Concrete nouns	*dog, building, tree, beach*
5.	Abstract nouns	*freedom, wisdom, strength*
6.	Compound nouns	*dining room, makeup, son-in-law*

Nouns can also be countable (something that can be counted – *chair, ship, book*) and non-count or uncountable nouns (things that cannot be counted - *coffee, snow, air*).

Exercise: Change the following **adjectives** into **abstract nouns**:

For example: *happy*   <u>happiness</u>
                      patient   _____
                      strong   _____
                      perfect   _____

Change the following **verbs** into **abstract nouns**:

For example: *to judge*   <u>judgment</u>
                      fly   _____
                      grow   _____
                      think   _____
                      speak   _____

DISCOVER: Make **noun compounds** out of the following phrases:

1.	A book about grammar	*a grammar book*
2.	A mine of gold	_____
3.	A person who keeps books	_____
4.	A salesman who travels	_____

5.   Checks for travelers   _____

6.   A board for ironing clothes   _____

7.   Seeing the sights   _____

8.   The lids that cover the eyes   _____

9.   A gown worn at night for sleeping   _____

10. A person who witnesses a scene
   with his own eyes   _____

11. Stew with lamb   _____

Nouns also exist in commonly used **expressions with participial adjectives**:

Present Participle as adjective	Past Participle as adjective
A stirring speech	*a revised edition*
A contributing cause	*a desired effect*
A booming economy	*an illustrated book*
Crushing costs	*accumulated assets*
A governing factor	*a recognized authority*

There are also expressions with Participial and Gerundive Modifiers. Students should work in pairs or small groups, explain what these expressions mean, and support their decisions with examples:

A breaking point	*a lost cause*
A winning personality	*a balanced budget*
A leading question	*a marked change*
A cutting remark	*a burned-out teacher*

EXERCISE. Ask the students to make up their own sentences using the following words:

Pleasing/pleased	*flattering/flattered*
Charming/charmed	*inspiring/inspired*
Annoying/annoyed	*revealing/revealed*
Surprising/surprised	*worrying/worried*

Many set expressions contain modifying elements. Participles may be preceded by adverbs or nouns, or nouns may modify other nouns.

ADVERB + PRESENT OR PAST PARTICIPLE

A high-ranking official	*a well-known secret*
A highly paid employee	*a beautifully dressed woman*
A far-reaching decision	*a far-fetched idea*

NOUN + PRESENT OR PAST PARTICIPLE

A heart-breaking decision	a heartfelt desire
A backbreaking job	a city-funded project
A fact-finding committee	a snow-clad mountain

EXERCISES IN MODIFYING COMPOUNDS AND EXPRESSIONS

1. An essay that has 500 words   _____

2. An apartment with four rooms   _____

3. An event that shook the world   _____

4. A training program that is fast paced _____

5. A house that has been newly renovated _____

(Adapted from Dunham & Vaden Summers,
English Integrated, 1986, pp. 11-17)

Exercise: Add –s to the countable nouns that can be made plural:

1. Information   _____

2. Lumber   _____

3. Luggage   _____

4. Machine   _____

5. Machinery   _____

6. Advice   _____

7. Committee   _____

8. Weather   _____

9. Slang   _____

10. Traffic   _____

Exercise: Fill in the blanks with the appropriate noun forms.

1. What is the (pronounce) _____ of this word?

2. The hurricane caused a great deal of (destroy) _____.

3. His (succeed) _____ was the result of hard work.

4. He gave a vivid (describe) _____ of his home town.

5. We must all try to find a (solve) _____ to the problem.

6. The manager's (decide) _____ was a surprise.

7. Everybody would like to see a (reduce) _____ in their taxes.

8. The superintendent is in charge of the (maintain) _____ of the building.

9. A (compare) _____ between the two cars raised unexpected questions.

10. You will have to find a good (explain) _____ for your action.

(Adapted from Marcella Frank's *Modern English Part I*, 1986, pp. 11-12)

ADJECTIVES

There are several types of adjectives:

1. Descriptive   beautiful, nice, tall

2. Quantitative   one, many, half, a lot

3. Demonstrative   this, that, these, those

4. Possessive   my, your, his, hers, ours

5. Interrogative   which, what, whose

6. Distributive   each, ever, either, neither, any

When more than one adjective comes before a noun, the adjectives are usually in a particular order:

Quantity - quality - size - age - shape - color - proper adjective - purpose

Jenny adopted a *beautiful big white* bulldog.
I love that really *old big green antique* car parked at the end of the street.
We bought a *wonderful old Italian* clock.

EXERCISE   Read the following **introductory passage** from John Steinbeck's short story entitled *The Chrysanthemums*, and identify the power of adjectives:

"The **high grey-flannel fog** of winter closed off the Salinas Valley from the sky and from all the rest of the world. On every side it sat like a lid on the mountains and made of the great valley a closed pot. On the **broad, level land floor** the gang plows bit deep and left the **black earth shining like metal** where the shares had cut. On the foothill ranches across the Salinas River, the **yellow stubble fields** seemed to be bathed in **pale cold sunshine**, but there was no sunshine in the valley now in December.

The **thick willow scrub** along the river flamed with **sharp and positive yellow leaves.**

It was a time of quiet and of waiting. The **air was cold and tender. A light wind** blew up from the south-west so that the farmers were **mildly hopeful** of a **good rain** before long; but fog and rain do not go together."

Here is another sample from Ernest Hemingway's first two sentences of his novel *A Farewell to Arms*:

"In the **late** summer of that year we lived in a house in a village that looked across the river and the plain to the mountains. In the bed of the river there were pebbles and boulders, **dry** and **white** in the sun, and the water was **clear** and swiftly **moving** and **blue** in the channels."

Adjectives and nouns ending in –*ate* pronounced /it/	Verbs ending in -*ate* pronounced /eit/
Accurate	to accommodate
Adequate	to anticipate
Affectionate	to appreciate
Appropriate	to celebrate
Certificate	to circulate
Chocolate	to communicate
Consulate	to concentrate
Delicate	to congratulate
Desperate	to contemplate
Fortunate	to cooperate
Immediate	to cultivate
Intimate	to decorate
Legitimate	to demonstrate
Passionate	to dominate
Predicate	to educate
Subordinate	to elevate
Syndicate	to eliminate
Temperate	to exaggerate
Ultimate	to hesitate
Unfortunate	to illustrate
Vertebrate	to imitate

Sometimes the same words can be both adjectives/nouns and verbs and the only difference would be their pronunciation:

Alternate	to alternate
Delegate	to delegate
Deliberate	to deliberate
Graduate	to graduate
Separate	to separate

Adjective suffixes

1. –able   *dependable, readable*
2. –ible   *sensible, visible*
3. –al   *spiritual, personal*
4. –ant   *pleasant, arrogant*
5. –ent   *efficient, confident*
6. –ary   *contradictory, imaginary*
7. –ful   *helpful, delightful*
8. –ic   *photographic, synthetic*
9. –ish   *childish, stylish*
10. –ive   *creative, perceptive*
11. –less   *useless, careless*
12. –like   *businesslike, lifelike*
13. –ly   *happily, basically*
14. –ous   *famous, dangerous*
15. –some   *awesome, troublesome*
16. –y   *healthy, easy*

Suggestion: Arrange the students in small groups and provide dictionaries. Students should be given the list and then asked to choose at least 3 suffixes and to find as many new words as possible. Students should then be encouraged to produce original sentences using the new words, first in a question, and then change the parts of speech in the answer.

For example:

Is he a *dependable* person?	Yes, you can always *depend* on him.
How *knowledgeable* is he?	I don't know, but he *knows* a lot about his job.
Are you eating *healthy* food?	_____
Was his advice *useful* in any way?	_____
_____?	Yes, they lived *happily* ever after.
_____?	No, it did not *please* everybody.
_____?	_____
_____?	_____
_____?	_____
_____?	_____
_____?	_____

NOTES

_____

_____

_____

_____

_____

Articles

The (definite article)

The basic meanings of **THE**:

This

That

The only one

Uses

People and things in the environment:

*We crossed **the** street at **the** intersection.*

A class as a whole:

The tiger is an animal.

With a ranking adjective:

The first lesson/the best book

To refer to something already mentioned:

I see two people walking in the street.

The man is holding the woman's hand.

Unique things:

The sun is shining brightly this morning.

With names of geographical areas and ships

The Arctic/The Atlantic Ocean/The Titanic

With names of libraries, museums, hotels

The New York Public Library/The Louvre/The Hilton

With groups of people:

The elderly/The poor/The needy

A, an (indefinite article)

Basic meaning of **A** or **AN**:

One

Uses

Any member of a group:

*My neighbor has **a** dog.*

For an unidentified member of a class:

*We saw **a** lion at the zoo.*

In the sense of **each**:

*One thousand dollars **a** month*

With WHAT A, SUCH A:

*What **a** nice day!*

***Such an** interesting question!*

With any countable nouns:

***A** pigeon flew around the balcony.*

EXERCISES IN THE USE OF ARTICLES

I. Use the following passage from Ernest Hemingway and use the correct articles:

"In ___ fall ____ war was always there, but we did not go to it any more. It was cold in ____ fall in Milan and ____ dark came very early. The ____ electric lights came on, and it was pleasant along ____ streets looking in ____ windows. There was much game hanging outside ____ shops and ____ snow powdered in ____ fur of ____ foxes and ____ wind blew their tails. ___ deer hung stiff and heavy and empty, and small birds blew in ____ wind and ____ wind turned their feathers. It was ____ cold fall and ____ wind came down from _____ mountain.

We were all at ___ hospital every afternoon, and there were different ways of walking across ____ town through _____ dusk to ____ hospital. Two of ____ ways were alongside canals, but they were long. Always, though, you crossed ____ bridge across ____ canal to enter ____ hospital. There was _____ choice of three bridges. On one of them ____ woman sold roasted chestnuts. It was warm, standing in front of her charcoal fire, and ____ chestnuts were warm afterward in your pocket. _____ hospital was very old and very beautiful, and you entered through ____ gate and walked across ____ courtyard and out ____ gate on ____ other side. There were usually funerals starting from _____ courtyard. Beyond _____ old hospital were ____ new brick pavilions, and there we met every afternoon and were all very polite and interested in what was ____ matter, and sat in _____ machines that were to make so much difference." (183)

(From Ernest Hemingway, *In Another Country*, [in] *Short Stories for Study*, 1946. New York: Henry Holt and Company)

II. Use the following groups of words and their articles in original sentences:

The United Nations   _____

The Police   _____

The University of Pennsylvania   _____

For the time being   _____

A useful gadget   _____

A few days ago   _____

The unexplained   _____

All the while   _____

The Wall Street Journal   _____

The majority   _____

Verbs

Some linguists call the verb the grammatical "center" of the sentence (Frank, *Modern English*, Part I, 1986, p. 41); others say it is "the leading word in a sentence" (Long, 1935, p. 172), and J. M. D Meiklejohn (1905) calls it the "cornerstone of the sentence." (6) Ann Hogue (2003) remarks that "verbs are the most changeable words in English"(4) and another author says: "Verbs are the wonderful words that give life to language." (Yates, 2006, p. 107))

"If you want something to be running, jumping, shouting, hitting, or exploding, it's the verb department you need to consult." (Sam Leith, *Write to the Point*, 2018, p. 58)

Verbs help us to **ask** and **answer** questions, **give commands and suggestions** and can be transitive and intransitive, main verbs or auxiliaries, regular or irregular, passive or active.

Transitive verbs require one or two objects, while intransitive verbs do not need a direct object. Some verbs can be transitive in one sentence and intransitive in another.

Transitive verbs:

accept	*cost*	*have*	*pick*
admit	*cover*	*hear*	*put*
allow	*demand*	*hold*	*raise*
beat	*destroy*	*include*	*realize*
bring	*discover*	*join*	*say*
build	*enjoy*	*kill*	*send*
buy	*expect*	*know*	*suppose*
carry	*express*	*lay*	*take*
catch	*feed*	*let*	*tell*
cause	*find*	*like*	*wear*
consider	*force*	*make*	
contain	*give*	*mean*	

Intransitive verbs

Act	*dream*	*live*	*sit*
Agree	*fall*	*look*	*sleep*
Appear	*go*	*matter*	*stand*
Arrive	*happen*	*occur*	*step*
Belong	*laugh*	*rain*	*talk*
Care	*lie*	*remain*	*think*
Come	*listen*	*rise*	*wait*

Verbs that can be **transitive and intransitive**

Move	*start*	*change*	*close*
Open	*stop*	*do*	*play*
Run	*live*	*wash*	*write*

DISCOVER: Ask your students to read the following passages, and check the verbs to see if they are **transitive** or **intransitive**:

"He was now having breakfast on the verandah of his room and he looked forward to spending a lazy day wandering about the pleasant town. He frowned slightly when a letter was brought in to him. On the evening of his arrival he had attended a large and dull dinner party at the Residency and on the day following another at the Club. He guessed that the letter was an invitation to a party of the same nature and he wondered whether there was any means by which he could politely refuse it. But though it was an invitation it was not of the sort he expected."

(Somerset Maugham, *Far Eastern Tales*, 1994, p. 123)

"They went back to the bungalow. Harold bathed himself and had a nap. After dinner they talked long and quietly. He admitted that before he married her he had occasionally drunk more than was good for him; in outstations it was easy to fall into bad habits. He agreed to everything that Millicent asked. And during the months before it was necessary for her to go to Kuala Solor for her confinement, Harold was an excellent husband, tender, thoughtful, proud and affectionate; he was irreproachable. A launch came to fetch her, she was to leave him for six weeks, and he promised faithfully to drink nothing during her absence. He put his hands on her shoulders." (166)

"Neil did not in the least know what to make of Darya Munro. She skipped over the first stages of acquaintance and treated him at once like someone she had known intimately all her life. It puzzled him. It seemed so reckless. When she met anyone his own instinct was to go cautiously. He was amiable, but he did not like to step too far before he saw his way before him. He did not want to give anyone his confidence before he thought himself justified. But with Darya you could not help yourself; she forced your confidence. She poured out the feelings and thoughts that most people keep to themselves like a prodigal flinging gold pieces to a scrambling crowd. She did not talk, she did not act like anyone he had ever known. She did not mind what she said. She would speak of the natural functions of the human animal in a way that brought the blushes coursing to his cheeks. (198)

Transitive	Intransitive
Attended	frowned
_____	_____
_____	_____
_____	_____
_____	_____
_____	_____

TWO-WORD VERBS - SEPARABLE

VERB	MEANING
Back up	support
Blow out	extinguish
Break down	disassemble
Bring up	raise (children, a topic in class)
Call off	cancel
Call up	telephone
Do over	do again
Figure out	understand
Fill out	complete
Get up	arouse from bed
Give up	abandon
Hand in	submit
Hang up	place on hook
Hold up	delay
Keep up	maintain
Leave out	omit
Let down	lower
Look over	review, examine
Look up	search for

Make out	distinguish
Make up	compose/invent/use cosmetics
Pack up	gather in a container
Pass out	distribute
Pick out	choose
Pick up	lift, collect
Put away	remove
Put off	postpone
Put on	don
Put out	extinguish
Take back	return
Take off	remove
Take up	raise, discuss
Talk over	discuss
Throw away	discard
Try on	test the fit and appearance
Try out	test
Turn down	reject/lower the volume
Turn in	deliver, submit
Turn off	stop power, shut off
Turn on	start power, put on

NON-SEPARABLE TWO-WORD VERBS

Back out of (something)	fail to keep a commitment
Break down	stop functioning
Break up with	end a relationship with
Break into	enter forcibly
Call on	ask (someone) to respond
Come back	return
Come over	visit
Come to	regain consciousness
Count on	depend on
Cross out	delete, eliminate
Fill in for (someone)	substitute
Find out	discover
Get along with	have a friendly relationship with
Get around	avoid
Get by	succeed with a minimum effort
Get over	recover
Get through	finish
Get up	arise

Go along	agree
Go away	leave
Go over	review
Keep on	continue
Look for	search
Look forward to	feel happy about some
Look into	investigate
Look like	resemble
Look out	beware
Look up	respect
Make out	succeed
Pass out	faint
Put up with	tolerate
Run into	meet accidentally
Run across	find accidentally
Run out of	exhaust
Settle on	decide, choose
Show up	appear
Take after	resemble
Take off	leave
Talk back	answer rudely
Wait on	serve

UNDERSTANDING AND USING TWO-WORD VERBS

DISCOVER: Ask your students to select from the following list of words the correct synonym for each of the italicized two-word verbs in the following sentences, and rewrite everything in their own words:

reject	resemble	appear	submit	choose
examine	stop functioning	cancel	complete	
raise	depend	review	test	abandon

1. Remember *to turn in* your income tax report before April 15th.

   _____

2. The two kids *take after* their mother very much in appearance.

   _____

3. How many people do you suppose will *show up* at the party tonight?

   _____

4. We think the committee *will turn down* his application.

   _____

5. If you like those apples, why don't you *pick out* one or two?

   _____

6. We need *to call off* the barbecue party because of the weather.

   _____

7. *Look* each word *over* carefully before you finish your assignment.

   _____

8. *Fill out* those forms with the correct information.

   _____

9. The computer *broke down* unexpectedly.

   _____

10. Jackie *brought up* a very interesting question.

    _____

11. You can *try out* your new idea in class tomorrow.

    _____

12. You can always *count on* me to help you.

    _____

13. My sister *gave up* a very good job to get married.

    _____

14. If we don't understand the new topic, our teacher will *go over* it with us.

    _____

UNDERSTANDING AND USING TWO-WORD VERBS

I. Fill in the blanks with the correct information using two-word verbs:

1. If the coat is too warm, I am going to take _____ _____.

2. You should do things on time. Don't put _____ _____ until later.

3. If you don't understand the question now, you will probably figure _____ _____ later.

4. Here is the application form you requested. Fill _____ _____ carefully.

5. If those words don't belong there, why don't you take _____ _____?

6. We all know he does not feel good about his failure, but we are sure he will get _____ _____ soon.

7. I can't find the pictures we took yesterday, but I have a feeling I will run _____ _____ later on.

8. Whenever you don't understand a new word, you can look _____ _____ in a dictionary.

9. Your question was quite embarrassing. Why did you bring _____ _____?

10. We arrived late because the bad weather held _____ _____.

11. I don't see how you can put up _____ with such bad working conditions.

12. If you go to next counter, the clerk there will wait _____ _____.

13. I submitted an application, but the committee turned _____ _____.

14. I missed two assignments. I am planning to make _____ _____ over the weekend.

15. This new concept is quite interesting. We have to look _____ _____ again.

16. These are very important details. Don't leave _____ _____!

17. If you find unnecessary things on our list, why don't you cross _____ _____?

18. Bobby is quite dependable. You can always count _____ _____ to help you.

II. Use the following two-word verbs with their prepositions in your own sentences:

To do away with _____

To feel up to _____

To go in for _____

To give in to   _____

To make up for   _____

To run out of   _____

To watch out for   _____

To keep up with   _____

To get along with   _____

To drop in on   _____

To hang on to   _____

To get away with   _____

To catch on to   _____

Verb Tenses

DISCOVER Ask the students to check their knowledge of verb tenses and write their own sentences using the following time words and expressions:

In a few minutes _____

Between 8:00 and 9:00 tonight _____

Ago _____

Right now _____

Just now _____

By the time _____

Yet _____

Every summer _____

Last night _____

Since I arrived _____

At this time _____

By the end of this month _____

While _____

For two semesters _____

Still _____

All day yesterday _____

At this same time tomorrow _____

So far _____

For a long time _____

This semester _____

Many times in the past _____

Thirty-eight hours a week _____

Up to now _____

Between 2003 and 2015 _____

Your own _____

The Future Tense

THE IDEA OF future in English is expressed in many ways, and that gives the speaker or the writer a chance to express various nuances of the language. Since our culture is a culture of people who like to project themselves into the future, future tenses may be formulated using a wide array of grammatical structures:

1. WILL and GOING TO may be used to show that we are planning to do something in the future or to make a prediction based on our opinion or life experience.

   Look at the sky. It looks like there's *going to be* a storm.

   Our meeting *will begin* at 10:00 a.m.

2. SIMPLE PRESENT can sometimes be used to show "fixed, unchangeable events."

   Please remember our classes *start* at 9:00 on weekdays next month.

   We'd better hurry. The movie *starts* at 8:00 p.m.

3. ALSO

   In time clauses and in *If* clauses, we use Simple Present, not Future:

   Don't forget to call you family *after you finish* the exam.

   If everything goes well, you will definitely reach the hill top before sunset.

4. PRESENT CONTINUOUS may also be used to indicate a future action:

   Are you *going* to the party, or *are* you *coming* with us to see the game?

5. TO BE TO + Infinitive is commonly used to show that an action is scheduled or likely to happen in the future:

   The President *is to address* the Senate tomorrow.

6. TO BE ABOUT TO + Infinitive should be used mostly in conversations when the speaker focuses on the very near future:

   We *are about to leave* for the mountains.

7. If we think or know something will happen soon, we resort to phrases like

    TO BE ON THE VERGE OF   TO BE ON THE BRINK OF

    TO BE DUE TO   TO BE SURE TO

    Doctors *are on the brink of discovering* a new drug for cancer.

    People in that area *are on the verge of starvation* if nothing is done right away.

8. When we talk about intentions, we may use certain verbs followed by a to-Infinitive:

    Do you *intend to buy* or *to lease* that car?

9. In similar cases, other verbs may be used to express future: **to agree, to aim, to expect, to hope, to plan, to promise, to propose, to resolve, to undertake, to want:**

    We are expecting to see the new movie star on Broadway next fall.

    I *hope to see* you the next time you come to New York.

PRACTICE

"Complete the text using the verbs given. Choose **will** ('ll) or **(be) going to** with each verb, depending on which is more appropriate.

1. A: I can't come during the day.

    B: I _____ you tomorrow evening, then. (*see*)

2. The method is quite simple, and I'm sure it _____ familiar to most of you already. (*be*)

3. Have you seen Karen recently? She _____ another baby. (*have*)

4. A: Did you get the theater tickets?

    B: No, I forgot all about them. I _____ them tomorrow. (*book*)

5. Wherever you go in Brazil, you _____ the people friendly. (*find*)

6. John says he _____ a politician when he grows up – and he's only 5 years old! (be)

7. Are these skis yours? _____ you _____ skiing? (*take up*)"

                        (Martin Hewings, *Advanced Grammar in Use*, 2005, p. 19)

"Underline the correct answers. In some cases both alternatives are possible.

1. You need to work much harder if you *have/are to have* any chance of passing the exam.

2. My sister *is to start/is about to start* a PhD in physics.

3. If you *enjoy/are to enjoy* romantic comedies, then this is a film you must see.

4. If the university *keeps/is to keep* its international reputation, it must first invest in better facilities for students.

5. Jim Brandon has denied that *he is to resign/is about to resign* as marketing manager.

6. If the railway system *is improved/is to be improved*, the government should invest substantial amounts of money now." (p. 25)

"Complete the sentences with these verb pairs. Use either the present simple or present continuous for the first verb. If both tenses are possible, write them both.

aim – to study	expect – to finish	~~look – to replace~~
intend - to move	propose – to deal	resolve – to give up
guarantee – to find		

1. My computer is now 5 years old, and I'*m looking to replace* it with a faster one.

2. In the first half of the course we'll study microbiology, and in the second half I _____ with genetic engineering.

3. We haven't completed the work yet, but we _____ it later this week.

4. I haven't done much work at college so far, but I _____ harder during the rest of the course.

5. Every New Year he _____ smoking, but by February he has started again.

6. We can't provide the spare parts ourselves, but we _____ a supplier who can.

7. At the moment I commute for over three hours a day, but I _____ closer to my work in the next few months." (27)

General Review Of
The Tenses

Write the correct form of the verb or verbs in parentheses in each sentence.

1. At present, my friend Arthur (write) a long novel about the Civil War.

2. I think his book (become) a "best seller" when it (publish) next year.

3. Arthur got the original idea for the book while he (go) to college.

4. When I saw Arthur last June, he (write) 125 pages of the book.

5. Arthur is very prolific. He (write) four books and 43 articles.

6. Although Arthur enjoys writing, he (like) to be a history teacher.

7. We would prefer that Mr. Hill (speak) to Mr. Hull himself.

8. I strongly suspected that Mr. Hull (speak, already) to Mr. Hall.

9. Mr. Hall will speak to Mr. Howell before he (leave) the office.

10. Mr. Howell, our director, (work) for this company nine years.

11. Mr. Hill interrupted Mr. Hull while he (speak) to Mr. Howell.

12. Do you think that the subways (run) behind schedule lately?

13. Yes, but at this time, much attention (devote) to that problem.

14. I wish that I (know) more about that particular problem than I do.

15. When you have read today's paper, you (understand) everything.

16. The plant earth (move) around the sun once every 365 days.

17. This fact (prove) by Brahe and Kepler more than 300 years ago.

18. We'll meet Alice at the corner. She (wait) when we (arrive).

19. As I (go) to work today. I saw Alice on her way downtown.

20. Whenever I meet Alice on the street, she (wear) something new

21. It (rain) very much in this part of the country every spring.

22. When I (leave) my office last night, it (rain, still) very hard.

23. The radio announcer said that it (be) cloudy and cold tomorrow.

24. Ever since Jim (win) that $60,000 contest, he (refuse) to work.

25. Jim will never look for a job unless some (force) him to do it.

26. If Jim (win, not) that contest, he (resign, not) from his good job.

27. When I discovered my camera (steal), I called the police right away.

28. The police think that the camera (take) sometime during the day.

29. If I (take) the camera with me yesterday, all of this (happen, not).

(From Grant Taylor, *Mastering American English*.1956. New York: McGraw-Hill Book Company, Inc., p. 166)

NOTES

_____

_____

_____

_____

_____

WOULD

WOULD FOR HABITUAL ACTIONS

1. On Saturdays, when I was a child, I would get up early, I would take the dog with me, and I would go for a walk around the block. In the afternoon I would go for a swim, or I would go fishing.

2. On Sundays when we were kids, my mother would gather us around the table, would sing a nice song, and would ask all of us to join her in chorus. We would laugh and she would serve our favorite food, the wonderful pancakes with strawberry and we would thank her.

3. We lived by the lake, and sometimes Dad would take us for a boat ride or would give us lessons in fishing.

WOULD IN INDIRECT SPEECH

1. He said, "I will see you after the meeting."

   _____

2. The Station Master said, "Don't worry! The train will arrive soon."

   _____

3. They said, "We will be back tomorrow."

   _____

WOULD in IF CLAUSES

1. If I have enough time tonight, I will definitely watch a ball game on TV.

   If I had enough time right now, I would _____.

2. If we have eggs, we will make a cake.

   If we had enough eggs, we would _____.

3. If I can get the keys, I will show you the cellar.

   If I had the keys, I would _____.

WOULD IN POLITE REQUESTS

1. **Do you want me to wrap these gifts for you?**

   If you would . . .

2. **Do you want me to call for a taxi?**

   If you would . . .

NOTES

_____

_____

_____

_____

_____

ADVERBS

This is how the *Cambridge Dictionary* defines the adverb: "*a word that describes or gives more information about another word, especially a verb, adjective, or another adverb, or about a phrase.*" These adverbs are important because they indicate time, manner, place, degree and frequency of something.

Types of adverbs

1.	**Manner** – modifies the verb	*quickly, anxiously, badly*
2.	**Place and direction** – modifies the verb	*around, away, down, toward*
3.	**Time** – modifies the verb	*tonight, recently, rarely*
4.	**Intensifying**	
	a. Degree –modifies an adjective or adverb	*very, absolutely*
	b. Emphasizing – modifies all parts of speech	*really* (unhappy), *even* (she)
5.	**Conjunctive adverb** – modifies the sentence	*moreover, therefore*
6.	**Sentence adverb** – modifies the sentence	*actually, unfortunately*

I noticed that **some ESL students avoid using adverbs,** and I was wondering why. I don't think I have a definite answer, but I guess it's because they don't know exactly where to put the adverbs in the sentence.

Suggestion: Work with your students, and challenge them to use at least one adverb in each of the following sentences, making sure they follow the correct word order:

1. Some students come to class late. (*Sometimes*)

2. My little sister failed to bring our mother a gift for her birthday. (*Never*)

3. My neighbor is regarded in the community.   (*Highly*)

4. They have expressed the same opinions about everything.   (*Always*)

5. You misunderstood what I've been telling you.   (*Completely*)

6. Our chemistry class has prepared the experiment.   (*Carefully*)

7. The professor has been invited to give a speech about data analysis.   (*Recently*)

8. The young man was accused of making the wrong statement.   (*Falsely*)

9. You should steam the vegetables for five minutes.   (*Slowly*)

10. I don't want to lose my advantage in the debate.   (*Obviously*)

Suggestion for more advanced students: Ask them to produce original sentences using the adverbs that required the reversed word order when they used at the beginning:

1. *Hardly ever*
2. *Seldom*
3. *No sooner*
4. *Scarcely*
5. *Not only*

ADVERBS OF FREQUENCY

I am	*always*	at home on Sundays
I can	*hardly*	understand what that man says.
Do you	*often*	play tennis?
They don't	*often*	go to bed late.
You don't	*usually*	arrive late, do you?
You should	*always*	try to be punctual.
She will	*occasionally*	offer to help.
We can	*generally*	get there in time.

Will he	*ever*	learn anything useful?
I wonder if they will	*ever*	improve.
I have	*rarely*	seen better work.
They can	*seldom*	find time for reading.
You must	*never*	do that again.

MID-POSITION ADVERBS

You	*almost*	managed it that time.
They	*already*	know about it.
His employers	*even*	offered him higher wages.
He	*just*	caught the train.
Mr. Green	*merely*	hinted at the possibility.
You	*nearly*	missed the bus.
I	*only*	wanted to ask you the time.
I	*quite*	understand.
We	*rather*	like it.
They	*soon*	found what they wanted.
She	*still*	hopes to get news of him.
I	*hardly*	know what to do.
Mr. White	*quite*	agreed with me.
The engine	*still*	makes a lot of noise.

(A.S. Hornby, *A Guide to Patterns and Usage in English,* 1970, pp. 182-185)

PRACTICE: Use the following **collocations in original sentences**:

... always drives ...   ... almost fell ...
... isn't usually ...   ... quickly my breakfast ...
... at the airport early ...   ... immediately after hearing the news...
... hardly followed the directions ... ... will probably be cancelled ...

Conjunctive Adverbs

Contrast   *However*

                       Nevertheless

                       Nonetheless

                       Still

                       On the contrary

Result or effect   *Hence*

                       Therefore

                       Consequently

                       As a result

Addition   *Moreover*

                       Furthermore

                       Also

                       Besides

                       In fact

Condition   *Otherwise*

Time   *Then*

                       Afterwards

                       Later (on)

Similarity   *Similarly*

                       Likewise

NOTES

_____

_____

_____

_____

_____

Exercises Using Conjunctive Adverbs

Complete and punctuate the following sentences:

1. Mom told me I must eat my vegetables _____ I could not have dessert.

2. Mom told me to eat my vegetables before having dessert _____ I ate dessert first.

3. Mom let me watch TV and talk on the phone _____ she said I could stay up as late as I wanted.

4. My brother passed all tests _____ he was number one in class.

5. I studied very hard _____ I passed the test with a very high score.

Finish the following:

1. Most of my friends hated math; **on the contrary,**

   _____

2. All the students paid attention in class today; **furthermore,**

   _____

3. George is brilliant when it comes to computers; **however,**

   _____

4. Some married students find it difficult to study at home; **consequently,**

   _____

5. At first, I wanted to join the student demonstration: **later on**

   _____

Provide the beginning of the following:

1. _____;   **otherwise**, I would have failed the final test.

2. _____;   **consequently**, I have a bad cold.

3. _____;   **therefore**, my sister was nominated for graduate scholarship.

4. _____;   **likewise**, a business manager
                              takes care of his company.

5. _____;   **then** I asked another question.

DISCOVER   Write original sentences and put together a short paragraph:

Some people think   _____ .

On the contrary,   _____ .

Moreover,   _____ .

In fact,   _____ .

Otherwise,   _____ .

Therefore,   _____ .

In conclusion,   _____ .

DISCOVER the use of adjectives vs. adverbs in this short passage:

"There in the mist, **enormous, majestic, silent, and terrible**, stood the
Great Wall of China. **Solitarily**, with the indifference of nature itself, it
crept up the mountain side and slipped down to the depth of the valley.
Menacingly, the **grim** watch towers, **stark and foursquare**, at due
intervals stood at their posts. **Ruthlessly**, for it was built at the cost of a
million lives and each one of those **great** stones have been stained with
the **bloody** tears of the captive and the outcast, it forged its **dark** way
through a sea of **rugged** mountains. **Fearlessly**, it went on its **endless**
journey, league upon league to the **furthermost** regions of Asia, in
utter solitude, **mysterious** like the **great** empire it guarded. There in the
mist, **enormous, majestic, silent, and terrible**, stood the **Great** Wall of
China."

(W. Somerset Maugham, *On a Chinese Screen*, 1990. New York:
Paragon House, p. 113)

Change the following adjectives into adverbs and then use them in a complete
sentence. Remember some words can be used as adjectives and adverbs.

Adjective	Adverb	Original sentence
Wrong	_____	_____
Hard	_____	_____
Interesting	_____	_____
Respectful	_____	_____

True   _____   _____

Fast   _____   _____

Sincere   _____   _____

Early   _____   _____

Fortunate   _____   _____

Late   _____   _____

Recent   _____   _____

NOTES

_____

_____

_____

_____

_____

EVEN - EVEN IF – EVEN THOUGH

Common mistakes:
*Even I know the answer, I cannot explain it in my own words.
He is a very nice guy. *Even though, I don't trust him.
The teacher got very angry; *even she told me to leave the classroom.
*Even she can't drive, she bought a car.

Even can be an adjective or an adverb, but our ESL students have problems with this word because in some languages EVEN, EVEN IF, and EVEN THOUGH are one word, not three.

As an adverb, EVEN is used to give special emphasis to a word or words.
Even *a child* can describe a car.
We had to do homework, **even** *on Sundays*.
It was so quiet, I could not hear anything, **not even** *a snowflake fall* on the grass.

As an adverb, EVEN can be **used to emphasize** IF and THOUGH, but it **cannot be used alone as a conjunction.**
We are going to take the test this afternoon **even if** we are not prepared.
You need to answer that question **even if** you think it's personal.

Even though is used to replace *although*:
I enjoyed the movie, **even though** it was quite long.

Even so is an adverb phrase, meaning *however*:
They seem to be very nice people. **Even so**, very few people trust them.

"Put in *even, even if,* or *even though*:

1. ___ *Even though* ___ she can't drive, she bought a car.
2. The bus leaves in two minutes. We won't catch it now _____ we run.

3. His Spanish isn't very good - _____ after three years in Mexico.

4. His Spanish isn't very good _____ he's lived in Mexico for three years.

5. _____ with the heat on, it was very cold in the house.

6. I couldn't sleep _____ I was very tired.

7. I won't forgive them for what they did _____ they apologize.

8. _____ I hadn't eaten anything for 24 hours, I wasn't hungry."

(Raymond Murphy, *Grammar in Use*, 2009, p. 219)

Pronouns

A pronoun is a part of speech that replaces a noun or a pronoun phrase. James W. Pennebaker wrote an article published in the **Harvard Business Review** entitled *Your Use of Pronouns Reveals Your Personality*. Basically, this is what he said in his finding:

"A person's use of function words – the pronouns, articles, prepositions, conjunctions, and auxiliary verbs that are the connective tissue of language – offers deep insights into his or her honesty, stability, and sense of self." (December 2011 issue)

Types of pronouns:

1.	Personal pronouns:	*I, me, you, he, him, she, her, it, we, us, they, them*
2.	Possessive pronouns:	*mine, yours, his, hers, its, theirs, ours, theirs*
3.	Demonstrative pronouns:	*this, that, these, those*
4.	Interrogative pronouns:	*who, whom, whose, which, what*
5.	Indefinite pronouns:	*all, another, any, everyone, several, some*
6.	Reflexive pronouns	*myself, yourself, himself, herself, itself*
7.	Relative pronouns:	*who, whom, whose, which, that*
8.	Reciprocal pronouns:	*each other, one another*

SUBJECT+PREDICATE AGREEMENT WITH INDEFINITE PRONOUNS
Indefinite pronouns do not refer to a specific person or thing; they refer to a person or thing not identified or possibly not even known. Most are always singular (*everyone, each, everything, everybody, everyone, someone, somebody,*

something, anyone, anybody, anything, no one, nobody, nothing); some are always plural (*both, many*); a few may be singular or plural (*all, any, some, none*).

ALL	EVERYBODY	NO ONE
ANOTHER	EVERYONE	NOTHING
ANY	EVERYTHING	ONE
ANYONE	FEW	OTHER
ANYTHING	MANY	OTHERS
BOTH	MORE	SEVERAL
EACH	MOST	SOME
EITHER	NEITHER	SOMEBODY
NOBODY	NONE	SOMETHING

Suggestion: Students should work in small pairs/groups and choose the correct form of the verb to agree with the subject(s):

1. All of the beaches was/were eroded by the winter storms.

2. Nothing in the garage sale cost/costs more than $5.00.

3. All the reviews of the new Broadway show was/were very good.

4. Each of the essay questions take/takes about twenty minutes to complete.

5. Some of the jury think think/thinks the accused is innocent.

6. There are many different ideas about food; some people prefer/prefers spicy dishes, but others don't/doesn't.

7. Everyone in our class was/were working hard to find the solution to the problem.

8. In the results of the survey, each statistic contradict/contradicts the other.

USING **OF** IN QUANTITY EXPRESSIONS

A. Quantity word followed by of + specific noun:

The verb agrees with the noun that precedes it.

Most of these **chairs are** new.

In this room, most of **the furniture is** new.

B. Quantity word followed by nonspecific nouns:

 The verb agrees with the noun that precedes it.

> Most **people visit** their families during major holidays.

> All **students are required** to show their ID cards when they enter the building.

C. The speaker refers to a specific thing:

> **Most of the books**

> **All of her money**

D. Specific nouns are preceded by a determiner: **those, my, the**, etc.

E. The speaker is not referring to a specific thing:

> **Most textbooks**

> **All visitors**

Suggestion: See if the students can use the preposition OF (THE) correctly in the following examples:

1. Most _____ products have labels stating where they were made.

2. Most _____ her clothes were gifts from her parents.

3. Some _____ students enjoy the challenge of new ideas.

4. Some _____ students in my class really enjoy working together.

NOTES

_____

_____

_____

_____

Suggestion: Alone or in small groups, students should be able to do the following exercise in matching:

1.	Some of the museums in the city	A.	contains a lot of violence.
2.	All of the bookstores at the mall	B.	are celebrated in every country.
3.	Some holidays like the New Year	C.	learn English overnight; it takes time.
4.	All industry	D.	is very violent.
5.	Most people with a positive attitude	E.	celebrate by exchanging gifts.
6.	Most of the technological advances	F.	somehow affects the environment.
7.	Some TV movies	G.	are open on Mondays.
8.	At Christmas, some people	H.	greatly affect people's daily lives.
9.	None of the films I want to see	I.	have posters of famous paintings.
10.	Not many students	J.	learn a new subject quickly.

Suggestion: Ask the students to finish the following sentences with the correct use of the verbs:

1. Most of the luggage _____
2. Everybody in the office _____
3. All of the information _____
4. Half of the cake _____
5. Neither of the neighbors _____
6. Each of the boys _____
7. Both of them _____
8. Everything the newspapers said _____
9. Everyone we know _____
10. Most of his furniture _____

QUESTION: What is the difference between ALMOST and MOST?

Almost describes **quantifiers** and shows **approximation**

Almost is an **adverb** meaning *nearly* qualifying verbs (He **almost** cried.); adjectives (The place was **almost** empty.); adverbs (He came **almost** immediately.); part of subject (**Almost** two years have passed.); part of object (The group donated **almost** nothing.).

Most describes **nouns** and shows **majority.**

Most is an **adjective** or pronoun meaning *the majority*:

Most cars have four doors.   **Most of** my friends like jazz.

NOTES

_____

_____

_____

_____

Some words are used as **various parts of speech**

About	We need to leave *about 6:00 a.m.*	(adverb)
	This is a book *about dogs.*	(preposition)
	The parade is *about to start.*	(adjective)
Above	Why don't you hang it *above the table?*	(preposition)
	Temperatures rose *above freezing.*	(adverb)
After	I go swimming every day *after work.*	(preposition)
	He changed his name *after* he left his country.	(conjunction)
	She came Sunday, and I got here the day *after.*	(adverb)
All	*All the children* gathered in the courtyard.	(adjective)
	We walked *all alone.*	(adverb)
	All are here.	(pronoun)
Before	I think I've seen you *before.*	(adverb)
	We'll know the result *before tomorrow.*	(preposition)
	The boss wants to talk to you *before* you go.	(conjunction)
Better	Your essay is *better than Jake's.*	(adjective)
	Better late than never.	(adverb)
	Small classes are a change for *the better.*	(noun)
Black	She was wearing a *black dress.*	(adjective)
	They *blacked* their faces before the show.	(verb)
	Among the colors, *black* is predominant.	(noun)
Both	I saw *both movies.*	(adjective)
	Both Joey *and* his sisters came to the party.	(conjunction)
	Both of my grandfathers were farmers.	(pronoun)

But	The car is old *but* reliable.	(conjunction)
	But me no *buts.*	(verb and noun)
	There's nobody here *but me.*	(preposition)
Content	The customs officer checked *the contents* of our bags.	(noun)
	I am not *content* with my essay.	(adjective)
	We have *to content* ourselves with what we have.	(verb)
Double	The manager asked me to work *double shifts.*	(adjective)
	The property *has doubled* in value.	(verb)
	The fall made him see *double.*	(adverb)
Down	I bent *down* to tie my shoes.	(adverb)
	They live *down the street.*	(preposition)
	We have never seen him so *down.*	(adjective)
	He *downed* his coffee and left the room.	(verb)
	We just bought a *down* pillow.	(noun)
Dry	The clothes *will dry* faster in the sun.	(verb)
	We were looking for a *dry spot.*	(adjective)
Express	You must *express* yourself very clearly.	(verb)
	The *express package* should arrive soon.	(adjective)
	Send it *express.*	(noun)
Fast	Jimmy is a *fast runner.*	(adjective)
	You *must fast* before the blood test.	(verb)
	We all observed *a fast* for several days.	(noun)
	They need to run *fast.*	(adverb)

Home	A *home run* meant victory.	(adjective)
	The man makes the house and the woman makes *the home*.	(noun)
	Is anybody *home*?	(adverb)
Inside	Go back *inside* and get your hat!	(adverb)
	Sources *inside the company* confirmed the results.	(preposition)
	The *inside box* looks very nice.	(adjective)
	The door was locked from *the inside*.	(noun)
Last	The first shall be *the last*.	(noun)
	Is this your *last response*?	(adjective)
	Does this jacket *last* longer?	(verb)
	When did you see her *last*?	(adverb)
Like	Nobody sings *like Jackie*.	(preposition)
	We *like* it.	(verb)
	We got a chance to meet people of *like minds*.	(adjective)
Near	Let's meet somewhere *near the library*.	(preposition)
	Is he a *near relative*?	(adjective)
	Is there a gas station *near* here?	(adverb)
Past	I know this from *past experience*.	(adjective)
	We now have to consider *the past*.	(noun)
	His house is just *past the bridge*.	(preposition)
Round	Draw a *round figure* here.	(adjective)
	The cars race *round and round*.	(adverb)
	A *round* of applause, please!	(noun)
	Let's *round* the troops.	(verb)

Since	I haven't seen him *since* he left.	(conjunction)
	I haven't seen him ever *since*.	(adverb)
	I haven't seen him *since the trial.*	(preposition)
That	I told him *that* he was right.	(conjunction)
	Nobody believed *that story.*	(adjective)
	Who told you *that*?	(pronoun)

DISCOVER

Provide dictionaries, and ask the students to figure out how many parts of speech they can find for the following words:

Either   except   iron   rest   right

_____

_____

_____

FUNCTION WORDS

IT IS vs. THERE IS

ESL students usually have problems when using these two structures. Some of them consider the two similar, while others simply translate from their native language what they think would be the equivalent in English. For languages where the verb TO BE is used sparingly or in certain expressions only, the challenge is even bigger.

Function word: THERE The word "there" is used as the false subject of certain English sentences. This means that the real subject appears later in the sentence.

There are many people waiting outside.

The logical subject of this sentence is "people,' but the speaker isn't focusing on the people themselves. Instead, he/she is talking about their existence: **there is, there are**. Therefore, "there" becomes the grammatical subject.

We should be very careful when using this grammar because the real subject (or noun) determines whether the verb is singular or plural.

There **is a book** on the desk.

There **are several books** on the desk.

We can also use other verb tenses and models with these structures:

a. **There have been many inquiries about this subject.**

b. **There could be another big snow tomorrow.**

c. **There will be plenty of time to finish the project.**

The question is easy to make by inversion:

Is there any cake left?   **Are there** any more questions?

The English language also has a common idiomatic noun clause that uses "there" as its subject:

There seems to be something wrong with his decision.
There appears to be a misunderstanding in this matter.

PRACTICE "Read the first sentence and then write a sentence beginning with *There* . . .

1.	The roads were busy today.	*There was a lot of traffic.*
2.	This soup is very salty.	*There . . . . . . in the soup.*
3.	The box was empty.	*. . . . . in the box.*
4.	The movie was very violent.	_____
5.	The shopping mall was very crowded.	_____
6.	I like this town – it's lively.	_____

(Raymond Murphy, *Grammar in Use*, 2011, p. 165)

Function word: IT

The word "it" is used as the subject of certain English sentences. In the following cases, it would be strange to use another word or it would be impossible without "it."

The first case includes:

a.	Time	**It is 2:45 p.m.**
b.	Distance	**It's only twenty miles from here.**
c.	Weather	**It was quite chilly this morning.**
d.	Temperature	**It's 85 degrees.**
e.	The inside or the outside environment	**It was very crowded on the bus.**

"It" is also used to answer questions with WHO (for identification)
A: Who's calling?
B: It's your brother.

"It" is used in certain collocations with adjectives:

Is it necessary to raise property taxes?
It's not easy to learn a foreign language.

Some noun clauses also begin with "it:"

It never occurred to me that he was going to ask this question.
It struck me that nobody else was leaving so early.
It looks like we are going to get some rain tonight.

Suggestion: Ask the students to produce their own original sentences:

1. Isn't it amazing _____ ?
2. It seems to us that _____ .
3. It's wonderful how_____ !
4. It didn't take much to _____ .
5. It takes a long time _____ .
6. It's quite easy_____

Suggestion: Work with the students and explain the following words. You or your students may want to use a dictionary:

Envy   *It is a desire to have what belongs to another.*

Efficiency   _____

Tardiness   _____

Enthusiasm   _____

Delight   _____

Bewilderment   _____

Boredom   _____

Entertainment   _____

Suggestion: Test the students' understanding of the two function words. Ask them to fill in the blanks with IT IS or THERE IS. Make sure they are using the correct tenses.

1. _____ _____ time to get up! _____ _____ already 8:00 a.m.
2. _____ _____ a lot of rain last weekend. _____ _____ floods everywhere.
3. _____ _____ very windy yesterday. _____ _____ impossible to go for a walk.
4. _____ _____ a funny smell here. _____ _____ gas I am smelling?
5. _____ _____ said that if you break a mirror you will be unlucky for seven years.
6. One weekend in January _____ _____ a heavy snow storm in our area. Luckily _____ _____ plenty of food in the refrigerator.
7. _____ _____ a swimming pool behind the garage?

8. Yes, _____ _____.

9. How deep _____ _____?

10. _____ _____ not a good idea to drive now when _____ _____ foggy outside.

11. _____ _____ lots of stories about this superstar, but _____ _____ not known exactly where he lives or where he spends his vacation.

12. Johnny says _____ _____ better to say nothing about our plans for the weekend.

13. _____ _____ very cold and windy last night.

14. Yes, _____ _____ heavy storms in our community.

15. We've done our best to solve the problem. _____ _____ nothing we can do expect wait and see what happens next.

16. As _____ _____ sunny after the rain this morning, they decided to go for a walk in the park.

PRACTICE "Are these sentences right or wrong? Change *it* to *there* where necessary.

1.	They live on a busy street. *It must be* a lot of noise.	*There must be a lot of noise.*
2.	Last winter it was very cold, and it was a lot of snow.	_____
3.	It used to be a church there, but it was torn down.	_____
4.	Why was she so unfriendly? It must have been a reason.	_____
5.	It's a long way from my house to the nearest store.	_____
6.	A: Where can we park the car?	_____
	B: Don't worry. It's sure to be a parking lot somewhere.	_____
7.	After the lecture, it will be an opportunity to ask questions.	_____

8. I like the place where I live, but it would be   _____
    nicer to live by the ocean.

9. I was told that it would be somebody to meet   _____
    me at the airport, but it wasn't anybody.

10. The situation is still the same. It has been no   _____
    change.

11. I don't know who'll win, but I'm sure to be a   _____
    good game."

(Raymond Murphy, *Grammar in Use*, 2011, p. 165)

FORMS OF OTHER

Another   Used as an adjective:

SINGULAR: I like these apples. Let me have *another one.*

PLURAL: *another five dollars, another ten miles, another two weeks*

Other   Used as an adjective:

Do you have any other questions?

The other   Meaning "the remaining of the two"   *the other hand*

Meaning "former or earlier"   *writing tools of other days*

Meaning "not long ago"   *the other night*

Others   Used as a pronoun (the plural form of *other*):

Some people think he is honest; *others* say he is not to be trusted.

Some like rap music; *others* like jazz.

The others   Meaning "the remaining"

One student failed, but *the others* passed.

Some other   Come and see me *some other* time.

Any other   *Any other* time but not today

Suggestion: Ask the students to provide the correct form of OTHER in the following cases:

1.   In just _____ three months, he will be a married man.

2.   I really can't go with you right now. It will have to be _____ time.

3.   Then we'll have to go on Friday. I don't have the time _____ day.

4. Most of the students have arrived and I am sure _____ will come soon.

5. Our instructor corrected a few papers, but she had no time to do _____.

6. Some people prefer pop music. _____ like classical music.

7. We invited six people to our party, but only four confirmed they were coming. _____ can't come.

8. Some people like apples, others like oranges, and _____ like bananas.

9. We get paid every _____ week.

10. I am afraid our little brother does not always play well with _____.

> "For *in* and *out, above, about, below*
> 'Tis nothing but a magic shadow show."
>
> Omar Khayam, *The Rubaiyat*

Prepositions

A PREPOSITION IS A part of speech that (usually) comes before a noun or a pronoun and expresses a temporal, spatial or other relationship.

SHORT LIST OF PREPOSITIONS

About	*before*	*despite*	*in*	*of*	*regarding*
Aboard	*behind*	*during*	*inside*	*off*	*round*
Across	*below*		*into*	*on*	
After	*beside*	*except*		*outside*	*through*
Among	*between*		*near*	*over*	*to*
Around	*beyond*	*for*	*next to*		*toward*
At	*by*	*from*		*past*	*with*

PREPOSITIONS OF TIME

On Sunday   **On** the weekend

In April   **in** the morning

At dawn   **at** 3:45 p.m.

Since 2015

For two days

Before midnight

Nine **to** five

From 9:00 a.m.

Till 5:00 p.m

By noon

PREPOSITIONS OF SPACE

In the living room

at the bus stop   **at** the movies

on the board   **on** the bus

beside the house   **by** the pool

between Boston and Washington, D.C.

behind the wall

over the fence

across the board

into the garden

towards the door

PHRASAL PREPOSITIONS

Regardless of
Irrespective of
As of
As per
In return for
As a result of
According to
Instead of
On behalf of
For the sake of
By way of
With reference to
In favor of
Owing to
Because of
In spite of
Due to
Prior to
Subject to
Ahead of
As well as
Short of
Out of
Contrary to
By means of

Suggestion: The list can go on the board or can be given out to the students. The assignment is the following: one group of students will choose 3 or 4 phrasal prepositions to be used at the beginning of the sentence. The other group will choose another set of phrasal prepositions and use them in the middle of original sentences.

For example:

Group 1:   *According to* our teacher, we have nothing to read over the weekend.

Group 2:   We are all *in favor of* extra points students should be given for originality.

Next,

Group 1 will teach the students in Group 2 how to use these structures at the beginning of the sentence.

Group 2 will teach the other students how to use these words in the middle of the sentence.

VERB-PREPOSITION COMBINATIONS + PREPOSITIONAL OBJECTS

1.	**Catch on to**	understand
2.	**Catch up with**	reach
3.	**Drop in on**	visit informally
4.	**Drop out of**	discontinue attendance or participation
5.	**Get along with**	be on good terms
6.	**Give in to**	surrender, yield
7.	**Go along with**	accept
8.	**Keep up with**	maintain the same pace/stay at the same level
9.	**Look down on**	consider as inferior
10.	**Look up to**	consider as superior
11.	**Put up with**	tolerate
12.	**Run out of**	exhaust a supply

Prepositional Phrase Structures

There are two kinds of prepositional phrases: *the basic* and *the idiomatic*. *Basic* prepositional phrases usually indicate *time* or *place* and are quite simple. Some examples are: *on top of the table, under the desk, at twelve o'clock*, etc. *Idiomatic* prepositional phrases often take the place of conjunctions. Some examples are: in spite of, by means of, on account of, etc.

Suggestion: Ask the students to work in pairs or small groups to finish the following sentences:

1. He was successful **by means of** _____.
2. We were able to enjoy our vacation **in spite of** _____.
3. **Regardless of** _____, she passed her license exam.
4. **In consideration of** _____, the judge reduced his sentence.

5. The new car is better than the old one **on account of**

_____

6. The ticket sales of the new show went up **as a result of**

_____

7. He was promoted **in view of** _____.

8. It isn't a very good plan. **For one thing,** _____.

In addition to the idiomatic prepositional phrases mentioned above, there are a few other kinds that are used in different ways. These include: _Sentence connectors, adverbials_, and _those that take a gerund or noun or pronoun._ Here is a short list of each type.

SENTENCE CONNECTORS	ADVERBIALS
In many respects (mainly)	**On purpose** (according to plan)
On the whole (generally speaking)	**By mistake** (not my intention)
By all means (certainly)	**On sale** (can be bought; lower price)
On the contrary (used to indicate the opposite situation)	**Off hand** (without having thought before speaking)
To some extent	**For good** (forever; not changing)

ADJECTIVE + PREPOSITION + GERUND or NOUN or PRONOUN

Afraid of	**concerned about**	**surprised at/by**	**upset over**
Fond of	**happy about**	**capable of**	**opposed to**
Disappointed in/with	**angry at (a person)**	**aware of**	**bored with**
Interested in	**worried about**	**conscious of**	**annoyed with**
Fearful of	**good at**	**ashamed of**	**delighted with**

VERB + PREPOSITION + GERUND or NOUN or PRONOUN

Agree with/on	**complain about**	**hear about**	**rely on**
Approve of	**consent to**	**laugh at**	**talk about**
Belong to	**consist of**	**listen to**	**wait for**
Believe in	**decide on**	**look at**	**wish for**
Care for	**depend on**	**pay for**	**work for**

Review of Prepositional Phrase Structures

These are some examples of each type:

1. **In many respects**, my new computer is better than my old one.
2. **By all means,** please come to my party tomorrow night.
3. I didn't break the window **on purpose**; it was an accident.
4. This machine is fixed **for good**; it shouldn't ever break down again.
5. Don't be **afraid of** the dark; there are no monsters!
6. I'm very **interested in** visiting the new supermarket this weekend.
7. This laptop **belongs to** that man.
8. I can't **consent to** paying that much money.

NOTE

In 1 and 2, the prepositional phrases introduce a sentence; in 3 and 4, the phrases are used as adverbs; in 5, 6, 7, and 8, they are used with either a noun or a gerund afterwards.

QUESTIONS FROM STUDENTS

_____

_____

_____

_____

_____

NOTES

_____

_____

_____

_____

_____

EXERCISES IN PREPOSITIONAL PHRASES

SUGGESTION Students can work in pairs/small groups and fill in the **correct prepositional phrase** in each sentence. In some cases, there may be several possible answers.

1. I am very _____ *fond of* _____ apples; I eat them all the time and I think they are delicious.

2. _____, I liked that movie very much. The only thing I didn't like was the music.

3. I'm not sure you broke the computer mouse _____, but I'd like you to be more careful in the future.

4. Are you _____ traveling to Greece on vacation this winter? I am sure it'll be a lot of fun.

5. I'm very _____ you. I was sure you'd be at the airport to pick me up, but I couldn't find you anywhere.

6. Let's go to Macy's on Saturday. There are many things _____ and I want to get a lot of things without spending too much money.

7. _____, I think the service at the hotel was very good, but the beds were a little too hard.

8. _____, I think that the plan wouldn't work at all. It's much too expensive and it would take too many people to do it.

9. We _____ going to the mountains on vacation after discussing the topic for quite a while.

10. I'd say _____ that we could send the package for under $10, but I never really thought about it before.

11. I'm _____ driving on the highway because people drive too quickly and dangerously there.

12. Colin resembles his grandfather _____.

13. _____, the weather here is like the weather in my country.

QUESTIONS FROM STUDENTS

_____

_____

_____

_____

_____

EXTRA PRACTICE WITH PREPOSITIONS IN IDIOMATIC EXPRESSIONS

More advanced students should try the following common idiomatic expressions:

1. I am going to settle the matter once and __for_____ all.

2. _____ case anybody calls, tell them I'll be back after lunch.

3. The dean said I had to take _____ least twelve credits a semester.

4. I think our neighbor's suggestion is ____ _____ the question.

5. She didn't seem to be excited _____ the least about the news.

6. He works very hard, or _____ any rate, he gives that impression.

7. I wish he would come _____ the point. We don't know what he wants.

8. Professor Jackson called my attention _____ that matter.

9. Miss Simpson makes most __ her clothes ____ hand.

10. _____ the most part, his explanations are quite clear.

11. The teacher said we had to learn those expressions _____ heart.

12. We had to postpone our barbecue party _____ account of the bad weather.

13. _____ long, you will be speaking like a native.

14. _____ the circumstances, the only thing we can do is wait.

15. _____ the event _____ trouble, call me right away.

16. Were you able to make use _____ the book I lent you last week?

17. What's the use _____ telling him the truth?

18. The elevator isn't running now. It must be _____ _____ order.

19. That is last year telephone directory. It must be _____ _____ date.

20. All _____ all, we had a good time during our last vacation.

21. First _____ all, you should present your idea to the other students in class.

22. The teacher said Tommy was _____ far the best student in class.

23. It's too bad he didn't take advantage _____ the opportunity.

24. This tool is quite sophisticated. _____ that case, you should use it very carefully.

25. _____ the time being, I suggest we shouldn't tell him anything.

26. Aren't you happy you came to the party _____ all?

NOTES

_____

_____

_____

_____

_____

AS vs LIKE

AS and LIKE are prepositions or conjunctions.

I worked *as a teacher.*   (I was a teacher.)
She is dressed *like a princess.*   (This is just a comparison; she is
not a princess.)

The prepositions **like** and **as** have different meanings.

Like = similar to   **As = in the role of**

Like is a preposition and is usually followed by a noun, a pronoun, or *–ing*. We use like to compare things.

I wish I could fly **like a bird**.   (I am not a bird)

As can be used as a preposition or as a conjunction. As a preposition, **as** is followed by a noun:

We sometimes use our basement **as a workshop.**

When used as a conjunction, **as** is followed by a sentence:

Nobody understands you **as I do.**

Like is sometimes used instead of **as** in informal English:

Like I said before . . .   INFORMAL
As I said before . . .   FORMAL

PRACTICE

Fill in the blanks using *as* or *like*:

1. Talking to him is _____ talking to a wall.

2. I like this jacket _____ is.

3. I will see you this afternoon _____ usual.

4. Getting a good answer from some students is _____ pulling teeth.

5. Please don't use my desk _____ an ashtray.

Use the following structures in original sentences:
As a last resort   like a native speaker   just as I thought   like a maniac

_____

_____

_____

Please check the Appendices for extra exercises with AS and LIKE

CONJUNCTIONS

COORDINATING

For	And	Nor	But	Or	Yet	So
f	a	n	b	o	y	s

SUBORDINATING

Cause and effect:	as		since	because	so that
Concession:	although		whereas	though	even though	while
Condition:	if		only if	unless	provided that	in case
Comparison:	rather than		whether	as much as	whereas
Time and place:	once	while	when	whenever	wherever	before	after

PRACTICE: Ask the students to read the following passage and underline and then make two separate lists: **one of coordinating conjunctions** and **the other one of subordinating conjunctions** as they are used in the story:

"In the early years of the fifth century of the Christian era a boy of sixteen was captured by the Roman soldiers in Gaul and enslaved in Ireland. The boy, who had come to know the more civilized customs of the Romans, looked about him in dismay and wonder at the state of barbarity of the native Celts. These warlike, superstitious people were the original inhabitants of the islands before the Romans first came to their shores under the leadership of Julius Caesar in 55 B.C. More than three hundred years of Roman rule had not civilized them even in Britain, and in Ireland they were still wilder. Led by their cruel Druid priests, who held them in bondage and even demanded human sacrifices from them, they roamed the mountains of Wales and Scotland and across the sea in Ireland. There, they kept their pagan ways and lived little differently than had the cave men of prehistoric times.

The boy, whose name was Saccath (or Sucat), worked for six years as a slave tending sheep in the Irish hills. He finally escaped to the coast and made his way home, but he couldn't rest for thinking of the sad state of the Irish people. He determined to dedicate his life to them and set about preparing himself for his future work by studying for the priesthood.

By that time the Romans had ceased to persecute Christians and had taken up the new religion themselves. If fact, it was they who did more than any others to spread Christianity throughout all the countries they governed and new lands they conquered.

When Saccath finished his studies and was ordained he asked to be sent to Ireland. His wish was granted, and through the good offices of St. Germanus he was made a bishop and sent on his mission. He organized the Christians who were already there and he made new converts. The hardships and dangers he faced among these cruel and barbaric people were great, but his patience was greater and he won many over to the gentler ways of Christianity. He established schools, and soon his pupils went out to help others. The Pope was so pleased with his work that he gave him the honorary name of Patricius, meaning 'noble.' We know him better as **Saint Patrick**, the patron saint of the country he started on its way to civilization.

Saint Patrick laid his foundations so well that in the following centuries his once wild and pagan country became one of the seats of learning for Europe. Perhaps the most important thing he taught the Irish was to write with Roman letters."

(Oscar Ogg, *The 26 Letters*, New York: The Thomas Y. Crowell Company, 1964, pp. 146-149)

"*Think and respond.* Read the following paragraphs. Use your dictionaries to find the meanings of the underlined words. Then, complete the sentences based on the reading, in writing.

Albert Einstein (1879-1955)

In his early years, Einstein showed no <u>obvious</u> sign of genius. He did not even talk until the age of three. In high school, in Germany, he hated the system of <u>rote</u> learning and the <u>drill sergeant</u> attitude of his teachers; as a result, he annoyed them with his <u>rebellious</u> attitude. One of his teachers remarked, 'You will never amount to anything.'

Yet, there were also <u>hints</u> of the man to be. At five, when he was given a compass, he was fascinated by the mysterious force that made the needle move. Before <u>adolescence,</u> Einstein went through a very religious period, and he frequently argued violently with his <u>freethinking</u> father, because his father <u>strayed</u> from the path of Jewish <u>orthodoxy</u>. However, Einstein calmed down after he began studying science, math, and philosophy on his own. He especially loved math. At age sixteen, he <u>devised</u> one of his first 'thought experiments.' These are experiments that an individual must do in the mind; they cannot be done in the laboratory.

Within a year after his father's business failed and the family moved to Northern Italy to start a new business, Einstein <u>dropped out</u> of school and <u>renounced</u> his German citizenship. He spent a year hiking in the Apennine Mountains of Italy, visiting relatives, and touring museums so that he could forget the bitter memories of his high school days in Germany. He then decided to enroll in the famous Swiss Federal Institute of Technology in Zurich. It is interesting to note that he failed the entrance exam because of <u>deficiencies</u> in botany and zoology as well as in languages. However, after a year's study at a Swiss high school, the institute admitted him. Eventually, he became a Swiss citizen.

Even at the Institute of Technology, however, Einstein's rebellious attitude continued. He <u>cut</u> lectures, read what he wanted to read, used the school's lab illegally, and made his teachers hate him. One of his teachers, mathematician Hermann Minkowski, who later made valuable contributions to Einstein's new physics, called him a 'lazy dog.' Einstein was able to pass his two major exams and graduate in 1900 because he borrowed the <u>scrupulous</u> notes of one of his classmates, Marcel Grossman, and <u>crammed</u> for the exams.

Complete the following sentences on a separate piece of paper.

1. **When** Einstein was in high school, . . .

2. **In spite of the fact that** his high school teachers said he would never be anything, . . .

3. **Until** he was three years old, . . .

4. **Even though** he failed the entrance exam to the Institute of Technology, . . .

5. His high school teachers in Germany didn't like him **because** . . .

6. **Before** he became a teenager, . . .

7. **After** he had studied for one year in the Swiss high school, ...

8. In school, he annoyed his teachers **whenever** . . .

9. Einstein had to take courses in botany, zoology and languages **before** . . .

10. He treated his teachers **as if** . . .

11. His father's business in Germany failed, so the family moved **in order that** . . .

12. **Although** he cut most of his classes at the institute, . . .

13. His attendance at the Institute of Technology was **so** poor **that** . . .

14. He borrowed his friend's lecture notes **so that** . . . "

(Carroll Washington Pollock, *Communicate What You Mean*, 1982, pp. 111-112)

SYNTAX

T HE WORD SYNTAX came into the English language from Greek via Latin and literally it means *"to arrange together."* Students should know that words function in groups of words, phrases, and sentences. Syntax deals with the order of words, the sequence of tenses, the way people use coordination and subordination to express their ideas and their thoughts. We can also add that, as opposed to morphology, which focuses on the word, syntax takes care of the details and intricacies of words used together to form clear, well-expressed opinions, arguments, or any other types of message that shapes our communication.

Education starts with questions. As Alexander Crombie said in his preface to the second edition of his opus entitled *Etymology and Syntax of the English Language* published in 1830, "Inquiry is necessarily the parent of knowledge." Students come to our classes and always manage to come up with ingenious questions that sometimes baffle even the most experienced language instructors. But that is a good thing because we must respond, to the best of our knowledge, with the correct explanations, clarifications, or simply a confirmation of what students question or sometimes perceive to be the heart of the matter.

Mario Pei wrote several books, one more important than the other one, and laid the foundations for an exhaustive presentation of language principles, historical development, and comparative analysis. He published *The Story of Language* in 1949 and revised it in 1965, and then in 1967 he came out with *The Story of the English Language*.

In his second edition (1965), *The Story of Language* had several new additions but kept some of its initial assets, one of which was the chapter dedicated to what he called "The Arrangement of Words." Here are some of his assessments regarding syntax:

'The unit of speech is neither the individual sound nor the individual word but the sentence, conveying a complete concept. Consequently, the unit of speech corresponds roughly to the unit of thought. Syntax deals with the arrangement of words in this longer, more complete unit of thought and speech. . . . The syntax of the common man is of an elementary variety as contrasted with that of the more cultured person.

Spoken-language syntax is normally less involved than written-language syntax. The ultimate in syntactic complexity is achieved by the political, literary, or scientific writer who needs precise linguistic distinctions to represent involved thought complexes." (132-133)

"Syntax, more than any other compartment of language, lends itself to the purposes of connected, complex thought and its communication. It is an essential part of that physiological-psychological machinery whereby man transfers his ideas to his fellow man." (136)

As far as syntax is concerned, we must say that a noun and a verb (in other books, a subject and a predicate) would be the most important parts of a sentence. But we must also add all the other necessary ingredients that make up a well-constructed thought in speaking and equally in writing.

Poly-semantic words
(words with several meanings)

POLY-SEMANTIC WORDS MAY create confusion in the classroom when students recognize certain words but in new contexts, the same words acquire a different meaning.

As part of syntax, let's consider three individual cases: *while, however,* and *otherwise.*

Depending on how these words are used, they may acquire various functions which may create those moments when teachers have to step in and provide clarification.

While
I. Meaning "during"
While J. F. Kennedy was in the White House, he created the Peace Corps.

II. Meaning "on the contrary"
Julie is tall, while her brother is a little shorter.

III. Meaning "although"
While we all know punctuality is important, we sometimes come in late.

However
I. Meaning "but"
I studied very hard for the test; however, I did not get the grade I expected.

II. Meaning "regardless," "in whatever way"
However you look at it, you can't say it's incorrect.

Otherwise
I. Meaning "if not," "or else"
He did not see the red light; otherwise, he would have stopped.

II. Meaning "in other respects," "apart from that"
How are you otherwise?

Suggestion: Ask your students to make a mental effort to understand the various circumstances when these words are used to express a variety of meaning depending on context. If they can complete the following sentences correctly, they should be able to leave the classroom with a clear understanding of what WHILE, OTHERWISE and HOWEVER are all about:

While

1. *While* I was waiting for the bus,

   _____.

2. *While* we were watching the news last night,

   _____.

3. *While* I was reading my email this morning,

   _____.

4. *While* some students think conversation is extremely necessary,

   _____.

5. *While* all my friends like to live in a big city,

   _____.

6. In New Jersey gambling casinos are legal, *while*

   _____.

7. *While* the research is important,

   _____.

8. *While* I know my essay is not perfect,

   _____.

9. *While* I fully understand your point of view,

   _____.

10. My elder brother likes to socialize, *while* my sister

   _____.

Otherwise

1. You'd better hurry; *otherwise*,

   _____.

2. Let's go now; *otherwise*,

   _____.

3. He is a little nervous, but *otherwise*

   _____.

4. _____; *otherwise*, I would have
   arrived earlier.

5. The apartment is quite small, but *otherwise*

   _____.

6. Don't waste your time now; *otherwise*,

   _____.

7. _____; *otherwise*, you can't drive.

However

1. This is a challenging situation; *however*,

   _____.

2. *However* hard we tried,

   _____.

3. We are very happy to attend this ceremony; *however*,

   _____.

4. _____; *however*, we will try again
   tomorrow.

5. The President was confident of success; *however*,

   _____.

6. *However* you look at this situation,

   _____.

7. _____; *however*, there was no
   need to call 911.

Challenge: Students should be asked to work in small groups and produce their own examples using these words in at least two examples per group.

PARALLEL STRUCTURES

PARALLELISM (FROM THE Greek roots meaning "beside one another') is the use of similar structures that are grammatically the same. It is used in spoken and written English to create some kind of a balance to our thoughts.

"When pairing ideas, underscore their connections by expressing them in similar grammatical form. Paired ideas are usually connected in one of three ways: (1) with a coordinating conjunction such as *and, but, or*; (2) with a pair of correlative conjunctions such as *either... or... not only... but also...* ; (3) with a word introducing a comparison, usually *than* or *as*.

(Diana Hacker, *A Writer's Reference*, Boston: Bedford Books of St. Martin's Press, p. 64)

"In matters of principle, **stand like a roc**k; in matters of taste, **swim with the current**."

Thomas Jefferson

"The inherent vice of capitalism is the unequal **sharing of blessing**; the inherent virtue of socialism is the equal **sharing of miseries**."

Winston Churchill

"My lack **of excitement**.
of curiosity,
of surprise,
of any sort of pronounced **interes**t,
began to arouse his distrust."

Joseph Conrad

"The air **must be** pure
if we are to breathe;
the soil **must be** arable
if we are to eat;
the water **must be** clean
if we are to drink."

Emerson

"**Persons attempting to find a motive** in this narrative will be prosecuted; **persons attempting to find a moral** in it will be banished; **persons attempting to find a plot** in it will be shot."

Mark Twain

"it was **the best of times**, it was **the worst of times**, it was **the age of wisdom**, it was **the age of foolishness**, it was **the epoch of belief**, it was **the epoch of incredulity . . .**"

Charles Dickens

Like father, like son.
Easy come, easy go.

DISCOVER Read the following passages and **underline the parallel structures and the well balanced words**:

"Seattle, which sits like Rome on seven hills, was endowed by nature with remarkable vistas of water and mountains, with weeping birches and monkey trees and dogwoods big as maples." - Russell Lynnes, "Seattle Will Never Be the Same," *Harpers*

"India is a poetic nation, yet it demands new electrical plants. It is a mystical nation, yet it wants new roads. It is traditionally a peaceful nation, yet it could, if misled, inflame Asia." - James A. Michener, "Portraits for the Future," *Saturday Review*

"We go to our libraries in order to read and take advantage of the experiences of others. I think we all realize that not every written word in a library is entirely true. Many different authors have here written what they think, what they have experienced, what they believe is true, and sometimes what they wish were true. Some are wrong, a few are right, and many are neither entirely wrong nor entirely right."

"We do not need to fear ideas, but the censorship of ideas. We do not need to fear criticism, but the silencing of criticism. We do not need to fear excitement or agitation in the academic community, but timidity and apathy. We do not need to fear resistance to political leaders, but unquestioning acquiescence in whatever policies those leaders adopt."- Henry Steele Commager, "The Problem of Dissent," *Saturday Review*

(Quoted in Hans P. Guth, *Concise English Book*, 1972, pp. 146–148)

Suggestion Ask the students to finish the following sentences by **adding parallel structures**.

1. Most of our classmates are friendly, _____ and _____.

2. The duties of a manager are to supervise his employees, _____ and _____.

3. Swimming relieves nervous tension and _____.

4. Some people relax by listening to music, by _____, and by _____.

5. At our local high school, classroom violence can result in expulsion, in _____ and in _____.

6. Many teachers commend their students by praising them in front of the whole class and by _____.

7. If you like basketball, you can attend each game and _____.

8. The attorney's purpose is to uncover the irregularities, _____ and _____.

9. The passenger was advised either to change his/her flight or _____.

10. The students got together, _____, and _____.

11. The new website claims to be more efficient, _____, and _____.

12. You can reach me not only via email, _____, but also _____.

ADJECTIVE CLAUSES

ADJECTIVE CLAUSES ARE dependent or subordinate clauses used as adjectives. Like adjectives, these clauses define, explain, describe, and modify nouns.

WHO identifies people
John F. Kennedy, **who** was the 35th president of the United States, graduated from Harvard University.
(WHOSE shows possession and WHOM functions as an object)
Students **whose** native language is English are studying across the hall.
He is the only person in **whom** you can really trust.

THAT describes people, animals, and things
All the customers **that**/who had complaints went to see the manager.
This is the book **that**/which I was talking about.
Everybody liked the idea **that** there were no classes on Saturday.

WHICH selects or repeats
Secretariat was the horse on **which** she rode for years.
Our teacher told us to re-write our essay, **which** I did last night.

WHEN describes time
This the time **when** people go to the beach.

WHERE describes places
This is the place **where** he was born.

WHY describes reason
The reason **why** he is so popular remains a secret.

Appositives and adjective phrases

An appositive is a noun or a pronoun (often) with modifiers. Appositives are usually placed after the noun or pronoun to explain it or to describe it.

Let us take a look at an example:

"The crops, judiciously chosen and carefully tended, paid the interest, made a reasonable living and left a few hundred dollars every year toward paying off the principal." (John Steinbeck, *The Long Valley*, 1968, page 111)

Students should try to finish the following sentences. If they are correct, explanations may or may not be necessary.

Noun phrase	Michelangelo, **the artist, ...**
Adjective phrase	The child, **afraid to be seen,** . . .
Present participle	The people, **waiting to be seated,** . . .
Past participle	The people **invited to the White House** . . .

Appositives are usually clauses reduced to phrases.

Clause	The man, **who was exhausted and hot**, continued to climb up the hill.
Phrase	The man, **exhausted and hot**, continued to climb up the hill.

Exercises using appositives

Students can work in pairs or small groups to finish the following sentences:

1. _____, the capital city of my country, _____.

2. _____, my favorite dish, _____ _____.

3. _____, the best place to spend a vacation in my country, _____

4. I would like to spend the rest of my life in _____ _____, the best place to live these days.

5. A lot of people in my country read _____, the most popular newspaper.

6. The Atlantic Ocean, _____, ...

7. Children and adults have a good time when they visit Disney World, _____.

8. The Amazon River, _____, . . .

9. I would like to visit Bombay, _____.

10. The Bermuda Triangle, _____, . . .

11. My friends have never been to the World Trade Center, _____.

12. _____, one of the most famous artists in the world, _____.

Combine the following sentences. Change the second sentence into an **appositive**.

1. I would like to speak to that person.
   That person is in charge of purchasing.

   _____

2. John no longer works here.
   John was his friend.

   _____

3. The father can't afford to live here anymore.
   The father is out of work.

   _____

4. My favorite teacher is Bob.
   Bob is a compassionate and understanding person.

   _____

5. My friend went back to Los Angeles.
   Los Angeles is the town where he can find a job easily.

   _____

6. Mr. Malone sold his car to my sister.
   Mr. Malone is an honest man.

   _____

7. The father decided to give up his business.
   He realized that is business venture was not successful.

   _____

8. Tom was confident as a teacher.
   He was very shy in real life.

   _____

Find the mistakes and rewrite the following sentences:

1. Chemistry difficult can be enjoyable.

   _____

2. Bill who a top graduate student was accepted at Yale University.

   _____

3. He has written many articles comment on the effect of climate change.

   _____

4. Anyone has a library card may check out books.

   _____

5. The young woman behind the counter the teacher.

   _____

6. Lincoln Center, the home of music, dance, and theater located on the Upper West Side.

   _____

7. His childhood home, is a well-built house, can be seen down the road.

   _____

NOUN CLAUSES

A **noun clause** is used in the same way a **noun** is used, and nouns may function as subjects, objects, objects of a preposition, and complements of an adjective.

The following subordinating conjunctions may be used to introduce noun clauses:

who	whatever	whenever	how much
whoever	which	why	how many
whom	whichever	whether (or not)	how long/often/soon
whomever	where	that	
whose	wherever	how	
what	when	however	

DISCOVER   Ask the students to change the underlined words into noun clauses:

Example:

The date of Sue's marriage is a secret.

When Sue is getting married is a secret.

1. "The president's destination is a secret.

   _____

2. The time of his departure was also a secret.

   _____

3. His ignorance of world affairs has surprised everyone in Washington.

   _____

4. His reason for taking the trip has been worrying his advisors.

   _____

5. The number of days he will stay is confidential.

   _____

6. The leaders he will meet with made everyone nervous.

   _____

7. His decision to go alone concerns the member of his cabinet.

   _____

8. His strange behavior has upset many people.

   _____

9. His future actions will certainly be of interest to everyone.

   _____

(Adapted from Carroll Washington Pollock, *Communicate What You Mean*, pp. 150-151)

COMBINING SENTENCES INTO ONE COMPLEX PASSAGE

CHALLENGE Combine each group of clauses into a single complex sentence, using the sentence printed in regular type for your independent clause. Subordinate all the other ideas by putting them in the constructions indicated in parentheses. You will find that you can fit the ideas into the independent clause in the same order in which they are printed.

A. (a) *The paint is still wet.* (adverb clause)
   (b) Ground glass is sprinkled on the highway lines.
   (c) *This reflects light at night.* (infinitive phrase)
   While the paint is still wet, ground glass is sprinkled on the highway to reflect light at night.

B. (a) Judge Elizabeth Fry sentence a man to jail.
   (b) *She was a strict jurist.* (appositive)
   (c) *He had continued to drive his car.* (adjective clause)
   (d) *His license had been revoked.* (adverb clause)

   _____

   _____

   _____

C. (a) *Patricia Gould rescued 157 people in 11 years.* (prepositional phrase with gerund)
   (b) *She is a lifeguard at Cedar Beach* (appositive)
   (c) She received her first thank-you note.
   (d) *It expressed gratitude for the rescue.* (participial phrase)

   _____

   _____

   _____

D. (a) The winning photograph showed a group of basketball players.
   (b) *They were 'frozen' in midair.* (participial phrase)
   (c) *They jumped for the ball.* (adverb clause)

   _____

   _____

   _____

E. (a) *Dolley Madison was the White House hostess.* (adverb clause)
    (b) She served her guests a custard.
    (c) *The custard was frozen.* (adjective – one word)
    (d) *It soon became popularly known as ice cream.* (adjective clause)

_____

_____

_____

F. (a) *He was hunting rare plants in the jungles of Indochina.* (elliptical adverb clause)
    (b) A French scientist discovered the ruins of a magnificent city.
    (c) *It had been abandoned for centuries.* (adjective clause)

_____

_____

_____

G. (a) The children earned money for the movies.
    (b) *They sold to recycling plants old newspapers.* (prepositional phrase with gerund)
    (c) *They had collected from their neighbors.* (adjective clause)

_____

_____

_____

H. (a) George Moore had a cat.
    (b) *He was an Irish novelist.* (appositive)
    (c) *It forced him to pay attention to it.* (adjective clause)
    (d) *It jumped on his desk and took his pen from his hand.* (prepositional phrase with gerund)

_____

_____

_____

I. (a) *This happened in the eighteenth century.* (prepositional phrase)
    (b) A Dutchman invented roller skates.
    (c) *He attached wheels to his ice skates.* (prepositional phrase with gerund)
    (d) *He could skate in warm weather.* (adverb cause)

    _____

    _____

    _____

J. (a) 'Lame ducks' are public officials.
    (b) *They are finishing out their terms.* (adjective clause)
    (c) *They have run for re-election and been defeated.* (adverb clause)

    _____

    _____

    _____

K. (a) The first airplane flight from a ship took place in 1910.
    (b) *Eugene Ely flew a land plane from a temporary wooden runway.* (adverb clause)
    (c) *He was an early American flyer.* (appositive)
    (d) *The runway was constructed on the deck of the U.S.S. Birmingham.* (participial phrase)

    _____

    _____

    _____

(Selected from Joseph C. Blumenthal, *English Workshop. Fifth Course,* Harcourt Brace Jovanovich, 1977, pp. 115-118)

IF

Conditional sentences type 2

He *smokes* too much; maybe that's why he *can't get rid* of his cough.
If he **didn't smoke** so much, he **could get rid** of his cough.
I *don't have* the right change, so we *can't get* tickets from the machine.
If I **had** the right change, we **could get** tickets from the machine.

1. She is very shy; that's why she does not enjoy parties.

    _____

2. They speak French to her, not English, so her English does not improve.

    _____

3. He doesn't work overtime, so he doesn't earn as much as I do.

    _____

4. We don't have any matches, so we can't light a fire.

    _____

5. I don't have too much time, so I read very little.

    _____

6. I don't know his email address, so I can't send him my best regards.

    _____

7. I live near my office, so I don't spend much time traveling to work.

    _____

8. You work too fast; that's why you make so many mistakes.

    _____

9. He doesn't help me, possibly because I never ask him for help.

    _____

10. Some people speak very quickly. That's why I can't understand them.

    _____

(Adapted from A.J. Thomson and A.V. Martinet, *A Practical English Grammar. Exercises 2.* Oxford: Oxford University Press, 1988, pp. 87-91)

Conditional Sentences Type 3

You *didn't tell* me we had run out of bread, so I *didn't buy* any.
If you **had told** me we had run out of bread, I **would have bought** some.
It *rained* all the time. That is why he *did not enjoy* his visit.
If it **hadn't rained** all the time, he **would have enjoyed** his visit.

1. We didn't visit the museum because we did not have enough time.

   _____

2. The examiner read the passage very quickly, so the candidates did not understand it.

   _____

3. We only came by bus because there were no taxis.

   _____

4. I didn't know your phone number, so I didn't call you.

   _____

5. I only came up the stairs because the elevator was not working.

   _____

6. We didn't listen carefully, and that's why we made so many mistakes.

   _____

7. It took us a long time to find the house because the streets were not clearly marked.

   _____

8. We got a lift, so we reached the train station on time.

   _____

9. They asked him to leave the dining room because he was not wearing a shirt.

   _____

10. She didn't know you were in the hospital, so she didn't visit you.

   _____

(Adapted from A.J. Thomson and A.V. Martinet, *A Practical English Grammar. Exercises 2.* Oxford: Oxford University Press, 1988, pp. 87-91)

INVERSION/REVERSED WORD ORDER

The regular word order is arranged according to the following pattern:

Subject + Predicate + Indirect Object + Direct Object + Adverbial

Sometimes changes appear in the word order depending on the intention, the emphasis, or the focus on various parts of the sentence.

1. When the subject is introduced **by there is/there are/was/were**:
    There are *twelve students* in this class.
    There will be *two hundred people* at the wedding tomorrow.

2. When the sentence begins with negative words or phrases:
    Nowhere in the world *will you find* a higher standard of living.
    Seldom *does he come* to class on time.
    At no time did anybody say a word about the accident.

3. When the sentence begins with **no sooner, hardly, scarcely**, etc.
    No sooner *had I arrived* than it started to rain.
    Scarcely *had she entered* the room when the phone rang.
    Hardly ever *do we agree* about this topic.

4. When the sentence begins with **only** followed by an adverbial (of time or place):
    Only then *did we realize* the meaning of his statement.
    Only once *did I complain* about the amount of work I had to do.
    Only in this city *will you find* such diversity of cultures.

5. When the sentence begins with *only* plus an IF clause:
    Only if you go to New York *will you get a chance* to see a Broadway show.

6. When the sentence begins with **so** followed by an adjective or adverb:
    So important *was the news* that we had to exchange messages right away.
    So extensive *was the damage* that the house had to be completely rebuilt.
    So seriously *was he injured* that he was taken to the hospital at once.

7. When the sentence begins with *such*:
    Such a powerful man *was he* that no one dared to oppose him.

8. In special cases when we agree in the positive or the negative:
    John likes jazz, and *so does his sister.*
    John likes jazz. *So do I.*
    John doesn't like jazz, and **neither** *does his sister.*
    John doesn't like jazz. **Neither** *do I.*

9. In sentences beginning with **not only**:
    Not only *is our car* old, but it is also out of style.

10. In sentences beginning with **neither . . . nor . . . :**
    Neither *is money* important to me, **nor** *is success* relevant to me.

11. In IF clauses when IF is omitted:
    Were I you, I would not buy that book.
    Should anyone call, please tell them I am out of town.
    Had I known about it, I would have told you.

12. In exclamatory sentences beginning with *there* or *here*:
    There *goes the last bus!* **Here** *comes the bride!*

13. When adverbials are used at the beginning of a sentence for emphasis:
    There *stood the tallest man* he had ever seen.
    Before them *lay a vast expanse* of desert.
    At the end of the trail *was a beautiful waterfall.*

14. With certain old subjunctive forms:
    Come what may!
    May you be happy!

Analyze the traditional Gaelic blessing:

May the road rise up to meet you.
May the wind be always at your back.
May the sun shine warm upon your face;
The rain fall soft upon your fields and,
Until we meet again, may God hold you
In the palm of his hand.

Compare with an Apache blessing:

May the sun bring you new energy by day
May the moon softly restore you by night
May the rain wash away your worries
May the breeze blow new strength into your being
May you walk gently through the world
And know its beauty all the days of your life.

EXERCISES USING INVERSION

"Write new sentences with a similar meaning beginning with one of these words and phrases.

Only if   barely   only with   ~~rarely~~   at no time   little

1. A new film has not often before produced such positive reviews.

    Rarely has a new film produced such positive reviews.

2. The public was never in danger

    _____

3. He only felt entirely relaxed with close friends and family.

    _____

4. The match won't be cancelled unless the pitch is frozen.

    _____

5. I didn't know then that Carmen and I would be married one day.

    _____

6. He had only just entered the water when it became clear he couldn't swim.

    _____

Now do the same using these words and phrases:
only once   only in   on no account   hardly   not only   not for one moment

1. You must not light the fire if you are alone in the house.

    _____

2. There was never any competitiveness among the three brothers.

    _____

3. I wasn't only wet through, I was freezing cold.

    _____

4. I have only ever climbed this high once before.

    _____

5. The audience had only just taken their seats when the conductor stepped on to the stage.

_____

6. He has only been acknowledged to be a great author in the last few years.

_____

Complete these sentences in any appropriate way. You can use the following words in your answers.

alike   boring   complicated   dominance   ~~interest~~   strength

1. *Such is the interest in Dr Lowe's talk that it will be held in a bigger lecture hall.*

2. Such _____ that few buildings were left standing in the town.

3. Such _____ that he hasn't lost a match for over three years.

4. So _____ that even their parents couldn't tell them apart.

5. So _____ that it even took a computer three days to solve it.

6. So _____ that most of the students went to sleep."

(Martin Hewings, *Advanced Grammar in Use*, 2005, p. 201)

REPORTED SPEECH

ARIANNE CELCE-MURCIA AND Diane Larsen-Freeman (1999) mention three ways of reporting statements or thoughts: **direct quotation, indirect reported speech, and paraphrase**. They do not spend too much time talking about the first one but emphasize the importance of the second one. The authors exemplify their opinion by giving several options for reporting somebody else's exact words.

> "ESL/EFL students must have a firm grasp of the categorical distinction between proper quotation and true paraphrase and how each is done." (687)

In her textbook entitled *Communicate What You Mean*, Carroll Washington Pollock (1982) dedicated close to twenty pages to the section of Reported Speech and gave ESL students useful advice in her introductory paragraphs:

> "In the English language, there are primarily two ways of reporting what a person has said: direct speech and indirect speech. In direct speech, we report the speaker's exact words, as in the following sentence:
>
> He said, 'It's late, so I'm going to bed.'

Notice that in writing a comma follows the introductory verb, and the person's words are placed between quotation marks. The quotation marks indicate that we are reporting exactly what the speaker said without changing any of his or her words. Notice also that the period, question mark, or exclamation point at the end of the statement is placed within the quotation marks.

In indirect speech, we do not give the speaker's exact words, but we keep the exact meaning of a remark or speech. Whereas direct speech is found in conversations, in books, in plays, and in quotations, indirect speech is normally used in live conversations and in written reports where we tell what an author has said.

When you begin academic work, you will discover that you will use indirect speech a great deal in both speaking and writing. In seminars and other small classes, your professors will expect you to contribute to classroom discussions by expressing your own ideas on the topics you are studying. However, your professors will also expect you to demonstrate an understanding of the information in textbooks, articles, and journals. Therefore, you will find that that you will be using indirect speech to report what others have written or said about the subject you are discussing in your classroom.

In like manner, you will discover that indirect speech will also be used in your written reports, term papers, and essay exams." (73)

According to Carroll Washington Pollock, there are several types of reporting: Reporting statements, yes/no questions, yes/no answers, information questions, demands, requests, exclamations, and mixed sentences.

Reporting Statements

Besides "say" and "tell," other verbs are available if we want to use various other possibilities:

Announce	declare	remark	reply	predict	deny
Complain	state	mention	answer	promise	explain

For example:

My friend said, "I have already finished reading that newspaper article.

My friend remarked that he had finished reading that newspaper article.

Reporting yes/no questions

These questions are reported by using "if" or "whether (or not)."

For example:

The students asked, "Do we have to attend the class after the finals?"

The students wanted to know if they had to attend the class after the finals.

The students wanted to know whether they had to attend the class after the finals.

The students wanted to know whether they had to attend the class after the finals or not.

Reporting yes/no answers

The words "yes" and "no" are not used in the reported speech statement.

For example:

He asked, "Can we take a break?" and the teacher said, "Yes."

He asked if they could take a break, and the teacher said (that) they could.

Reporting information questions

Careful attention must be paid to the correct word order in the statement.

For example:

He asked, "When do you want to start your essay?"
He asked me when I wanted to start my essay.

Reporting commands

Commands usually change into infinitives:

Command: *Sit down!*   The teacher told me *to sit down.*

Verbs that are used to introduce commands: *tell, order, command, warn, direct*

1. The insurance company said, "Send your premium check as soon as possible!"

2. The insurance company *told us to send* our premium check as soon as possible."

Reporting requests

A request can be made politely by using structures such as "will you,' "would you," "can you,' or "could you."

1. The cashier said, "Can you swipe your card and sign the transaction?"

2. The cashier *asked me to swipe* my card and sign the transaction.

Reporting exclamations

Exclamations usually become statements in reported speech.

1. He said, "Thanks a lot!"   He *thanked* me.

2. They said, "What a nice day!"   They *said it was* a nice day.

3. She said, "You must be joking!"   She *did not believe* me.

Reporting mixed types

Read the following passage from Truman Capote's *Breakfast at Tiffany's* and change it into reported speech:

"One night, it was long past twelve, I woke up at the sound of Mr. Yunioshi calling down the stairs. Since he lived on the top floor, his voice fell through the whole house, exasperated and stern. 'Miss Golightly! I must protest!'

The voice that came back, welling up from the bottom of the stairs, was silly-young and self-amused. 'Oh, darling, I *am* sorry. I lost the goddamn key.'

'You cannot go on ringing my bell. You must please, please have yourself a key made.'

'But I lose them all.'

'I work, I have to sleep,' Mr. Yunioshi shouted. 'But always you are ringing my bell.'

'Oh, *don't* be angry, you *dear* little man: I *won't* do it again. And if you promise not to be angry' – her voice was coming nearer, she was climbing the stairs – 'I might let you take those pictures you mentioned.'(15)

_____

_____

_____

_____

_____

_____

_____

PUNCTUATION

RUSSELL BAKER, WINNER of the Pulitzer Prize for his book *Growing Up* and for his essays in *The New York Times,* wrote an article regarding punctuation entitled *How to Punctuate*, which attracted the attention of many ESL teachers and students. Here is an excerpt from it:

"When you write, you make a sound in the reader's head. It can be a dull mumble — that's why so much government prose makes you sleepy — or it can be a joyful noise, a sly whisper, a throb of passion.

Listen to a voice trembling in a haunted room:

"And the sulken, sad, uncertain rustling of each purple curtain thrilled me — filled me with fantastic terrors never felt before . . ."

That's Edgar Allan Poe, a master. Few of us can make paper speak as vividly as Poe could, but even beginners will write better once they start listening to the sound their writing makes.

One of the most important tools for making paper speak in your own voice is punctuation.

When speaking aloud, you punctuate constantly — with body language. Your listener hears commas, dashes, question marks, exclamation points, quotation marks as you shout, whisper, pause, wave your arms, roll your eyes, wrinkle your brow.

In writing, punctuation plays the role of body language. It helps readers hear the way you want to be heard.

'Gee, Dad, have I got to learn all them rules?'

Don't let rules scare you. For they aren't hard and fast. Think of them as guidelines.

Am I saying, "Go ahead and punctuate as you please"?

Absolutely not. Use your own common sense, remembering that you can't expect readers to work to decipher what you're trying to say.

There are two basic systems of punctuation:

1. The loose or open system, which tries to capture the way body language punctuates talk.

2. The tight, closed structural system, which hews closely to the sentence's grammatical structure.

Most writers use a little of both. In any case, we use much less punctuation than they used 200 or even 50 years ago. (Glance into Edward Gibbon's *Decline and Fall of the Roman Empire,* first published in 1776, for an example of the tight structure system at its most elegant.)

> No matter which system you prefer, be warned: Punctuation marks cannot save a sentence that is badly put together. If you have to struggle over commas, semicolons, dashes, you've probably built a sentence that's never going to fly, no matter how you tinker with it. Throw it away and build a new one to a simpler design. The better your sentence, the easier it is to punctuate."
>
> (*The New York Times*, February 11, 2006)

Lynne Truss in her famous # 1 British Bestseller *Eats, Shoots & Leaves,* Gotham Books (2003) says this about this subject:

> "Punctuation has been defined many ways. Some grammarians use the analogy of stitching: punctuation as the basting that holds the fabric of language in shape. Another writer tell us that *punctuation marks are the traffic signals of language*: they tell us to slow down, notice this, take a detour, and stop. I have even seen a rather fanciful reference to the full stop and comma as "the invisible servants in fairy tales – the ones who bring glasses of water and pillows, not storms of weather or love." But best of all, I think, is the simple advice given by the style book of a national newspaper: that punctuation is "a courtesy designed to help readers to understand a story without stumbling." (7)

When we write, as students or teachers, we are going to use approximately 30 main punctuation marks, although not more than a dozen are important and absolutely necessary.

Capitalization

- Every sentence begins with a capital letter.
- The first person singular, *I*, is always capitalized.
- Proper names of people, cities, countries, states, universities, buildings, etc. are capitalized.
  Isaac Newton   *New Jersey*   *Iowa*   *Yale University*
- Names of languages and adjectives of nationality are capitalized.
  Tagalog   *German*   *Persian*
- Names of college and university courses are capitalized.
  Fundamentals of Communication 101

- The days of the week, the holidays, and the months of the year are capitalized.
  Tuesday Easter December

- Names of religions and deities are capitalized.
  Christianity Buddha Shinto Mohammed

- Names of hotels, bridges, ships are capitalized.
  The Carlyle The George Washington Bridge The Lusitania

- Names of islands, rivers, mountains, lakes, bays, waterfalls are capitalized.
  The Philippines The Mississippi Lake Michigan Hudson Bay

- Names of museums and libraries are capitalized.
  The Metropolitan Museum The 42nd Street Library

- Names of institutions, foundations, and organizations are capitalized.
  The United Nations The Clinton Foundation

- Professional titles used with the names of that person are capitalized.
  Professor Moore

- All the words in titles (except prepositions, articles, and conjunctions) are capitalized.
  Using Poetry across the Curriculum

The Period

a. The period is used to mark the end of a sentence.
    We have just started to talk.

b. The period comes after most abbreviations.
    Ms.   Mr.   M.A.

c. A period comes after numerals or letters in a vertical list.

    1. Dogs   a. Dogs
    2. Horses   b. Horses
    3. Cats   c. Cats

The Comma

a. A comma comes between two independent clauses joined by coordinating or correlative conjunctions: *and, but, so, or, for, nor, yet*:
    I came here with my family two weeks ago, **and** *we are planning to stay for at least six months.*

*The suspect admitted his crime, **but** he never mentioned why he did it.*

*The explanation was not clear, **so** we asked the teacher to give us more details.*

*You can send him a text message, **or** you can call him right away.*

*We left the beach after the party, **for** there was nothing else to do.*

*The message was not addressed to anybody in particular, **nor** was it easy to understand.*

*The joke was sarcastic and a little bit too long, **yet** everybody laughed.*

b. In subordination, a comma is needed after a dependent clause:

When everything was said and done, the visitors got dressed and left.

c. A comma is necessary to set off the one or ones spoken to in a direct address:

Let's face it, Jack, you are the only one who knows the answer.

d. Appositives are usually set off by commas.

New York City, *the best place to spend a vacation,* is already a world destination for tourists.

e. A comma is recommended between two adjectives before a noun when the word and would not change the meaning.

She greeted her guests with wide, open arms.

f. A comma is used with non-restrictive adjective clauses, especially in sentences beginning with *who, which, where:*

My brother, *who was the only one present,* did not say anything to contradict me.

g. A direct quotation is set off by commas.

"Will you," *he said,* "come to see me as soon as possible?"

h. Commas are used to separate items in a specific date.

Monday, March 26, 2018, was the day they started to build their house.

i. A comma separates the name of the city from the county and state.

John Steinbeck was born in *Salinas, Monterey County, California,* on February 27, 1902.

j. Commas are used between words, phrases, or clauses in a series.

We went shopping, and we bought *tomatoes, cabbage, lettuce, pears, and meat.*

The Question Mark

All information and yes/no questions are used with a question mark.
Why are you asking such questions?   *Are you kidding me?*

The Exclamation Point

Also known as the exclamation mark, the exclamation point is used after words, expressions, or sentences showing strong feeling, emotion, or high volume.
Watch out!   *Great news!*   *This is hilarious!*

"I once left a publisher for the sole reason that he tried to change my semicolons to periods." Milan Kundera, Czech writer, 1988

The Semicolon

1. Semicolons are not interchangeable with commas and periods. Conjunctive adverbs like *furthermore, however, moreover,* etc. combine two independent clauses that are separated by a semicolon.

   The teacher did his best to clarify the story; *however,* the students were not satisfied.

2. A semicolon is sometimes used to join two short independent clauses.

   The singular form is tooth; the plural form is teeth.

The Colon

The Colon is a punctuation mark used to precede a list of items, a quotation, or an explanation.
   The following flowers can be sent as gifts: lilies, roses, tulips, chrysanthemums, etc.
   A **colon** is also used with ratios, titles and subtitles of books, city and publisher in bibliographies, Biblical citations, in business salutations and in formal letter writing or other types of correspondence.

1. Ratios: 1:5
2. Titles and subtitles of books: *Modern English. Part I: Parts of Speech*
3. City and publisher   New York: Scribner

4.	Biblical citations	Psalm 25:4
5.	Business salutations:	To Whom It May Concern:
6.	Formal letter writing:	Attention: Human Resources
7.	Correspondence	cc: Building Management

Quotation Marks

In 2017, John McPhee, a staff writer at *The New Yorker*, collected several of his essays and offered some of the insights he gathered during his career while teaching at Princeton University. Among his subchapters, one title might attract attention because it deals with a unique topic: Elicitation. After interviewing famous people like Woody Allen or Jackie Gleason, he goes deeper into a 1991 Supreme Court decision to defend the idea that quotations must be exact and unedited. To make his point, he quotes Justice Anthony M. Kennedy:

"In some sense, any alteration of a verbatim quotation is false." (quoted in McPhee, *Draft No. 4. On the Writing Process*, 2017, p. 101) And then the author keeps pressing his support of exact quotations by adding the following passage from Justice Kennedy:

> "In general, quotation marks around a passage indicate to the reader that the passage reproduces the speaker's words verbatim. They inform the reader that he or she is reading the statement of speaker, not a paraphrase or other indirect interpretation by an author. By providing this information, quotations add authority to the statement and credibility to the author's work." (103)

 Tips For our ESL classroom purposes, the following is just a mini guide to help teachers see the whole picture regarding quotation marks and their usage:

1. Quotation marks, also known as quotes, quote marks, speech marks, inverted commas or talking marks, are used in pairs in various writing systems to render the exact words of a speaker:

   "I am going to ask you a very important question," said the teacher.

   She asked, "What do you mean by that?"

2. When there is a quotation within a quotation, the outside quotation will be indicated by double quotation marks, whereas the inside one comes with single quotation marks.

   "The weatherman said, 'We are going to have plenty of sunshine over the weekend.'"

3. Sometimes quotation marks are used around single words for emphasis, but only when quoting a word or term someone else used.

I did not understand what they meant by "filthy."

4. There are cases when certain words are used with quotation marks to describe words.

"A trickle of water" means a very small quantity of water that flows slowly.

5. Periods and commas go inside closing quotation marks. Colons and semicolons go outside. Question marks and exclamation points go inside if they go with the quotation but outside if they refer to the whole sentence.

"Where is Tom?" she asked.

Are we going to sing "The Star Spangled Banner"?

6. The so-called "scare quotes" are known to have appeared in the 1960s. According to some journalists, they are just dirty punctuation tricks. Here is one example:

"Imagine a busy manager, quickly skimming over an editorial. He might come across a phrase like 'the deficit,' and suppose it's a bad thing, or 'affordable' health care, and suppose it's a good thing. The scare quotes would usually signal the shortcut for the writers, allowing them to wallow in their ideological prejudices without spelling out their empirical premises." (Clark, 2010, p. 87)

The Apostrophe

1. We use apostrophes in contractions:

We *won't* be able to get there before noon. I *shouldn't* say that.

2. We use an apostrophe flowed by **s** (**'s**) to form the possessive of singular nouns and of plural nouns that do not end in **s**. We also use it to form the plural of numbers and letters.

My sister's grades were quite good. She only got *A's* and *B's*.

Exxon is spelled with *two X's*.

Walk in *two's*, not *three's*.

3. When we form the possessive of plural nouns already ending in -**s** or -**es,** we only add an apostrophe.

The teacher read all her students' essays.

4. Indefinite pronouns like **one, other, somebody, nobody** etc. also use an apostrophe to show possession.

That *is nobody's* business.

This must be *somebody else's* book.

Parentheses

Sometimes writers want to insert additional information that can be a word, a group of words, an expression, or a whole sentence. That can be done for clarification, amplification or simply for addition by using a pair of parentheses.

We use the parentheses in the following cases:

1. To set off structurally independent elements.

The patterns were statistically significant *(see Figure 5)*.

2. To set off reference citations in text.

Dumas and Dore *(1991)*

3. To introduce an abbreviation.

Effect of the galvanic skin response *(GSR)*

4. To set off letters that identify items in a series within a sentence or paragraph.

The subject areas included *(a)* synonyms associated with cultural interactions, *(b)* descriptors for ethnic group membership, and *(c)* psychological systems and outcomes associated with bicultural adaptation.

5. To enclose a citation or page number of a direct quotation.

The author stated, "The effect disappeared within minutes" *(Lopez, 1993, p. 311)*, but she did not say which effect.

(Adapted from the Publication Manual of the American Psychological Association, Sixth Edition, 2010, p. 93)

The Asterisk

The star-shaped symbol (approximately 5,000 years old – the oldest mark of punctuation – according to Keith Houston in his *Shady Characters: The Secret Life of Punctuation Symbols, and Other Typographical Marks,* W. W. Norton & Company, 2014) comes from the Greek word *asteriskos,* meaning "a little star." A diminutive of *aster,* meaning "star," the asterisk (*) is used in printing or writing to edit swear words or to signal something is important, interesting, or considered ungrammatical or unacceptable. The author or the person using the asterisk will put it before the word to attract attention to a spelling or grammar mistake, but if someone else notices the problem, that person will add the asterisk at the end of the word.

Examples: *I enjoy to ski. Luck* (meaning the word was misspelled originally)

The asterisk is sometimes used in advertising to indicate extra information:
    Tech toys for the holidays!
    *available in certain stores only

EXERCISES IN PUNCTUATION

SUGGESTION Ask the students to read the following passage from Hemingway's Soldier's Home and insert the correct punctuation:

one morning after he had been home for about a month his mother came into his bedroom and sat on the bed she smoothed her apron

i had a talk with your father last night harold she said and he is willing for you to take the car out in the evenings

yeah said krebs who was not fully awake take the car out yeah

yes your father has felt for some time that you should be able to take the car out in the evenings whenever you wished but we only talked it over last night

i ll bet you made him krebs said

no it was your father s suggestion that we talk the matter over

yeah I ll bet you made him krebs sat up in bed

will you come down to breakfast harold his mother said

as soon as i get my clothes on krebs said

This is the original passage:

One morning after he had been home for a month his mother came into his bedroom and sat on the bed. She smoothed her apron.

"I had a talk with your father last night, Harold," she said, "and he is willing for you to take the car out in the evenings."

"Yeah?" said Krebs, who was not fully awake. "Take the car out? Yeah?"

"Yes. Your father has felt for some time that you should be able to take the car out in the evenings whenever you wished but we only talked it over last night."

"I'll bet you made him," Krebs said.

"No. It was your father's suggestion that we talk the matter over."

"Yeah. I'll bet you made him," Krebs sat up in bed.

"Will you come down to breakfast, Harold?" his mother said.

"As soon as I get my clothes on," Krebs said.

(Ernest Hemingway, *Soldier's Home*, [in] *The Bedford Introduction to Literature*, Ninth Edition, 2011, Boston: Bedford/ St. Martin's, p. 189)

NOTES

_____

_____

_____

_____

_____

Speaking/Conversation

TIPS FOR ESL INSTRUCTORS:

1. ESL students should be encouraged to speak as much and as often as possible.
2. Every culture has its own ways of conducting conversation.

p. 351

3. "Conversation is a two-way thing, involving give and take, action and reaction."   p. 354
4. Communicating effectively in English means targeting stress, intonation, and speech rhythm, as well as consonants and vowels.

p. 357

TIPS FOR ESL STUDENTS:

There are certain strategies that our students should be made aware of:

1. Use eye contact.
2. Look for clues that your listener does not understand what you are saying.
3. Don't be afraid to ask to make sure you are being understood.
4. When your listener asks WHAT? You probably need to do something more than repeat yourself.
5. Talk more slowly in English than you do in your native language.
6. Don't worry about mistakes.   p. 360

During Mark Twain's visit to Heidelberg he attended a play with a friend. During the intermission the bored friend said he was leaving and asked if Twain wanted to leave with him. "No," said Twain, I think I'll stick around and wait for the verb." In many constructions in German, the main verb doesn't appear until the end of the sentence.

(Adapted from M. Agar, *The Language Shock. Understanding the Culture of Conversation*, 1994)

"Language is itself the most exhilarating of games, an endless contest in which we are engaged all our lives, pure fun for the mind. It can be, at its best, a game infinitely more complex than chess, or at other times athletic, world-class soccer, team against team." (Thomas, 1990, p. 114)

Most ESL classes should be conducted as conversations, and our students should be encouraged to speak as much and as often as possible.

"A conversation is the central, nearly defining activity of social living. [...] Most of our conversations are exchanges of signals demonstrating the reality and closeness of the participants, holding them in companionship. We depend heavily on small-talk for our cohesion; the weather, the time of day, the turn of seasons, the current births and deaths, topics used not so much for any intrinsic interest as for just holding us together.

From time to time, conversations turn to matters of significance, and large social decisions emerge. The older meaning of CONVERSATION is of interest here. The word came from IE (Indo-European) root *wer*, meaning *to turn, to move around a place, to frequent a neighborhood*. Doing these things together was the origin of our word, not talking, certainly nothing like small-talk. CONVERSATION was the word for the behavior of people, their manner of life together. Later the meaning expanded to indicate one's associates, a circle of acquaintances. Only recently did talking take over the word, although the earlier meanings still resound inside. A conversation piece is not really an item of furniture or an eccentric piece of sculpture displayed to stir up talking; it was a genre of painting depicting groups of human beings simply being social, one way or another, maybe talking, maybe not. These paintings were enormously popular in their time, but the fashion faded away. [...]

I wish we could have CONVERSATION back with its early meaning. One of the nicest things about us is our pleasure in simply being *together*, talking to each other about one thing or another but not necessarily talking at all, just there in an amiable arrangement, a *conversation.*"(35-36)

According to David Crystal (2005), there are many ways of telling the language story, but his approach goes a different way with a focus on 'how' rather than 'what,' 'why,' 'where,' or 'when.' In his book entitled *How Language Works*, he presents his personal account, and in Chapter 42, *How conversation works*, he says:

"Of the many types of communicative act, most study has been devoted to conversation, seen as the most fundamental and pervasive means of conducting human affairs. It turns out, upon analysis, to be a highly structured activity, in which people tacitly operate with a set of basic conventions. A comparison has even been drawn with games such as chess; conversations, it seems, can be thought of as having an opening, a middle, and an end game. The participants make their moves and often seem to follow certain rules as the dialogue proceeds. But the analogy ends there. A successful conversation is not a game; it is no more than a mutually satisfying linguistic exchange. Few rules are ever stated explicitly (some exceptions are *Don't* interrupt! And *Look at me when I'm talking to you*). Furthermore, apart from in certain types of argument and debate, there are no winners.

For a conversation to be successful, in most social contexts, the participants need to feel they are contributing something to it and are getting something out of it. For this to happen, certain conditions must apply. Everyone must have an opportunity to speak; no one should be monopolizing or constantly interrupting. [. . .] They need to have a sense of when to speak or stay silent; when to proffer information or hold it back; when to stay aloof or become involved. They need to develop a mutual tolerance, to allow for speaker unclarity and listener inattention: perfect expression and comprehension are rare, and the success of a dialogue largely depends on people recognizing their communicative weaknesses, through the use of rephrasing (e.g. *Let me put that another way*) and clarification (e.g. *Are you with me?*). "(267-268)

Every culture has its own way of conducting conversations, and that might be the first thing ESL students notice when they are immersed into a new culture. Before addressing the topic of conversation, students should be asked to present their own life experiences and talk about differences in communication styles that they noticed while studying English as a Second Language.

The following excerpt comes from Nancy Masterson Sakamoto's textbook entitled *Polite Fictions* (1982):

"After I was married and had lived in Japan for a while, my Japanese gradually improved to the point where I could take part in simple conversation with my husband, his friends and family. And I began to notice that often, when I joined in, the others would look startled, and the conversational topic would come to a halt. After this happened several times, it became clear to me that I was doing something wrong. But for a long time, I didn't know what it was.

Finally, after listening carefully to many Japanese conversations, I discovered what my problem was. Even though I was speaking Japanese, I was handling the conversation in a Western way.

Japanese-style conversations develop quite differently from Western-style conversations. And the difference isn't only in the languages. I realized that just as I kept trying to hold Western-style conversations even when I was speaking Japanese, so my English kept trying to hold Japanese-style conversations even when they were speaking English. We were unconsciously playing entirely different conversational ballgames.

A Western-style conversation between two people is like a game of tennis. If I introduce a topic, a conversational ball, I expect you to hit it back. If you agree with me, I don't expect you simply to agree and do nothing more. I expect you do add something – a reason for agreeing, another example, or an elaboration to carry the idea further. But I don't expect you always to agree. I am just as happy if you question me, or challenge me, or completely disagree with me. Whether you agree or disagree, your response will return the ball to me.

And then it is my turn again. I don't serve a new ball from my original starting line. I hit your ball back again from where it has bounced. I carry your idea further, or answer your questions or objections, or challenge or question you. And so, the ball goes back and forth with each of us doing our best to give it a new twist, an original spin, or a powerful smash.

And the more vigorous the action, the more interesting and exciting the game. Of course, if one of us gets angry, it spoils the conversation, just as it spoils a tennis game. But getting excited is not at all the same as getting angry. After all, we are not trying to hit each other. We are trying to hit the ball. So long as we attack only each other's opinions, and do not attack each other personally, we don't expect anyone to get hurt. A good conversation is supposed to be interesting and exciting.

If there are more than two people in the conversation, then it is like doubles in tennis, or like volleyball. There's no waiting in line. Whoever is nearest and quickest hits the ball, and if you step back, someone else will hit it. No one stops the game to give you a turn. You're responsible for taking your own turn.

But whether it's two players or a group, everyone does his or her best to keep the ball going, and no person has the ball for very long.

A Japanese-style conversation, however, it not at all like tennis or volleyball. It's like bowling. You wait for your turn. And you always know your place in line. It depends on such things as whether you are older or younger, a close friend or a relative stranger to the previous speaker, in a senior or junior position, and so on.

When your turn comes, you step up to the starting line with your bowling ball and carefully bowl it. Everyone else stands back and watches politely, murmuring encouragement. Everyone waits until the ball has reached the end of the alley and watches to see if it knocks down all the pins, or only some of them, or none of them. There is a pause while everyone registers your score.

Then, after everyone is sure that you have completely finished your turn, the next person in line steps up to the starting line with a different ball. He doesn't return your ball, and he does not begin from where you ball stopped. There is no back and forth at all. All the balls run parallel. And there is always a suitable pause between turns. There is no rush, no excitement, no scramble for the ball.

No wonder everyone looked startled when I took part in Japanese conversations. I paid no attention to whose turn it was and kept snatching the ball halfway down the alley and throwing it back at the bowler. Of course, the conversation died. I was playing the wrong game.

This explains why it is almost impossible to get a Western-style conversation or discussion going with an English student in Japan. I used to think that the problem was their lack of English language ability. But I finally came to realize that the biggest problem is that they, too, are playing the wrong game.

Whenever I serve a volleyball, everyone just stands back and watches it fall, with occasional murmurs of encouragement. No one hits it back. Everyone waits until I call on someone to take a turn. And when that person speaks, he doesn't hit my ball back. He serves a new ball. Again, everyone just watches it fall.

So I call on someone else. This person does not refer to what the previous speaker has said. He also serves a new ball. Nobody seems to have paid any attention to what anyone else has said. Everyone begins again from the starting line, and all the balls run parallel. There is never any back and forth. Everyone is trying to bowl with a volleyball.

Now that you know about the differences in the conversational ballgames, you may think that all your troubles are over. But if you have been trained all your life to play one game, it is no simple matter to switch to another, even if you know the rules. Knowing the rules is not at all the same thing as playing the game.

Even now, during a conversation in Japanese I will notice a startled reaction and belatedly realize that once again I have rudely interrupted by instinctively trying to hit back the other person's bowling ball. It is no easier for me to 'just listen' during a conversation than it is for my Japanese students to 'just relax' when speaking with foreigners. Now I can truly sympathize with how hard they must find it to carry on a Western-style conversation."

(Quoted in Smalley, Ruetten and Kozyrev, *Refining Composition Skills*, Boston: Heinle & Heinle, 2001)

ESL students can usually acquire the basic rules of speaking and, depending on their proficiency level, carrying on a conversation is not a big issue. As long as the communication process goes on, even with minor errors, what is important is that there is a message. And as long as the interlocutors understand what is being said, the message goes through.

Are there any secrets? *Reader's Digest, Write Better, Speak Better* (1972) contains a whole chapter dedicated to **the secrets of conversation.**

"Conversation, in part, is self-expression. It provides us opportunities for asserting our individuality, telling the world just how we feel, or 'letting off steam.' Talk of this sort is pleasurable and valuable. It is like tinkering with a hot rod, or breeding tropical fish, or puttering around with painting or novel writing. It serves as a sort of safety valve and comes easily to almost everybody.

However, when conversation is entered into merely to 'get something off your chest' it makes very bad conversation. It is too one-sided. No number of monologues ever add up to *real conversation*. When everyone wants to shoot baskets, the ball doesn't get passed around enough for a good game.

At its best, conversation means the pooling of information, the sharing of interests, the bringing together of ideas.

Conversation is a two-way thing, involving give and take, action and reaction. Indeed it is a many-way thing – the communication of many ideas among many people." (391)

Pronunciation skills need a little bit of help, but it all starts with making students aware that English does NOT have too many spelling or pronunciation rules. After learning a set of vocabulary words, ESL students expect to pronounce new words following the rules of the words they already know. Bill Bryson in the **Pronunciation** section of his book *Mother Tongue (1990)*, says:

"No other language in the world has more words spelled the same way and yet pronounced differently. Consider just a few:

Heard – beard
Road – broad
Five – give
Fillet – skillet
Early – dearly
Beau – beauty
Steak – streak
Ace – mustache
Low – how
Doll – droll
Scour – four
Four – tour
Grieve – sieve
Paid – said
Break – speak." (84-85)

The language changes and with it, vocabulary words may change their meaning, and this may affect pronunciation. "English spelling is so irrational," says Guy Deutscher (2005), mostly because sounds, meanings and structures all seem to have changed.

"Just have a go at reading the following poem out loud as quickly as you can:

I take it you already know
Of tough and bough and cough and dough?
Others may stumble, but not you,
On hiccoughs, thorough, lough, and through?
Well done! And now you wish perhaps,
To learn of less familiar traps?
Beware of heard, a dreadful word
That looks like beard and sounds like bird.
And dead – it's said like bed, not bead –
For goodness sake, don't call it 'deed.'
Watch out for meat and great and threat
(They rhyme with suite and straight and debt);
A moth is not a moth in mother,
Nor both in bother, broth in brother.
And here is a match for there
Nor dear and fear for bear and pear.
And then there's does and rose and lose –

Just look them up – and goose and choose,
And cork and work, and word and sword,
And do and go, and thwart and cart –
Come! Come! I've hardly made a start!"
(From the *Manchester Guardian*, 1954)

(Quoted in Guy Deutscher, *The Unfolding of Language*, 2005, p. 53)

It's not easy for an ESL student to fully comprehend a native speaker, especially when there is a discrepancy between the written word and what the students expect to hear.

"Australians will tell you they come from 'Stralia.' While Torontoans will tell you they come from 'Tronna.' In Iowa it's 'Iwa' and in Ohio it's 'Hia.' People from Milwaukee say they're from 'Mwawkee.' In Louisville it's 'Loovl,' in Newark it's 'Nerk,' and in Indianapolis it's 'Naplus.' People in Philadelphia don't come from there; they come from 'Fuhluffia.' (Bryson, 1990, p. 88)

"In Baltimore (pronounced 'balamer'), an eagle is an 'igggle,' a tiger is a 'tagger,' water is 'wooder,' a power mower is a 'paramour," a store is a 'stewer,' clothes are 'clays,' orange juice is 'arnjoos,' a bureau is a 'beero,' and the Orals are of course the local baseball team." (89) (The official name of the basketball team is *Baltimore Orioles*.)

As a practical exercise, students in your class should be asked if they have found any huge discrepancies between the written form and what they would have expected to hear. Also, another practical exercise would be to discuss how people pronounce the letter cluster OUGH in the following words:

Through   *Though*   *Thought*   *Tough*   *Plough*   *Thorough*   *Hiccough*

If this works, also try: -EA-

Leaf as in	barren leaves
Lead (verb)	lead on!
Lead (noun)	unleaded gasoline
Plead	Do you plead guilty?
Tread	Tread lightly!
Seal (verb and noun)	sealed with a kiss
Feature	special features
Ream	a ream of paper
Stream	music streaming
Beau	Does your sister have a beau?
Lean	lean cuisine
Leap	quantum leap

In order to function in the classroom when speaking is needed, ESL students must learn how to meet the particular speech communication needs. Since cultures treat this subject differently, so do our ESL students. In a regular ESL classroom, teachers may encounter several nationalities at the same level of study, and treat them accordingly. In the preface to *Speech Communication Made Simple* (2000), Paulette Dale and James Wolf argue that foreign students will be better prepared if they know, among other things, how to develop their confidence, the use of body language, eye contact, posture, voice, if they want to communicate properly with each other, separately or in groups.

Public speaking is that area where our students will have to learn how to present information orally, how to express their opinion, how to listen and how to lead and participate in class discussions. Whether the speech is simply informative or persuasive, students can develop skills that will shape their performances in many ways, not only in the company of their peers, but also in real life situations. Speaking is of utter importance, and **Daniel Webster** (1782-1852), U.S. Senator who represented New Hampshire and Massachusetts in the United States House of Representatives, made it very clear when he said:

"If all my talents and powers were to be taken from me by some inscrutable Providence, and I had my choice of keeping but one, I would unhesitatingly ask to be allowed to keep the Power of Speaking, for through it, I would quickly recover all the rest."
(Quoted in the Introduction to *Speech Communication Made Simple*, page x)

As far as public speaking is concerned, **eye contact**, **facial expressions**, **posture, gestures**, all will convey the message that the speaker is confident, has prepared his speech, and will do so after careful combining words with visual aids and other ancillary material.

According to Dale & Wolf, "The speech delivery style of Europeans and Asians tends to be very formal. Speakers of those cultures often read oral presentations from carefully written manuscripts.

On the other hand, American speakers are generally more informal relative to speakers in other cultures. American audiences prefer a natural, spontaneous delivery that conveys a lively sense of communication. They don't relate well to speakers who read from a manuscript. If you use an outline of your ideas instead of a prepared text, your speech will not only sound more natural, but you will also be able to establish better rapport with your listeners and keep their attention. [. . .]

The language and style you use when making an oral presentation should not be the same as the language and style you use when writing. Well-written information that is meant to be read does not work as well when it is heard. It is therefore important for you to adapt written texts or outlines for presentations. [. . .]

Good speakers are much more informal when speaking than when writing. They also use their own words and develop their own speaking styles. Whenever possible, they use short words. Listeners appreciate it when speakers use simple, everyday words in a presentation. One advantage is that it is much easier for speakers to pronounce short words correctly. Another is that long and sophisticated vocabulary choices make listening more difficult." (28)

Outlines, transitions, tonality, pronunciation, intonation, to name just a few ingredients, will make the speech a success. If students do a quick 5-minute informative presentation of their choice of subjects, or if they are required to plan and prepare a speech in a small group or in front of the whole class, the first and most important idea is that they must understand how to go from their culture to the level of communication that makes intercultural communication a viable tool in learning. Students, like teachers, learn from each other. They also acquire the habit of teaching each other and competing with each other.

Sue Miller (2010) addresses the parallel topic of communicating effectively in English by targeting stress, intonation, and speech rhythm, as well as consonants and vowels, in her comprehensive book entitled *Targeting Pronunciation* with its suggestive subtitle, *Communicating Clearly in English*. The second edition starts with a question: What is clear, effective speech? And the explanation is the answer:

"To become an effective speaker, you need to develop your pronunciation and language skills together. Good oral communication skills include clear pronunciation as well as accurate grammar and vocabulary. How clearly do you think you communicate in English? Decide which of the following six levels of speech effectiveness best fits your speech:

Level 1	People understand only a few words of my speech. Conversations in English as not possible.
Level 2	People understand less than half of what I say. I frequently need to repeat things. My vocabulary and grammar are limited. Conversations are slow and difficult.
Level 3	People understand more than half, but not nearly half, of what I say. I need to repeat and clarify many things. There are problems with my pronunciation, sentence structure, and vocabulary. Conversations proceed in spite of interruptions.
Level 4	People understand most of what I say. My pronunciation and occasional errors in grammar or vocabulary are noticeable, and they occasionally interfere with communication. Conversations proceed with minimal interruptions.

Level 5   My speech is fully understandable. Although my accent and any isolated variations in vocabulary, grammar, or pronunciation may be noticeable, they do not interfere with communication. Conversations proceed smoothly.

Level 6   My speech is nearly native with a barely detectible accent. I use correct grammar and appropriate vocabulary. My communication is clear, fluent, and effective." (4)

Targeting Pronunciation focuses on the student pronunciation training without changing the sounds and rhythm patterns of the original language. The author is convinced that ESL students probably need to work on their English speech rhythm and intonation, expect to make some mistakes, but eventually improve their accent, speak clearly and effectively by gaining confidence when speaking English.

When it comes to pronunciation targets, Sue Miller argues that ESL students should discuss the following conversation strategies:

1. **"Use eye contact**. Conversations are easier to understand when you are looking at the other person. Furthermore, to native speakers of English, eye contact establishes trust and confidence. It makes your listener feel that you are interested and attentive.

2. **Look for clues that your listener does not understand what you are saying**. Does your listener seem annoyed or unfriendly? This may be a clue that he or she does not understand what you are saying. Is your listener responding inappropriately to your questions or comments? This may not be due to your accent. It could be happening because you are not using the right words.

3. **Don't be afraid to ask to make sure you are being understood**. You might say, *Can you understand me*? Or *Please tell me if I say anything that you don't understand*. This puts everyone at ease.

4. **When your listener asks *what*? you probably need to do something more than repeat what you said**. Think about ways you can say it more clearly. Try changing the word stress or focus. Frequently, just by lengthening the stressed syllable and raising its pitch, a word will be easier to understand. Emphasizing the focus words more strongly can often make a whole sentence easier to understand.

5. **Provide extra information**. Rephrase what you said using different words. Explain the meaning. For example, "*I work at a senior center, a place where older people go*." Use gestures. Spell or write down unfamiliar words.

6. **Pay attention to the stressed words**. They provide most of the meaning whether you are the listener of the speaker.

7. **Talk more slowly in English than you do in your native language**. Pause more often. Slow down at the ends of sentences and on focus words.

8. **Find out how to pronounce frequently misunderstood words and phrases**. This might be your address or workplace name.

9. **Don't worry about mistakes**. Hearing your own mistakes is a sign of progress. If you make a mistake, correct it casually without apologizing. If this is n to comfortable, make a mental note of your mistake. Later when you are practicing, say that word or phrase correctly." (99)

Another perspective comes from Nancy Ellen Zelman (2005), who focused her *Conversation Inspirations* on conversational fluency for students studying English. Although the book can be used in many other situations where the target is language acquisition or understanding modern American culture, the author also recommends it, adapted, for dealing with other languages. What makes this book so useful are the topics grouped into five conversational activities, accompanied by relevant information regarding their usage in the classroom. According to the author, the topics (that can be written on index cards) may be used in free and/or controlled conversations. The proficiency level targeted would be intermediate, but quick adjustments could make them available to beginning students as well.

The introduction to *Conversation Inspirations* sets forth the procedure for **monitored conversation:**

1. "Call two students up to the front of the class and ask them to sit in two chairs facing each other, while the rest of the class is seated in a semicircle. The students seated in the 'hot seats' get a conversation card.

2. Explain that the two students up front must speak to each other for three minutes, talking about the situation or topic on the card.

3. Explain that the cards merely function to promote linguistic interaction, and that what is important is not the topic *per se*, but the language used by the two students.

4. Then explain the responsibility of the monitoring students, which is to listen to the students in the hot seats for inappropriate speech, mispronunciation, and incorrect grammar. When a mistake is heard, the listeners write down (as best they can) the phrase or

sentence in which the mistake was made. The listener's job is to practice responsible listening. Explain that this is just as important as the speakers' jobs because as awareness of mistakes is the first step toward avoiding the same mistakes in one's owns speech.

5. As an alternative, assign half the class to listen to one of the speakers, and the rest of the class to the other.

6. One of the listeners gets the job of timekeeper. When the pair in front is ready and has decided on who plays which part in the role play, the timekeeper says 'Go' and the speakers converse.

7. At the end of three minutes, the timekeeper says 'Stop.'

8. Call upon the listeners one at a time to identify the mistakes that they have heard.

9. The student who has made the mistake tries to correct it, but it unable to do so, the other listeners may be called upon to make the correction.

10. If no one is able to correct the mistake, the teacher may then explain the problem. The teacher can then ask all students to write the mistake in their notebooks and next to it a large 'X.' Then correct the mistake and have all students write the correct form in their books.

Note: A few of the role-plays require more than two people to participate in the 'hot seats.' The procedure detailed above can easily be modified to accommodate three speakers." (viii-ix)

Examples of topics from *Conversation Inspirations*:

Section	Topic
1. Famous people	"Find out if Christopher Columbus has any second thoughts about discovering America." (25)
2. Dating	"Tell your fiancé that you want to call off your engagement." (13)
3. Personal experience	"Is there anything that you tried at one time that you would never try again?" (74)
4. Family	"Do you think it is better to be part of a large family or a small one? Is there an ideal size?" (60)

> "All good books are alike in that they are truer than if they had really happened and after you are finished reading one you will feel that all that happened to you and afterwards it all belongs to you; the good and the bad, the ecstasy, the remorse and sorrow, the people and the places and how the weather was."
>
> Ernest Hemingway

Literature

 TIPS to DISCOVER LITERATURE

1. Why literature?

   Literature is the **best form of culture to find language in action**.

   p. 363

2. Values in literature are the same as values in life.   p. 364

3. What do story tellers to attract readers?

   "In the first place, they never waste words. Second, they generally deal with a single event or episode, making other events in the story decidedly less important. And in the third place, all of them strive to make this chief episode and its surroundings so real that we can never forget them."   p. 364

4. How does literature affect us all?

   Literature produces in us "an attitude toward our fellow human beings, an understanding of ourselves, or feelings of deep moral obligation that are valuable to humanity under any conceivable circumstances."

   p. 366

5. How can we use literature in an ESL class?

Here are suggestions of short stories and tasks that can go with each one of them:

The Vacation (Ray Bradbury)	Find collocations and figurative language
Locomotive 38, the Ojibway (William Saroyan)	Use correct quotation marks.
A Day's Wait (Ernest Hemingway)	Change a dialogue into reported speech.
The Dream (Somerset Maugham)	Change the ending of the story.
The Gift of the Magi (O. Henry)	Discover the conflict.
The Story-Teller (Saki)	Which of the two is the story-teller of the title and why?
The Chrysanthemums (John Steinbeck)	Write an imaginary biography of your favorite character.

> "Languages are the pedigree of nations."
>
> Samuel Johnson

It's always a good idea to try some literature in an ESL classroom. **Why literature?** If you ever tried to use a poem or a short story in your classroom, I am sure you realized how your students reacted to the usage of vocabulary words, how the characters developed from the beginning to the end, how they discovered figurative meaning, or how they would have predicted the turn of events, the climax, and maybe even the resolution.

I learned a long time ago that **literature is the highest level of culture** transcribed to the pages of a book. Language is the mirror of a nation's culture, and if you pay attention to how language delivers the author's message, how the conflict develops, how the characters change, literature is still the **best form of culture to find language in action**.

During the summers in the 1990s, I worked at our language center located at Lincoln Center in New York City. I was in the elevator one day when one of our students was holding a book in her hands and talking to a visitor from another language center. It made me so happy to hear that our young student was telling her friend that she really liked the idea of reading a complete book.

I also remember that one day, after a group of latecomers joined our program, another student walked into our offices and asked if they could read a play by Tennessee Williams. I had to ask why, but she was much faster when she said that her roommate was already reading the same play in her class and liked it a lot. It was sometime in the morning, and I had to walk to a bookstore at lunchtime and buy a class set of *Cat on a Hot Tin Roof.*

I was looking for, if not the perfect, at least the best introduction to the literature section of this book. Taking into consideration the limited time in the classroom and the limited space we have at our disposal in this book, I think Mary Ellen Chase (1968) is the one who nailed it when she campaigned for the values in literature:

> "Just what do *values* in literature mean? What is a value? Why did Plato, the great Greek Philosopher, teach the young men of Athens that there are certain values in human life which can never be destroyed or even changed? Justice is one such value, he said. Truth is another. Courage is a third. Such values, he taught, have existed since man began to live, and they will remain as long as life lasts. He taught also that people cannot make the most of themselves or get the best that life has to offer them unless they recognize such values and live by them.
>
> Values in literature are the same as values in life. For literature at its best *is* life. It is not just about life; it is life itself. [. . .] When we read anything at all, if we are good readers, we look for these values. [. . .]
>
> We can always judge the value of any piece of literature by the number of genuine emotions or thoughts which it calls forth from us. If it demands new feelings, new understandings, we can be sure that it has value." (1-2)

Why short stories? **The short story is a particularly American form of art**. People in this country like stories, and you can see that in all types of writing, especially in the short story. It was in American magazines especially that short stories began to appear. Writers like Irving, Poe, and Hawthorne established the form of the short story; and Poe was the first critic, as well as one of the first great writers of short stories.

Mary Ellen Chase wrote this comment about reading short stories:

> "Good readers read not only for what an author says but for how he says it; in other words, they are aware of form as well as content. Short stories, precisely because they are short, are fine examples of form.
>
> All writers of short stories have certain qualities in common. In the first place, they never waste words. Second, they generally deal with a single event or episode, making other events in the story decidedly less important. And in the third place, all of them strive to make this chief

episode and its surroundings so real that we can never forget them. When you read stories, you may find it helpful to keep these qualities in mind. How has the writer make every word count? Which episodes are introduced to serve a more important end? How does the author impress the chief event upon us – the event to which the other episodes have lent support?

Look for patterns and shapes in a story. When you find them – and find similar ones occurring in other stories – you will have discovered that much more to enjoy in reading." (223)

Somerset Maugham, one of the great writers of all time, said that a short story is "a piece of fiction that has a unity of impression and that can be read in a single sitting."

Schakel and Ridl (2005) compiled their *Approaching Literature in the 21st Century* with a focus on helping students to discover literature and to build confidence by analyzing literary works. They also encourage learners to interact with individual pieces of literature, mainly because they can find pleasure in reading and responding to what they read.

"Students sometimes ask what the 'point' or 'message' of a story is. In discussing literature, we try to avoid words like *point* or *message*, because they make it seem like stories are written just to get an idea or moral lesson across. It seems to us stories are written to depict *an experience* or capture *a character*, not mainly to convey an idea (essays and lectures do that). If so, a more helpful place to start is to ask what is striking, what stands out, about the experience or the character described in the story. Usually students can talk or write helpfully about a story by looking at a central character or experience and identifying what seems interesting or unusual or problematic about it." (7)

For each short story, students should be assigned various tasks, such as paying attention to collocations or vocabulary in context, looking for figurative language, looking for the way the author is using grammar, or looking for why the characters do what they do, etc.

"In the evaluation of a novel, poem, play, or short story, as well as in the evaluation of sermons, moral exhortations, political speeches, and directive utterances generally, the usefulness of the given piece of writing as a 'map' of actual 'territories' is often secondary – sometimes quite irrelevant. If this were not the case, *Gulliver's Travels, Alice in Wonderland, The Scarlet Letter,* or Emerson's *Essays* would have no excuse for existence.

Second, when we say that a given piece of affective writing is true, we do not mean 'scientifically true.' We may merely mean that we agree with the sentiment; we may also mean that we believe that an attitude has been accurately expressed; again, we may mean that the attitudes evoked seem such as will lead us to better social or personal conduct.

The word 'true' has many meanings. People who feel that science and literature or science and religion are in necessary conflict do so because they habitually think in opposites of black and white. To such people, it science is 'true,' then literature or religion is nonsense; if literature or religion is 'true,' science is merely 'pretentious ignorance.' What should be understood when people tell us that certain statements are 'scientifically true' is that they are useful and verifiable formulations, suitable for the purposes or organized cooperative workmanship. What should be understood when people tell us that the plays of Shakespeare or the poems of Milton or Dante are eternally true is that they produce in us attitude toward our fellow human beings, an understanding of ourselves, or feelings of deep moral obligation that are valuable to humanity under any conceivable circumstances." (Hayakawa, 1990, pp. 85-86)

ESL students will definitely benefit from reading literature in the classroom or in their own leisure time as long as they are advised, encouraged, and challenged properly. They usually remember reading a short story better than all the other types of skills – again, if the stories are short, interesting, motivating, entertaining, and above all – challenging. Students like to be challenged, and if we manage to find the appropriate types of literature to match their comprehension level, ESL teachers will eventually see how their students blossom and grow. It's difficult to say who will savor and appreciate such ventures because, as teachers we sometimes go back to our favorites and re-read passages or complete books, which after decades might look a little bit different, but enjoyable nonetheless.

Appendices

APPENDIX 1
Samples of lesson plans

IN HER WELL-KNOWN book entitled *Teaching Language in Context,* Alice Omaggio Hadley (1993) "attempted to assist readers interested in classroom language learning in the process of clarifying their own beliefs about language teaching and learning." (vii)

In presenting three "traditional methods," the author also provided lesson plans for each type of method.

The Grammar-Translation Method – Lesson Plan

"The lesson plan that follows is based on a description given by Rivers (1981, pp. 1-2) of a typical grammar-translation class. Before class begins, the students, seated in rows with books open, are about to begin a new section. On the page before them is a *reading selection*, preceded by several columns of *vocabulary* listed with native-language equivalents. The lesson proceeds as follows:

9:00–9:05   Short vocabulary quiz. Students write out the new words as the teacher reads the native-language translation.

9:05-9:15   Various students are asked to read aloud in the target language from the reading selection in the book. After several minutes, the teacher reads a few sentences aloud to the students and then asks them to spend a few minutes reading the rest of the passage silently.

9:15-9:25   Students begin to translate the sentences of the passage into their native language. Occasionally the teacher offers help when students stumble.

9:25-9:40   The core of the lesson now begins with the grammar explanation. On the blackboard, the teacher has placed an outline of the uses of the past tense, examples of which are drawn from the reading passage. The rules are explained in detail in the native language. If students are not familiar with the grammatical terminology, time is taken out to teach it. Students copy the explanations andrules, as well as the examples and various exceptions, into their notebooks.

9:40-9:50   The rest of the lesson is spent on written tasks, such as writing out verb paradigms and filling in the blanks in grammatical exercises. Some time is also spent in translating sentences, usually consisting of non-sequiturs seeded with the grammar point of the lesson, from the native language to the new one. Students who do not complete these tasks before class ends are asked to complete them for homework, as well as memorize the vocabulary list preceding the reading in the next section of the book." (90-91)

APPENDIX 2
The Direct Method – Lesson Plan

THE FOLLOWING DESCRIPTION of a direct method class is based on one given by Rivers (1981, p.3).

9:00-9:10   The teacher comes into the classroom and immediately begins speaking in the target language, greeting students and asking about classroom objects. Students answer in the target language. The teacher continues to ask questions and occasionally gives commands. As the students obey these orders, they recount in the target language exactly what they are doing and the class then tells the teacher what has happened (using part time in their account of the actions just performed.)

9:10-9:25   The lesson develops next around a picture, which the teacher uses to teach the core vocabulary. Various actions and objects are discussed in reference to the activity depicted in the picture. The teacher demonstrates those activities and concepts that are not immediately apparent through mime and waits until the class seems to understand. The students then repeat the new words and phrases and try to form their own sentences in response to the teacher's questions. (This is done with little or no corrective feedback and the students' responses are often quite inaccurate.)

9:25-9:45   Once the vocabulary has been taught and absorbed, the teacher asks the students to read a passage on a similar theme aloud from their text. The teacher models the sentences to be read first and the students mimic either in chorus or individually. The passage is never translated, but the teacher assures comprehension by asking questions in the target language. If difficulties arise, the teacher might explain briefly in the target language while the students take notes.

9:45-9:50   The lesson concludes with a song. When the class ends, the students leave with a sense of accomplishment, since they have been actively involved all period." (93)

APPENDIX 3

Audiolingual Methodology – Lesson Plan

THE FOLLOWING LESSON, based on a description given by Rivers (1981, pp. 4-6), is typical of an ALM class day:

9:00-9:15   The class repeats the lines of a new dialogue, following the teacher's model. To illustrate the meaning of the sentences, the teacher makes stick-figure sketches of the people in the dialogue on the board and points to them as the lines are said. First, everyone repeats the line in chorus. When a pair of sentences has been repeated well in chorus, the teacher divides the class into two groups and the same lines are repeated, with one group responding to the other's line in turn. Next, individual rows of students take a dialogue line and repeat it. Finally, the teacher calls on individuals to repeat the new sentences in front of the class.

9:15-9:40   The teacher moves on to the pattern drilling phase of the lesson, in which structures that were used in the dialogue are now drilled one by one. The class first chorally repeats the drill sentence after the teacher's model. Then they do transformations of the sentence according to the teacher's cues. Transformations may include minimal changes in vocabulary or involve a morphological manipulation of some type. Seven or eight changes of this type are effected by the class in chorus. When the class has had enough practice that they are performing the transformations easily, the teacher asks students to identify what the sentences have in common. The rule, when satisfactorily inducted, is then further drilled through more pattern practice in smaller groups and finally with individual response.

9:40-9:50   A chain drill is used as a final consolidating activity. Students ask one another questions or give one another cues, going down a row from student to student in a chain of stimulus and response. The teacher indicates the homework for the next class session, which consists of listening to lab tapes and practicing more patterns and recorded dialogues, as well as transcribing several times certain words or phrases from the text.

Throughout the entire lesson, the teacher has insisted on absolutely correct forms. Any and all errors have been corrected on the spot, often with a request that other students repeat the correct response in chorus, followed by a repetition from the student who made the error originally. The class has been teacher-centered throughout the 50-minute period; the students' role has been to respond to the teacher's stimulus." (97-98)

APPENDIX 4

Communicative Language Teaching Approach – Sample Classroom Activities

"Because CLT is a comprehensive approach and not a method, it is difficult to characterize it by any one sample lesson plan. However, the kinds of classroom activities that would be representative of CLT include interactive language games, information sharing activities, task-based activities, social interaction, and functional communication practice. Savignon (1983) suggests designing the curriculum to include language arts (or language analysis activities), language-for-a-purpose (content-based and immersion) activities, personalized language use, theater arts ((including simulations, role-plays, and social interaction games), and language use beyond the classroom (including inviting L2 speakers into the classroom and planning activities that take learners outside the classroom to engage in real-world encounters). She gives many examples of communicative language teaching ideas that can be used to generate a classroom atmosphere conducive to the development of communicative competence in all skill areas." (105) According to Diane Larsen-Freeman (1986), there are several well-known language-teaching methods and she did a thorough investigation to reach extremely valuable conclusions. In her preface, the author argues that a method includes both "principles" and "techniques."

"The principles involve five aspects of second- and foreign-language teaching: he teacher, the learner, the teaching process, the learning process, and the target language/culture. Taken together, the principles represent the theoretical framework of the method. The techniques are the behavioral manifestation of the principles – in other words, the classroom activities and procedures derived from an application of the principles." (xi) In Chapter Nine, Larsen-Freeman summarizes the Communicative Approach as follows:

Observations	Principles
1. The teacher distributes a handout that has a copy of a sports column from a recent newspaper.	Whenever possible, 'authentic language" - language as it is used in a real context – should be introduced.
2. The teacher tells the students to underline the reporter's predictions and to say which ones they think the reporter feels most certain of and which he feels least certain of.	Being able to figure out the speaker's or writer's intentions is part of being communicatively competent.

Observations	Principles
3. The teacher gives the students the directions for the activity in the target language.	The target language is a vehicle for classroom communication, not just the object of study.
4. The students try to state the reporter's predictions in different words.	One function can have many different linguistic forms. Since the focus of the course is on real language use, a variety of linguistic forms are presented together.
5. The students unscramble the sentences of the newspaper article.	Students should work with language at the discourse or supra-sentential (above the sentence) level. They must learn about cohesion and coherence, those properties of language which bind the sentences together.
6. The students play a language game.	Games are important because they have certain features in common with real communicative events – there is a purpose to the exchange. Also, the speaker receives immediate feedback from the listener on whether or not she has successfully communicated. Having students work in small groups maximizes the amount of communicative practice they receive.
7. The students are asked how they feel about the predictions.	Students should be given an opportunity to express their ideas and opinions.
8. A student makes an error. The teacher and other students ignore it.	Errors are tolerated and seen as a natural outcome of the development of communication skills. Students' success is determined as much by their fluency as it is by their accuracy.
9. The teacher gives each group of students a strip story and a task to perform.	One of the teacher's major responsibilities is to establish situations likely to promote communication.

Observations	Principles
10. The students work with a partner to predict what the next picture in the strip story will look like.	Communicative interaction encourages cooperative relationships among students. It gives students an opportunity to work on negotiating meaning.
11. The students are to do a role-play. They are to imagine that they are all employees of the same company.	The social context of the communicative event is essential in giving meaning to the utterances.
12. The teacher reminds the students that one of them is playing the role of the boss and that they should remember this when speaking to her.	Learning to use language forms appropriately is an important part of the communicative competence.
13. The teacher moves from group to group offering advice and answering questions.	The teacher acts as an advisor during communicative activities.
14. The students suggest alternative forms they would use to state a prediction to a colleague.	In communicating, a speaker has a choice not only about what to say, but also how to say it.
15. After the role-play is finished, the students elicit relevant vocabulary.	The grammar and vocabulary that the students learn follow from the function, situational context, and the roles of the interlocutors.
16. For their homework, the students are to listen to a debate on the radio or watch it on television.	Students should be given opportunities to develop strategies for interpreting language as it is spoken by native speakers. (Littlewood, 1981) (128-130)

APPENDIX 5

Vocabulary Lesson Plans (1)

Word Formation Game (Paul Nation (Ed.), 1994, p. 187)

Levels Intermediate +	Students have no difficulty understanding the patterns of word formation, and in fact frequently invent existing but unfamiliar words. This game requires students to work in teams which are told they cannot use real words as game entries. To comply with this rule, team members are forced to exchange information about existing vocabulary in the process of producing new words.
Aims Study four processes of word formation in English Practice creating words	**Procedure** 1. Divide the class into teams. The game works most effectively if teams have equally mixed English proficiency levels. 2. Explain the following word formation processes (McManis, Stollenwerk, & Zheng-Shen, 1987) to the class: a. An acronym is the result of combining the first sounds or letters of principal words in a phrase. *Radar* is an acronym for "radio detecting and ranging," while *scuba* represents "self-contained underwater breathing apparatus." b. Blending is a process that combined parts of existing words to produce new words. *Clash* is derived from "clap" and "crash"; *because* came from "by" and "cause." c. Compounding combines entire words to produce new vocabulary items, such as *flashlight, doorknob*, and *headache*. d. Clipping produces short words from longer words, such as *phone* from "telephone" and *gas* from "gasoline."

Class time 45-60 minutes for 15-20 students	3. Have each team gather and make as many words as possible using the processes. After approximately 20 minutes of deliberation, one member of each team writes the team's entries on the blackboard.
Preparation time None **Resources** Optional handout (see Appendix below)	4. Ask the class as a whole to decide if each entry follows a rule of word formation. Teams must supply definitions. The teacher or any class member may note whether the entry is an existing word. A team wins by making up the largest number of new words. Students usually need to be reminded that the point of the game is to create words, not to list familiar vocabulary. A team must have entries in all categories and be able to give definitions for each entry.
	Give one point for known words and two points for well-made created words.
Caveats and Options **Appendix: Optional** **handout for students:** **Word Formation Game**	## Directions 1. The purpose of this game is to explain some of the ways that new words enter the English language. You can increase your vocabulary by understanding the patterns of word formation.
	2. The teacher will divide the class into teams.
	3. Team members make up new words to fit the word formation rules. The team that makes up the most words wins. Every word must follow a rule of word formation. (Some of the words will turn out to be real words anyway.)
	4. A team cannot win unless it has made at least one word for every category.
	5. Be prepared to give a definition for each word your team creates.
	6. After you have worked with your team for 20 minutes, one person from each team will write its list of words on the blackboard. The class as a whole will decide if each entry conforms to a rule. The teacher is the judge in case of a difference of opinion. Real words will be identified at this time.

	Category A - Compound words are new words created by combining two existing words, such as *flashlight* (flash + light), *rainbow* (rain + bow), *toothbrush* (tooth + brush), and *doorknob* (door + knob).
	Category B – Acronyms are the result of combining the first sounds or letters of important words in a phrase. *Radar* is an acronym for "radio detecting and ranging." *Scuba* comes from "self-contained underwater breathing apparatus."
	Category C – Blending is a process which creates new words by combining parts of other words. *Clash* is derived from "clap" and "crash." *Because* is a blend of "by" and "cause."
	Category D – Clipping produces new words by shortening an existing word, such as *phone* from "telephone" and *gas* from "gasoline."
Reference Contributor	McManis, C., Stollenwerk, D., & Zheng-Sheng, Z. (Eds.). (1987). Language Files (4th ed.) Reynoldsburg, OH: Advocate Publishing Group. Michele Kilgore is an ESL instructor at Georgia State University.

NOTES

_____

_____

_____

_____

_____

Vocabulary Lesson Plans (2)

Levels Intermediate+	This activity involves students working with a group of words and trying to find connections between them. Procedure
Aims Develop a deeper understanding of word meanings	1. Choose a group of 10-15 words that you want students to review. These could be taken from anything the students have been studying. The words should be of a similar part of speech to enable students to make connections more easily. For example: *style, comfort, sample, combination, service, guarantee, advertisement, parade, index.*
Class time 25 minutes	2. Divide the class into groups. Ask groups to think of connections between the words on the list. Can they arrange the word into groups, and explain the connections between them? Give an example to help them get started, such as one from the list above:
Preparation time 5 minutes	3. *Comfort* and *service* can go together. They can both be used to describe a hotel. A hotel should provide comfort, and the service should be good.
Resources List of words to review	4. *Sample* and *advertisement* can go together. When you want to buy something in a store, you will see advertisements for different things (paint, carpets, curtains), often with different samples for you to choose from.
	5. Set a time limit for the activity: 10-15 minutes.
	6. Ask group leaders to present their group's combinations to the class. Who could make the most connections between the words on the list?
Contributor	Ronald Jackup is a freelance ESL teacher and writer.

Connections (Paul Nation, Ed. 1994, p. 130)

APPENDIX 6

ARGUMENTATIVE ESSAY (SAMPLE)

"Why Foreign-Language Study Should Be Required" by Nia Tuckson

Introduction Thesis

'What do you call someone who speaks three languages? Trilingual. What do you call someone who speaks two languages? Bilingual. What do you call someone who speaks only one language? American.' As this old jokes illustrates, many Americans are unable to communicate in a language other than English. Given our global economy and American companies' need to conduct business with other countries, this problem needs to be addressed. <u>A good first step is to require all college students to study a foreign language.</u>

Evidence: First point in support of thesis

After graduation, many students will work in fields in which speaking (or reading) another language will be useful or even necessary. For example, healthcare professionals will often be called on to communicate with patients who do not speak English; in fact, a patient's life may depend on their ability to do so. Those who work in business and finance may need to speak Mandarin or Japanese; those who have positions in the military or in a foreign service may need to speak Persian or Arabic. A working knowledge of one of these languages can help students succeed in their future careers, or it can also make them more employable.

Evidence: Second point in support of thesis

In addition to strengthening a resume, foreign-language study can also give students an understanding of another culture's history, art, and literature. Although such knowledge may never be 'useful' in a student's career, it can certainly enrich the student's life. Too narrow a focus on career can turn college into a place that trains students rather than educates them. In contrast, expanding students' horizons to include subjects beyond those needed for their careers can better equip them to be lifelong learners.

Evidence: Third point in support of thesis

When they travel abroad, Americans who can speak a language other than English will find that they are better able to understand people from other countries. As informal ambassadors for the United States, tourists have a responsibility to try to understand other languages and cultures. Too many Americans assume that their own country's language and culture are superior to all others. This shortsighted attitude is not likely to strengthen relationships between the United States and other nations. Understanding a country's language can help students to build bridges between themselves and others.

First opposing argument

Some students say that learning a language is not easy and that it takes a great deal of time. College students are already overloaded with coursework, jobs, and family responsibilities, and a new academic requirement is certain to create problems. In fact, student may find that adding just six credits in language study will limit their opportunities to take advanced courses in their majors or to enroll in electives that interest them. However, this burden can be eased if other, less important course requirements – such as physical education – are eliminated to make room for the new requirement.

Second opposing argument

Some students may also argue that they, not their school, should be able to decide what courses are most important to them. After all, a student who struggled in high school French and plans to major in computer science might understandably resist a foreign-language requirement. However, challenging

Refutation

college language courses might actually be more rewarding than high school courses were, and the student who struggled in high school French might actually enjoy a college-level French course (or take another language). Finally, a student who plans to major in computer science may actually wind up majoring in something completely different – or taking a job in a country in which English is not spoken.

Conclusion

Entering college students sometimes find it hard to envision their personal or professional futures or to imagine where their lives may take them. Still, a well-rounded education, including foreign language, can prepare them for many of the challenges that they will face. Colleges can help students keep their options open by requiring at least a year (and preferably two years) of foreign-language study. Instead of focusing narrowly on what interests them today,

Concluding statement

American college students should take the extra step to become bilingual – or even trilingual in the future."

(Quoted in Kirszner & Mandell, *Practical Argument*, 2011, pp. 14-16)

APPENDIX 7

CONVERSATION LESSON PLAN

Warm up

Discuss the following questions as a class:
If you had a serious problem, whom would you go to for help?
Would you be willing to discuss anything with that person?
What if he/she were the problem? Could you talk to him/her openly about it?
How honest are you when discussing unpleasant subjects?

Vocabulary Preview/Pronunciation

spouse	*merchandise*	*insomnia*
confront	*snorkeling*	*vice versa*
gambling	*upset*	*tactfully*
best man	*maid of honor*	*scratch*
collision	*amazing*	*incredible*
ridiculous	*disgusting*	*co-worker*
picky	*bad breath*	*geometry*

Conversation Starters

Example:
A: *What's new?*
B: *Not much. How about you?*
A: *I just got a new job.*
B: *Congratulations! That's great . . .*

Asking for Advice

What do you think I should do?
What should I do about . . . .?
What would you do (in this situation)?

Your objective

You and your partners are best friends. Either you or your friend has a problem. Act out (role play) the following situations in which you give your friend advice or vice versa. You have approximately four minutes for each situation. Your teacher will tell you when to change to a new partner.

The Situations

1. Your friend would like to be a movie star, but you don't think he/she has enough talent. Advise him/her to choose another profession. (Start: "Guess what?...)

2. You borrowed your best friend's gold watch (worth $3,000) last week and lost it. You have looked everywhere, but cannot find it. What do you tell him/her? (Begin: "I don't know how to tell you this, but . . .")

3. Your best friend's spouse called and asked you to talk to your friend about his/her gambling problem. Discuss the problem with your friend. (Begin: "Can I talk to you for a minute? . . .)

(Adapted from Glen Alan Penrod, *Touchy Situations*, Delta Publishing House, 2002, pp. 14-20)

APPENDIX 8

INFORMATIVE SPEECH PREPARATION CHECKLIST

Name: _____ Topic: _____

Due Date: _____

_____ Chose narrow, specific, achievable topic.

_____ Consulted outside sources:

     _____ Interviews   _____ Books   _____ Magazines

     _____ Newspapers _____ Dictionaries _____ Encyclopedias

     _____ Encyclopedic dictionaries _____ Professional journals

     _____ Internet

_____ Chose organizational pattern.

_____ Prepared outline.

_____ Prepared body.

_____ Prepared preview.

_____ Prepared attention-getting opener.

_____ Prepared summary.

_____ Prepared memorable concluding remarks.

_____ Prepared transition after introduction.

_____ Prepared transition before summary.

_____ Prepared transitions in body.

_____ Prepared visual aids:

     _____ Objects _____ Charts and diagrams _____ Demonstrations

_____ Practiced speech with visual aids at least three times.

(Paulette Dale and James C. Wolf, *Speech Communication Made Simple*, 2000, p.86)

APPENDIX 9

INFORMATIVE SPEECH EVALUATION FORM

Speaker _____   Topic _____

Date: _____

DELIVERY	RATING	COMMENTS
Eye Contact	1 2 3 4 5	_____
Volume of Voice	1 2 3 4 5	_____
Rate of Speech	1 2 3 4 5	_____
Enthusiasm	1 2 3 4 5	_____
Adherence to time limit	1 2 3 4 5	_____

CONTENT	RATING	COMMENTS
Attention-Getting Opener	1 2 3 4 5	_____
Preview	1 2 3 4 5	_____
Organization	1 2 3 4 5	_____
Supporting Materials	1 2 3 4 5	_____
Visual Aids	1 2 3 4 5	_____
Transitions	1 2 3 4 5	_____
Summary	1 2 3 4 5	_____
Concluding Remarks	1 2 3 4 5	_____

ADDITIONAL COMMENTS

_____
_____
_____
_____
_____

RATING KEY

1 = Poor   2 = Fair   3 = Acceptable   4 = Good   5 = Excellent

(Paulette Dale and James C. Wolf, *Speech Communication Made Simple*,
2000, p. 190)

APPENDIX 10

VOCABULARY ENERGIZERS

AUSPICIOUS

"The word 'auspicious' derives from the Latin *avis* ('bird') and *specio* ('see'). The ancient Romans believed that the flight, feeding habits and songs of birds foretold the future. The Romans even dissected birds, for they thought the birds' internal organs predicted events. The priests who observed the birds were called *auspices* ('bird watchers'). If all the signs were good, then the occasion would be *auspicius*, meaning 'favorable' or 'of good omen.' Hence, today if a young writer produces a well-reviewed best seller, his career is off to an auspicious or promising start. A student who gets all 'A's' in his/her first semester has an auspicious beginning in college. Bright sunrise, fragrant flowers, and melodious birds are auspicious of the wonderful day to come. Etymologically related to 'auspicious' is the word 'auspices.' If you are under someone's auspices, you have their favor, support, or sponsorship." (p. 54)

MENTOR

"When Odysseus – crafty hero of the Greeks who conceived the idea of the Trojan horse – went to fight in the Trojan War, he left his wife and infant son in the charge of his trusted friend Mentor. Since Odysseus did not return ten years later with the other Greeks after the war ended but remained away for still another ten years, many thought he was dead. Hordes of suitors came to ask his wife Penelope to marry them, but she kept putting them off. Mentor could not prevent this rowdy bunch from eating Odysseus' livestock, drinking his wine, and molesting the servants. Finally, Athena – goddess of wisdom and protector of Odysseus – assumed the form of Mentor and told Odysseus' son Telemachus to seek his father. This wise counsel, of course, came from Athena rather than Mentor. Nevertheless, Mentor's name has become synonymous with wise, loyal, and protective guardianship.

Socrates was the mentor of Plato, Plato the mentor of Aristotle, and Aristotle the mentor or Alexander the Great. Another famous mentor was the wizard Merlin, the teacher and protector of King Arthur. American playwright Lorraine Hansberry (1930-1965), famous for her drama *A Raisin in the Sun*, gratefully acknowledged her mentor, the inspiring high school teacher who introduced her to the plays of Sean O'Casey and William Shakespeare." (pp. 65-66)

PRECOCIOUS

"'Precocious' derives from Latin *prae* ('before') and *coquere* ('cook'). Latin *praecoquere* meant 'cook beforehand' or 'ripen beforehand.' 'Precocious' entered the English language to refer to flowers and fruits that ripened early. Now we apply 'precocious' to children and youth whose mental or artistic qualities are far more developed than in others of their age. We sometimes hear of precocious mathematical wizards who enter college while other children of their age are still in elementary school. The precocious Mozart composed music at the age of five. (p. 92)

(From David Popkin, *Vocabulary Energizers*, Nashville, Tennessee:
Hada Publications, 2003)

APPENDIX 11
The Wisdom of Proverbs

He who rides a tiger cannot dismount

In *Chinese Proverbs* (1875), William Scarborough recorded the earliest version of this saying in English as "He who rides a tiger is afraid to dismount." The implication here is that some things, once started, cannot be easily or safely stopped, and it was to that point that Archibald Colquhoun wrote in *The Mastery of the Pacific* (1902), "The colonies . . . are for her [France] the tiger which she has mounted . . . and which she can neither manage nor get rid of." (p. 84)

Love is blind

On the self-deceptions wrought by love, the Spanish novelist Miguel de Cervantes wrote in *Don Quixote* (1615), "Love looks through spectacles which make copper appear gold, rich poverty, and weak eyes distill pearl." Similarly, Benjamin Franklin noted "There are no ugly loves, nor handsome prisons," in Poor Richard's Almanack (1737). The saying "Love is blind" is far older yet, with Plato rendering it for the first time in *Laws* (c. 375 B.C.) as "Love is blind as regards the beloved." (p. 118)

Seeing is believing

According to this old maxim, you can in fact believe your eyes. The Greek playwright Aristophanes recorded what was probably the earliest such saying in *The Ecclesiazusae* (c. 393 B.C.) as "I saw it and believed." Centuries later a manuscript (1609) by Simon Harward contained the English version, "Seeing is Believing," and just a few years later, John Clarke's *Paroemiologia Anglo-Latina* (1639) quoted the exact wording of the current version: "Seeing is believing." (p. 159)

Too many cooks spoil the broth

"Broth" here is a metaphor for any sort of undertaking, while the cooks are those who will have a say in how it is to be done (and who will presumably ruin things because of their conflicting opinions.) Apparently already a common proverb in the sixteenth century, the saying was first recorded in John Hooker's *Life of Sit Peter Carew* (c. 1580) as "The more cookes the worse pottage." (p. 185)

(Adapted from Stuart Flexner and Doris Flexner, *Wise Words and Wives' Tales*, New York: Avon Books, 1993)

APPENDIX 12

Vocabulary in Context   TEST

Using context clues for help, circle the letter of the best meaning for each word or words.

4. After the American Civil War, trolleys and streetcars greatly expanded workers' mobility, permitting them to move beyond a walking distance from factories.

    a. pay   c. ability to move
    b. skills   d. interests

5. What people say may not reflect accurately what they are actually feeling. It is sometimes necessary to resort to clues other than their spoken words to understand them fully.

    a. remove from   c. make use of
    b. make light of   d. ignore

6. Individual political organizations often join together to form coalitions to increase the support for their issues.

    a. partnership   c. contests
    b. lines   d. questions

7. The possibility of developing a top seller is so alluring that American companies spend billions of dollars a year trying to create new products to improve old ones.

    a. dangerous   c. attractive
    b. final   d. unreasonable

8. Toddlers are naturally inquisitive. It is because they are so curious about their surroundings that they are so eager to explore everything.

    a. unreliable   c. curious
    b. clumsy   d. tired

9. After X-rays were discovered in 1895, there were some preposterous reactions. For example, London merchants sold x-ray-proof underwear.

    a. logical   c. dangerous
    b. ridiculous   d. delayed

10. Using sign language, chimpanzees can convey such ideas as 'candy sweet' and 'give me a hug.'

    a. reject   c. think of
    b. accept   d. communicate

11. America has often been called a 'melting pot' into which people of many different cultures assimilate.

    a. learn   c. avoid
    b. leave   d. blend

(Langan, pp. 33-36)

APPENDIX 13

Exercises in Inference
"Mystery 2: Ruth's Birthday"

A multitude of small accidents had delayed Ruth Mundy. The battery in her car had gone dead and she had to call a cab; she had mislaid the key to the strong box! Just as the taxi pulled up she located it. Hastily snatching from the dresser drawer two twenty-dollar bills, one old and crumpled, one crisp and new, she thrust them loosely into her bag. In her hurry, the perfume bottle on the dresser upset, spilling perfume on her lovely moire purse! If this kept up she'd be late for her birthday party! Now, where was that book she was to return? She was sure she had put it on the dresser! Finally locating it under her coat on the bed, she grabbed it and ran.

Once in the taxi she opened her bag and fumbled for her vanity case. Its clasp opened and she stuck her finger in the paste rouge. Another casualty! Well, it didn't get on anything else, that was one break. Removing all traces of the rouge with her handkerchief, she threw it away. Arriving at the Mayflower Hotel she handed the driver a bill. While she waited for the change Professor Fordney alighted from his car and greeted her with a "Hello Ruth."

Acknowledging the greeting she turned to the driver. "You've made a mistake. This change is for five. I gave you a twenty."

"O no, lady! You gave me five dollars!" Fordney listened amused while Ruth excitedly proved she'd given the driver a twenty-dollar bill. "How's that, Professor?" she laughed.

How did Ruth prove her story? _____

Mystery 3: The Ex-Wife Murder

"Who shot her?" cried Rogers as he rushed into the hospital three minutes after his ex-wife dies from a bullet through her head.

"Just a minute," Professor Fordney said, "I'd like to ask you a few questions . . . routine, you know. Although divorced for the past six months, you have been living in the same house with your ex-wife, have you not?"

"That's right."

"Had any troubles recently?"

"Well . . . yesterday when I told her I was going on a business trip, she threatened suicide. In fact, I grabbed a bottle of iodine from her as she was about to drink it. When I left last evening at seven, however, telling her I was spending the night with friends in Sewickley, she made no objections. Returning to town this afternoon," he continued, "I called my home and the maid answered."

"Just what did she say?"

" 'Oh, Mr. Rogers, they took poor mistress to St. Anne's Hospital 'bout half an hour ago. Please hurry to her!' She was crying so I couldn't get anything else out of her; then I hurried here. Where is she?"

"The nurse here will direct you," responded the Professor. "A queer case this, Joe," said Inspector Kelley, who had been listening to the conversation. "These moderns are a little bit too much for me! A man and woman living together after being divorced six months!"

"A queer case, indeed, Jim," sighed Fordney. "You'd better detain Rogers. If he didn't shoot her himself, I'm confident he knows who did."

Why did Professor advise the Inspector to detain Rogers? _____

(Silberstein, Dobson, and Clark, pp. 141-142)

APPENDIX 14

AS vs. LIKE

I. Complete the sentences using *like* or *as* + the following:

a beginner	blocks of ice	~~a palace~~	a birthday present
a child	a church	winter	a tour guide

1. This house is beautiful. *It's like a palace.*

2. My feet are really cold. They're _____.

3. I've been playing tennis for years, but I still play _____
   _____.

4. Margaret once had a part-time job _____
   _____.

5. I wonder what that building with the tower is. It looks
   _____.

6. My brother gave me this watch _____a long
   time ago.

7. It's very cold for the middle of the summer. It's _____
   _____.

8. He's 22 years old, but he sometimes behaves _____
   _____.

II. Put in *like* or *as*. Sometimes either word is possible.

1. We heard a noise ____*like*_____ a baby crying.

2. Your English is very fluent. I wish I could speak _____ you.

3. Don't take my advice if you don't want to. You can do _____
   you like.

4. You waste too much time doing things _____ sitting in cafés
   all day.

5. I wish I had a car _____ yours.

6. You don't need to change your clothes. You can go out _____
   you are.

7. My neighbor's house is full of lots of things. It's _____ a
   museum.

8. We saw Kevin last night. He was very cheerful, _____ always.

9. Sally has been working _____ a waitress for the last two months.

10. While we were on vacation, we spent most of our time doing active things _____ sailing, water skiing, and swimming.

11. You're different from the other people I know. I don't know anyone _____ you.

12. We don't need all the bedrooms in the house, so we use one of them _____ a study.

13. The news that Sue and Garry were getting married came _____ a complete surprise to me.

14. _____ her father, Catherine has a very good voice.

(Raymond Murphy, *Grammar in Use*, 2011, p. 229)

APPENDIX 15

Johann Wolfgang von Goethe, *Actions and Words*

"Art is long, life short, judgment difficult, opportunity transient. To act is easy, to think is hard; to act according to our thought is troublesome. Every beginning is cheerful; the threshold is the place of expectation. The boy stands astonished, his impressions guide him; he learns sportfully, seriousness comes on him by surprise. Imitation is born with us; what should be imitated is not easy to discover. The excellent is rarely found, more rarely valued. The height charms us, the steps to it do not; with the summit in our eye, we love to walk along the plain. It is but a part of art that can be taught; the artist needs it all. Who knows it half, speaks much and is always wrong; who knows it wholly, inclines to act and speaks seldom or late. The former have no secrets and no force; the instructions they can give is like baked bread, savory and satisfying for a single day; but flour cannot be sown, and seed corn ought not to be ground. Words are good, but they are not the best. The best is not to be explained by words. The spirit in which we act is the highest matter. Action can be understood and again represented by the spirit alone. No one knows what he is doing while he acts aright; but of what is wrong we are always conscious. Whoever works with symbols only is a pedant, a hypocrite, or a bungler. There are many such, and they like to be together. Their babbling detains the scholar; their obstinate mediocrity vexes even the best. The instruction which the true artist gives us opens the mind; for where words fail him, deeds speak. The true scholar learns from the known to unfold the unknown, and approaches more and more to being a master."

(*The Treasure Chest. An Anthology of Contemplative Prose*. Edited by J. Donald Adams, New York: E. P. Dutton & Company, Inc., 1946, pp. 97-98)

APPENDIX 16

LIST OF IRREGULAR VERBS

Present and Infinitive	Past	Past Participle
awake	awoke	awoken
be	was/were	been
bear (bring forth)	bore	born
bear (carry)	bore	borne
become	became	become
begin	began	begun
bend	bent	bent
bite	bit	bitten
bleed	bled	bled
blow	blew	blown
break	broke	broken
bring	brought	brought
build	built	built
burn	burned/burnt	burned/burnt
burst	burst	burst
buy	bought	bought
catch	caught	caught
choose	chose	chosen
cling	clung	clung
clothe	clothed/clad	clothed/clad
come	came	come
cost	cost	cost
creep	crept	crept
cut	cut	cut
deal	dealt	dealt
dig	dug	dug
dive	dove/dived	dived
do	did	done
draw	drew	drawn
dream	dreamed/dreamt	dreamed/dreamt
drink	drank	drunk
drive	drove	driven
eat	ate	eaten
fall	fell	fallen
feed	fed	fed
feel	felt	felt
fight	fought	fought
find	found	found
flee	fled	fled
fling	flung	flung
fly	flew	flown
forbid	forbade/forbad	forbidden

forget	forgot	forgotten
forsake	forsook	forsaken
freeze	froze	frozen
get	got	got/gotten
give	gave	given
go	went	gone
grind	ground	ground
grow	grew	grown
hang (suspend)	hanged/ hung	hung
hang (kill)	hanged/hung	hanged
have	had	had
hear	heard	heard
hide	hid	hid/hidden
hit	hit	hit
hold	held	held
hurt	hurt	hurt
keep	kept	kept
kneel	knelt	knelt
know	knew	known
lay	laid	laid
led	led	led
leap	leaped	leaped/leapt
leave	left	left
lend	lent	lent
let	let	let
lie (tell a lie)	lied	lied
lie (recline)	lay	lain
light	lit/lighted	lit/lighted
lose	lost	lost
make	made	made
mean	meant	meant
meet	met	met
pay	paid	paid
prove	proved	proved/proven
put	put	put
read	read	read
rid	rid	rid
ride	rode	ridden
ring	rang	rung
rise	rose	risen
run	ran	run
say	said	said
see	saw	seen
seek	sought	sought
sell	sold	sold
send	sent	sent

set	set	set
shake	shook	shaken
shine	shone	shone
shoot	shot	shot
show	showed	showed/shown
shrink	shrank	shrunk/shrunken
shut	shut	shut
sing	sang	sung
sink	sank	sunk/sunken
sit	sat	sat
sleep	slept	slept
slide	slid	slid
sling	slung	slung
speak	spoke	spoken
speed	sped	sped
spend	spent	spent
spin	spun	spun
spread	spread	spread
spring	sprang	sprung
stand	stood	stood
steal	stole	stolen
stick	stuck	stuck
sting	stung	stung
stink	stink/stank	stunk
strike	struck	struck
string	strung	strung
swear	swore	sworn
sweep	swept	swept
swell	swelled	swelled/swollen
swim	swam	swum
swing	swung	swung
take	took	taken
teach	taught	taught
tear	tore	torn
tell	told	told
think	thought	thought
throw	threw	thrown
understand	understood	understood
wake	woke	woken
wear	wore	worn
weep	wept	wept
wet	wet	wet
win	won	won
wind	wound	wound
wring	wrung	wrung
write	wrote	written

LIST OF PREPOSITIONAL VERBS

To accuse of	The thief *was accused of* stealing a passenger's purse.
To (dis)approve of	Her parents *disapprove of* her staying out late at night.
To allude to	He mentioned the subject once but never *alluded to* it again.
To advise of/about	A good lawyer *can advise you of/about* your rights.
To agree on	We seem *to agree on* the usage of this term.
To agree with	I *agree with* you.
To argue with	He *argued with* his neighbor about the garbage.
To believe in	We all *believe in* having a good time at the party.
To burden with	I *don't want to burden you with* all my difficulties.
To beware of	We *should beware of* those who flatter.
To blame for	The manager *was blamed for* not taking the proper precautions.
To call for	Do you hear someone *calling for* help?
To count on	You *can count on* me to help you.
To conform to	Some people *don't want to conform to* society's regulations.
To cope with	He is so sensitive he *cannot cope with* all his problems.
To confide in	She has always *confided in* her husband.
To convict of	He *was convicted of* a crime he had not committed.
To consent to	The suspect *consented to* a cross examination.
To come to	These groceries *come to* twenty dollars.
	Then idea *came to* me while watching TV.
To call on	We *called on* the Hendersons the last time we visited Chicago.
To dispense with	Let's *dispense with* all formalities!
To depend on	The outcome of the test *depends on* several factors.
To differ from	The new batch of cookies *differs from* the first one.

To dream of/about	She *has always dreamed of/about* going on a safari.
To deal in	He *deals in* modern paintings and sculptures.
To deal with	We *don't want to deal with* people like them.
To deviate from	His ideas *deviate sharply from* the traditional ones.
To deprive of	Nobody *can be deprived of* the rights guaranteed by law.
To emerge from	Many distinguished men *have emerged from* the slums.
To excel in	My sister *excels in* all sports.
To end in	That project *ended in* failure.
To engage in	The two friends *engaged in* a long conversation.
To escape from	Some prisoners *have escaped from* prison.
To flee from	The prisoners *were fleeing from* their pursuers.
To fight for/against	People *have often had to fight for* their freedom.
To hear of	The landlord *would not hear of* reducing the tenant's rent.
To insist on	The scientist *insisted on* the accuracy of his results.
To interfere in	You *should never interfere in* other people's business.
To interfere with	We hope you *are not going to interfere with* that project.
To inflict on	The punishment *inflicted on* him was too severe.
To immunize against	Vaccines are available *to immunize people against* many diseases.
To keep on	He *kept on* working there for thirty years.
To look for	I can't find my flash drive. I *have looked for* it everywhere.
To laugh at	Don't embarrass him by *laughing at* his mistakes in English.
To mourn for	She *mourned for* her deceased husband for a long time.
To plot against	Someone who *plots against* his own country is a traitor.
To persevere in	If you persevere, you are *bound to succeed in* your studies.

To participate in	We wonder why he does not want *to participate in* class debates.
To plan on	A situation arose which they *had not planned on*.
To protect from	Cyclists must wear helmets *to protect their heads from* injury.
To recover from	She *has finally recovered from* the shock of the news.
To retire from	My friend finally *retired from* the diplomatic service.
To reflect on	True understanding comes from *reflecting on* your experience.
To reprimand for	He *was reprimanded for* traveling without his family's permission.
To reproach for	She *reproached me for* not giving her notice of my visit.
To rescue from	It took a long time *to rescue everybody from* the sinking ship.
To resort to	Officials fear that extremists *may resort to* violence.
To result in	The trial *resulted in* an acquittal.
To rule over	That dictator *rules over* his people with an iron hand.
To smell of	The whole room *smells of* gas.
To speak of/about	The man *spoke about* the days he spent in the army.
To stare at	The little boy *stared at* the toys in the store window.
To struggle against	We must continue *to struggle* against poverty.
To subscribe to	My brother *subscribed to* many online magazines.
To substitute for	Margarine *may be substituted for* butter in this recipe.
To succeed in	The passenger *succeeded in* finding an empty seat.
To think of/about	Lately he *has been thinking of/about* her a great deal.
To talk of/about	I *can't talk about* things I don't understand.
To transform into	They *have transformed that old house into* an antique shop.
To vote for	Which candidate *are you going to vote for*?
To warn of/about	He *has already been warned about* the dangers of heavy smoking.
To yield to	You *must yield to* traffic coming from your right.

APPENDIX 18

MINI-GUIDE TO PRONUNCIATION (1)

The pronunciation of the suffix -ed in the Past

1. /t/ is added to verbs which end with the following **voiceless** consonants:

/p/   /k/   /s/   /sh/   /ch/   /f/

dipped	helped	jumped
talked	asked	barked
kissed	rinsed	pulsed
washed	wished	trashed
reached	touched	trashed
laughed	stuffed	triumphed

2. /d/ is added to verbs which end with **vowels** or with the following **voiced** consonants:

/b/   /g/   /v/   /z/   /dg/   /m/   /n/   /r/   /l/   /th/

enjoyed	lied	slayed
climbed	barbed	bobbed
begged	dragged	tagged
loved	lived	saved
raised	gazed	liaised
indulged	ridged	hinged
climbed	dimmed	summed
warned	banned	burned
starred	cared	stared
travelled	called	curled
bathed	breathed	clothed

3. /id/ is added to verbs which end in /t/ or /d/:

wanted	translated	parted
added	handed	folded

PRACTICE   Arrange the following verbs in 3 groups depending on their pronunciation:

Used, liked, tried, picked, entered, earned, boiled, illustrated, passed, needed, camped, banked, crossed, lasted, lifted, sobbed, behaved, spelled, rushed, studied, lasted, lifted, searched, tempted, walked, poured, guarded, played, curved, wagged, acted, touched, dubbed, mailed, limited, loathed

Group 1 /t/   Group 2 /d/   Group 3 /id/

_____   _____   _____

MINI-GUIDE TO PRONUNCIATION (2)

The pronunciation of the suffix /s/ in the 3rd person singular of verbs, noun possessives, and noun plurals

1. /s/ is added to words which end in voiceless consonants

/p/   /t/   /k/   /f/   /th/

stops	drops	helps
fits	treats	tents
asks	marks	tasks
laughs	gulfs	cuffs
sloths	berths	

2. /z/ is added to words ending in voiceless consonants

/b/   /d/   /g/   /v/   /m/   /n/   /l/   /r/   /th/

tabs	bulbs	clubs
modes	codes	roads
icebergs	legs	drugs
lives	carves	valves
gems	climbs	elms
bins	barns	warns
travels	camels	halls
cars	stars	clusters
clothes	lathes	

3. /iz/ is added to words ending in

/s/   /z/   /sh/   /ch/

classes	glasses	busses
roses	causes	prizes
washes	galoshes	dashes
watches	matches	bunches

PRACTICE Arrange the following words in 3 groups depending on their pronunciation:

acts, gifts, glimpses, lungs, winds, lenses, sneezes, urges, taxes, bins, grasps, fits, boards, dumps, teases, prices, alarms, thorns, mines, airs, bears, courts, cups, cubs, sends, cents, delights, Paul's, jokes, disturbs, roots, wilts, dwarfs, grapes, arches, scripts, corpses

Group 1 /s/   Group 2 /z/   Group 3 /iz/

_____   _____   _____

References

Agar, Michael. 1996. *The Language Shock. Understanding the Culture of Conversation.* Perennial.

Axelrod, Rise B, Charles R. Cooper, and Alison M. Warriner. 2005. *Reading Critically Writing Well.* Boston/New York: Bedford/St. Martin's.

Ayto, John. 2011. *Bloomsbury Dictionary of Word Origins.* Revised Edition. Arcade.

Azar, Betty Schrampfer. 1992. *Fundamentals of English Grammar.* Englewood Cliffs, NJ: Prentice Hall-Regents.

Azar, Betty Schrampfer. 1999. *Understanding and Using English Grammar.* Pearson Education.

Baker, Ann and Sharon Goldstein. 2008. *Pronunciation Pairs.* Cambridge: Cambridge University Press.

Baker, Russell. "How to Punctuate." *The New York Times.* February 11, 2006.

Barzun, Jacques. 1984. "What if-? English versus German and French." *Oxford Book of Essays,* 1991.

Beeching, Cyril Leslie. 1989. *A Dictionary of Eponyms.* Third Edition. London: The Library Association Publishing Ltd.

Berlitz, Charles. 2005. *Native Tongues.* Edison, N.J.: Castle Books.

Blackstone, Bernard. 1965. *A Manual of Advanced English for Foreign Students,* London: Longmans, Creen and Co. LTD.

Bloom, Harold. 2000. *How to Read and Why.* Scribner.

Bloom, Harold. 2002. *Genius. A Mosaic of One Hundred Exemplary Creative Minds.* New York: Warner Books.

Blumenthal, Joseph C. 1977. *English Workshop. Fifth Course.* New York: Harcourt Brace Jovanovich.

Bradbury, Ray. 1965.*The Machineries of Joy.* New York: Bantam Books.

Bower, G. H. and M. C. Clark. 1969. "Narrative Stories as Mediators for Serial Learning." *Psychonomic Science* 14: 181-182.

Bryson, Bill. 1990. *The Mother Tongue. English and How It Got That Way.* New York: William Morrow and Company, Inc.

The Bedford Introduction to Literature. 2011. Ninth Edition. Boston: Bedford/ St. Martin's.

Burgess, Anthony. *A Mouthful of Air.* 1992. New York: Morrow and Company, Inc.

Cambridge Advanced Learner's Dictionary. 2008. 3rd Edition. Cambridge: Cambridge University Press.

Capote, Truman. 1980. *Breakfast at Tiffany's.* New York: Signet.

Carruthers, Mary. 2008. *The Book of Memory.* Cambridge: Cambridge University Press.

Celce-Murcia, Marianne and Diane Larsen-Freeman. 1999. *The Grammar Book. An ESL/EFL Teacher's Course.* Second Edition. Boston, Massachusetts: Heinle & Heinle Publishers.

Chase, Mary Ellen, Arno Jewettt and William Evans. 1968. *Values in Literature.* Boston: Houghton Mifflin Company.

Chesla, Elizabeth. 2000. *Write Better Essays in Just 20 Minutes a Day.* New York: Learning Express.

Chevalier, Jean and Alain Gheerbrant. 1996. *A Dictionary of Symbols.* London: Penguin Books.

Clark, Raymond, Patrick R. Moran and Arthur A. Burrows. 2008. *The ESL Miscellany. A Treasury of Cultural and Linguistic Information.* Brattleboro, Vermont: Pro Lingua.

Clark, Roy Peter. 2010. *The Glamour of Grammar.* New York, Boston, London: Little, Brown and Company.

Cole, Tom. 2006. *The Preposition Book.* University of Michigan Press.

Cook, Ann. 2009. *American Accent Training.* Barron's Educational Series.

Coomber, James E. and Howard D. Peet. 2000. *McDougal Littell Wordskills. Blue Level.* Evanston, Illinois: McDougal Littell, A Houghton Mifflin Company.

Coomber, James E. and Howard D. Peet. 2000. *McDougal Littell Wordskills. Purple Level.* Evanston, Illinois: McDougal Littell, A Houghton Mifflin Company.

Coulmas, Florian. 1996. *The Blackwell Encyclopedia of Writing Systems.* Oxford: Blackwell Publishers Ltd.

Crombie, Alexander. 1830. *The Etymology and Syntax of the English Language.* The Third Edition. London: John Taylor www.books.google.com.

Crovitz, H. F. 1979. "Memory Retraining in Brain-Damaged Patients." *Cortex,* 15, 131-134.

Crystal, David. 1992. *The Cambridge Encyclopedia of Language.* Cambridge: Cambridge University Press.

Crystal, David. 2004. *The Stories of English*. Woodstock & New York: The Overlook Press.

Crystal, David. 2006. *How Language Works*. Woodstock & New York: Overlook Press.

Crystal, David. 2014. *Words in Time and Place*. Oxford: Oxford University Press.

Dale, Paulette and James C. Wolf. 2000. *Speech Communication Made Simple*. Second Edition. White Plains, NY: Longman.

Deutscher, Guy. 2010. *Through the Language Glass*. New York: Picador.

Deutscher, Guy. 2005. *The Unfolding of Language. An evolutionary tour of mankind's greatest invention*. New York: Henry Holt and Company.

Dinesen, Isak. 1992. *Out of Africa*. Modern Library.

Dunham, Henrietta C. and Catherine Vaden Summers. 1986. *English Integrated, An Advanced Reader/Grammar for Learners of English*. Boston, Massachusetts: Heinle & Heinle Publishers.

Elster, Charles Harrington. 2014. *Word Workout*. New York: St. Martin's Griffin

Emerson, Ralph Waldo. 1870. *Prose Works*. Vol 1. Boston: Fields, Osgood & Co.

Emery, Donald W., John M. Kierzek and Peter Lindlom. 1985. *English Fundamentals*. New York: MacMillan Publishers.

Espy, Willard R. 1987. *Thou Improper, Thou Uncommon Noun*. New York: Clarkson N. Potter Publishers.

Essinger, James. 2007. *Spellbound*. New York: Bantam Dell.

Finocchiaro, Mary and Christopher Brumfit. 1983. *The Functional-Notional Approach: from Theory to Practice*. Oxford: Oxford University Press.

Flesch, Rudolph. 1949. *The Art of Readable Writing*. New York: Harper & Brothers Publishers.

Flexner, Stuart and Doris Flexner. 1993. *Wise Words and Wives' Tales*. New York: Avon Books.

Forsyth, Mark. 2011. *The Etymologicon. A Circular Stroll through the Hidden Connections of the English Language*. London: Icon Books Ltd.

Frank, Marcella. 1986. *Modern English. Part 1: Parts of Speech*. Second Edition. Pearson.

Frank, Marcella. 1986. *Modern English. Part 2: Sentences and Complex Structures*. Second Edition. Pearson.

Gamon, David and Allen D. Bragdon. 1998. *Building Mental Muscle. Conditioning Exercises for the Six Intelligence Zones*. Cape Cod and San Francisco: Brain Waves Books.

Gilbert, Judy B. 2012. *Clear Speech*. Cambridge: Cambridge University Press.

Goethe, Johann Wolfgang. 2015. *Wilhelm Meister's Apprenticeship*. CreateSpace Independent Publishing Platform.

Gordon, Karen Elizabeth. 1983. *The Well-Tempered Sentence*. New Haven and New York: Ticknor & Fields.

Grant, Linda. 2017. *Well Said*. Cengage Learning.

Hacker, Diana. 1995. *A Writer's Reference*. Third Edition. Boston: Bedford Books of St. Martin's.

Hadfield, Jill and Zoltan Dornyei. 2011. *Motivating Learning*. London and New York: Routledge.

Hartfiel, V. Faye, Jane B. Hughey, Deanna R. Wormuth, and Holly L. Jacobs. 1985. *Learning ESL Composition*. Rowley, Massachusetts: Newbury House Publishers, Inc.

Hayakawa, S. I. 1990. *Language and Thought*. Fifth Edition. San Diego: Harcourt Brace Jovanovich, Publishers.

Hayden, Rebecca E., Dorothy W. Pilgrim, and Aurora Quiros Haggard. 1956. *Mastering American English*. Englewood Cliffs, New Jersey: Regents/Prentice Hall.

Hemingway, Ernest. 2014. *A Farewell to Arms*. Reprint Edition. Scribner.

Hewings, Martin and Sharon Goldstein. 1998. *Pronunciation Plus*. Cambridge: Cambridge University Press.

Hewings, Martin. 2005. *Advanced Grammar in Use*. Cambridge: Cambridge University Press.

Hobbs, James B. 1993. *Homophones and Homographs. An American Dictionary*. Second Edition. Jefferson, North Carolina, and London: McFarland & Company, Inc., Publishers.

Hodges, Raymond W., Irene C. MacCaskills, and Mary Pimentel. 1984. *College Word Study*. Providence, Rhode Island: P.A.R. Incorporated.

Hogue, Ann. 2003. *The Essentials of English*. White Plains, N.Y.: Pearson Education.

Hornby, A. S. 1970. *A Guide to Patterns and Usage in English*. London: Oxford University Press.

Houston, Keith. *The Mysterious Origins of Punctuation*. http://www.bbc. culture/story/20150902-the-mysterious-origins of punctuation.

International Encyclopedia of Linguistics. 2003. William J. Frawley, Editor in Chief. Oxford University Press.

Jackson, H. J. 2001. *Readers Writing in Books*. New Haven: Yale University Press.

Jason, Kathrine and Holly Posner. 1995. *Explorations in American Culture*. Boston, Massachusetts: Heinle & Heinle.

Jean, Georges. 1987. *Writing. The Story of Alphabets and Scripts*. New York: Harry N. Abrams, Inc.

Jeffries, Linda and Beatrice Mikulecky. 2009. *Reading Power*. Pearson Longman.

Joshi, Manik. 2017. *English Sentence Exercises. Word Order in Sentences*. eBook.

Keller, Helen. 2002. *The Story of My Life*. Signet Classics.

Kenneally, Christine. 2007. *The First Word*. New York: Viking.

Kirkpatrick, Betty. 1996. *Clichés. Over 1500 Phrases Explored and Explained*. New York: St. Martin's Griffin.

Kirszner, Laurie G. and Stephen R. Mandell. 2011. *Practical Argument. A Text and Anthology*. Boston: Bedford/St. Martin's.

Lado, Robert. 1964. *Language Teaching: A Scientific Approach*. London: MacGraw Hill.

Langan, John. 1999. *Ten Steps to Advancing College Reading Skills*. Marlton, NJ: Townsend Press.

Lazar, Gillian. 2003. *Meanings and Metaphors. Activities to practice figurative language*. Cambridge: Cambridge University Press.

Le Goff, Jacques. 1993. *Intellectuals in the Middle Ages*. Willey-Blackwell.

Lee, Harper. 1993. *To Kill a Mockingbird*. New York: HarperCollins.

Leith, Sam. 2018. *Write to the Point*. New York: The Experiment.

Littlewood, W. 1981. *Communicative Language Teaching*. Cambridge: Cambridge University Press.

Lloyd, Donald J. 2017. "Snobs, Slobs, and the English Language" *The American Scholar*. Routledge.

Long, Mason. 1935. *The New College Grammar*. New York: The Ronald Press Company.

Longman Advanced Dictionary of American English. 2007. Pearson Education.

Lorayne, Harry and Jerry Lucas. 1974. *The Memory Book*. New York: Ballentine Books.

Manguel, Alberto. 1996. *A History of Reading*, New York: Viking.

Markwardt, Albert H. 1958. *American English*. New York: Oxford University Press.

Maugham, Somerset M. 1938. *Cosmopolitans*. New York: The Sun Dial Press, Inc.

Maugham, Somerset M. 1990. *On a Chinese Screen*. New York: Paragon House.

May, Rollo. 1991. *The Cry for Myth*. New York, London: W.W. Norton & Company.

McLean, Michelle. 2011. *Essays & Term Papers*. Pompton Plains, NJ: Career Press.

McCrum, Robert, William Cran and Robert MacNeil. 1986. *The Story of English*. New York: Elisabeth Sifton Books. Viking.

McPhee, John. 2017. *Draft No. 4. On the Writing Process*. New York: Farrar, Straus and Giroux.

Meiklejohn, J. M. D. 1905. *A Short Grammar of the English Tongue with Three Hundred and Thirty Exercises*. London: Meiklejohn and Holden.

Meyers, Jeffrey. 2008. *Samuel Johnson. The Struggle*. New York: Basic Books.

Miller, Sue. 2005. *Targeting Pronunciation. Communicating Clearly in English*. Houghton Mifflin.

Mindell, Phyllis, Ed. D. 1993. *Power Reading*. Englewood Cliffs, NJ: Prentice Hall.

Morgan, John and Mario Rinvolucri. 2004. *Vocabulary*. Oxford: Oxford University Press.

Murphy, Raymond. 2011. *Grammar in Use*. Cambridge: Cambridge University Press.

Nation, Paul (Ed.) 1994. *New Ways in Teaching Vocabulary*. Bloomington, Illinois: Pantagraph Printing.

The New Encyclopedia Britannica. 1986. Chicago: The University of Chicago.

The Norton Reader. An Anthology of Nonfiction. 2012. Linda H. Peterson, General Editor. New York: W. W. Norton & Company.

Ogg, Oscar. 1964. *The 26 Letters*. New York: The Thomas Y. Crowell Company.

Omaggio Hadley, Alice. 1993. *Teaching Language in Context*. Second Edition. Boston, Massachusetts: Heinle & Heinle Publishers.

Orion, Gertrude. 2011. *Pronouncing American English*. Cengage Learning.

Oshima, Alice and Ann Hogue. 1991. *Writing Academic English*. Longman Academic English.

Oster, Judith. 1987. *From Reading to Writing. A Rhetoric and Reader*. Second Edition. Bostonand Toronto: Little, Brown and Company.

The Oxford Book of Essays. Chosen and Edited by John Gross. 1991. Oxford, New York: Oxford University Press.

Parfitt, Matthew. 2012. *Writing in Response*. Boston/New York: Bedford/St. Martin's.

Pearsall Smith, Logan. 1933. *On Reading Shakespeare*. New York: Harcourt, Brace and Company.

Pei, Mario. 1967. *The Story of the English Language*. Philadelphia and New York: J. B. Lippincott Company.

Pei, Mario. 1965. *The Story of Language*. Philadelphia & New York: J. B. Lippincott Company.

Pennebaker, James W. "Your Use of Pronouns Reveals Your Personality." *Harvard Business Review*. December 2011.

Penrod, Glen Alan. 2002. *Touchy Situations. A Conversation Text for ESL Students*. Delta Publishing House.

Peoples, Lorraine. 2011. *You Can Teach Someone to Read*. 2nd Edition. Gilbert, Arizona: GLoBooks Publishing LLC.

Perkins Wilder, Lina. 2010. *Shakespeare's Memory Theatre. Recollection, Properties, and Character*. Cambridge: Cambridge University Press (books. google.com).

Piozzi, Hester Lynch Thrale. 1794. *British Synonymy*. G.G. and J. Robinson Publishers.

Popkin, David. 2003. *Vocabulary Energizers. Stories of Word Origins*. Nashville, Tennessee: Hada Publications.

Publication Manual of the American Psychological Association. Sixth Edition. 2010. Washington, DC: American Psychological Association.

Reader's Digest. Write Better, Speak Better. 1972. Pleasantville, New York: The Reader's Digest Association, Inc.

Richards, Jack C. and Theodore S. Rodgers. 1986. *Approaches and Methods in Language Teaching*. Cambridge: Cambridge University Press.

Rivers, Wilga M. 1981. *Teaching Foreign Language Skills*. 2nd ed. Chicago: University of Chicago Press.

Rosa, Alfred and Paul Eschholz. 2015. *Models for Writers. Short Essays for Composition*. Twelfth Edition. Boston, New York: Bedford/St. Martins.

Rottenberg, Annette T. 1997. *Elements of Argument*. Boston: Bedford Books.

Sacks, David. 2005. *Language Visible. Unraveling the Mystery of the Alphabet from A to Z*. New York: Broadway Books.

Sakamoto, Nancy. 1982. *Polite Fictions. Why Japanese and Americans Seem Rude to Each Other*. Kinseido.

Saroyan, William. 2013. *My Name Is Aram*. Mineola, New York: Dover Publications, Inc.

Savignon, Sandra. 1972. *Communicative Competence: An Experiment in Foreign-Language Teaching*. Center for Curriculum Development.

Schakel, Peter and Jack Ridl. 2005. *Approaching Literature in the 21st Century. Fiction – Poetry – Drama*. Boston, New York: Bedford/St. Martins.

Short Stories for Study. 1946. New York: Henry Holt and Company.

Silberstein, Sandra, Barbara K. Dobson, and Mark A. Clarke. 2002. *Reader's Choice*. Ann Arbor: The University of Michigan Press.

Simpson, John. 2016. *The Word Detective. A Life in Words: from Serendipity to Selfie*. London: Little, Brown.

Skarmeta, Antonio. 1987. *Burning Patience*. Pantheon.

Smalley, Regina L. and Mary K. Ruetten. 1995. *Refining Composition Skills. Rhetoric and Grammar*. Fourth Edition. Boston: Heinle & Heinle.

Spence, Jonathan D. 1984. *The Memory Palace of Matteo Ricci*. New York, NY: Viking Penguin.

St. Augustine. 1984. *The Confessions. The City of God. On Christian Doctrine*. Chicago: Chicago University Press.

Stannard Allen, W. 1979. *Living English Structure*. London: Longman Limited Group.

Stavans, Ilan. 2005. *Dictionary Days. A Defining Passion*. Saint Paul, Minnesota: Graywolf Press.

Steinbeck, John. 1986. *The Long Valley*. New York: Penguin Books.

Stewart, Edward C. *American Assumptions and Values: Orientation to Action* [in] *Toward Internationalism*. Second Edition. 1997. Boston: Heinle & Heinle.

Strumpf, Michael and Auriel Douglas. 2004. *The Grammar Bible*. New York: Henry Holt and Company.

Success with Words. A Guide to the American Language. 1983. Pleasantville, New York/Montreal: The Readers' Digest Association, Inc.

Sudlow, Michael. 1989. *Exercises in American English Pronunciation*. Excellence in Education Publications.

Sullivan, Howard and Norman Higgins. 1983. *Teaching for Competence*. New York and London: Teachers College, Columbia University.

Sundem, Garth, Jan Krieger, and Kristi Pickiewicz. 2008. *10 Languages You'll Need Most in the Classroom*, Thousand Oaks: Corwin Press.

Thomson, A.J. and A.V. Martinet. 1986. *A Practical English Grammar. Exercises I, II*. Oxford: Oxford University Press.

The Treasure Chest. An Anthology of Contemplative Prose. 1946. Edited by J. Donald Adams. New York: E. P. Dutton & Company, Inc.

Truss, Lynne. 2003. *Eats, Shoots & Leaves. The Zero Tolerance Approach to Punctuation.*New York: Gotham Books.

Webster's Dictionary of Synonyms. 1951. Springfield, Mass.: G. & C. Merriam CO., Publishers

Webster's Universal Dictionary of the English Language. 1937. Cleveland. O./ New York, N.Y. : The World Syndicate Publishing Company.

Why Do We Say It? The Stories behind the Words, Expressions and Clichés We Use. 1985.Secaucus, NJ: Castle.

Williams, Phil. 2016. *Word Order in English Sentences*. Rumian Publishing

Yang, Charles. 2006. *The Infinite Gift*. New York: Scribner.

Yates, Frances A. 1966. *The Art of Memory*. Chicago: The University of Chicago Press.

Yates, Jean. 2006. *English Vocabulary for Beginning ESL Learners*. New York: McGraw Hill.

Zelman, Nancy Ellen. 2005. *Conversation Inspirations*. Pro Lingua Associates.

Zobel, H. B. "How History Made the Constitution." *American Heritage*. March 1988. Volume 39. Issue 2.

Index

Made in the USA
Middletown, DE
25 June 2022